全面突破新托业
NEW TOEIC
660分

廖迪安 著

使用说明 | User's Guide

突破托业 660分!

本书专为突破托业考试的考生而设计!
以最省力的方式,帮你冲过考试关获得就业机会!

突破 1

图片即情境,情境就是考题!

托业考试是以职场环境为背景的英语沟通考试,官方明文公布了多达 13 种考试取材范围。作者根据多年考试的经验,将这些范围重新统整分成 6 个章节、36 个单元,只要掌握这些情境,就能够掌握考题要点。

[问题]
没有具体考试范围,怎么知道要背哪些单词?

想要考取好成绩,单词不需要背很多,但要背"对"!
本书一张图片列举出 8 个在情境中可明确指出的单词,以及 8 个可通过情境延伸记忆的单词,每个单词不仅有中英文,更随机补充同义词、衍生词、衍生短语。

词性对照表

| n 名词 | v 动词 | a 形容词 | ad 副词 |
| p 介词 | pr 代词 | ph 短语 | abbr 缩写 |

使用说明 | User's Guide

突破 2

重点试题练习，一举攻破托业！

都已经没办法长时间专心准备考试了，难道为了考到最低录取门槛的 660 分，还要去买一套全真模拟试题回家练习吗？

本书每个情境皆附上重点模拟试题（Part 1、Part 3 或 Part 4、Part 7），什么是重点模拟试题？
就是最有"投资回报率"的题目！

[听力题]
Part 1：看图选择正确的描述，这么容易拿分的 10 道题，怎么可以放弃！
Part 3 或 Part 4：题型皆为听完一段英语后，回答试卷上的 3 个问题，应考技巧类似，一次就能攻破 60 道题！

[阅读题]
Part 7：看得懂一篇文章并了解其意，就能掌握"文章理解"的题型。而能看得懂文章，也就能够轻松掌握以考单词填空、语法概念为主的 Part 5 和 Part 6 了！

突破 3

用 36 张照片，掌握托业考试！

背单词、做试题，是上考场前的准备工作。
只要掌握考试情境，并熟悉这个情境在考试中会出现的方式以及内容，就能迅速掌握考试重点、掌握托业考试！

★ 本书附赠音频为 MP3 格式

660分

003

托业考试介绍 | NEW TOEIC

什么是托业考试?

　　TOEIC即Test of English for International Communication（国际交流英语考试）。托业考试是针对英语非母语人士所设计的英语能力测验，测验分数反映受测者在国际职场环境中与他人以英语沟通的熟练程度。参加托业考试不需具备专业的知识或词汇，因为考试内容以日常使用的英语为主。托业考试是在以职场为基准点的英语能力测验中世界顶级的考试。全球每年有超过500万人报考托业考试，在150个国家中有超过14 000家的企业、学校或政府机构采用托业考试为依据，同时在全球超过150个国家中是最被广泛接受且最方便报考的英语考试之一。

托业听力阅读考试成绩与沟通能力对照

TOEIC 成绩/分	语言能力
905~990	英语能力十分近似于英语母语人士，能够流畅有条理地表达意见、参与谈话，主持英语会议、调和冲突并做出结论，语言使用上即使有小瑕疵，亦不会造成理解上的困扰
785~900	可有效地运用英语满足社交及工作所需，措辞恰当、表达流畅。在某些特定情形下，如面临压力紧张、讨论话题过于冷僻艰涩时，仍会显现出语言能力不足
605~780	可以用英语进行一般社交场合的谈话，能够应付例行性的业务需求；参加英语会议时，能听取大部分要点。 无法流利地以英语发表意见、做辩论，使用的词语、句型也以一般常见的为主
405~600	掌握少量相关语言，可以从事英语相关程度较低的工作。 文字沟通能力尚可，会话方面稍显词汇不足、语句简单
255~400	语言能力仅仅局限在简单的一般日常生活对话，同时无法做连续性交谈，亦无法用英语工作
10~250	只能以背诵的句子进行问答而不能自行造句，尚无法将英语当作沟通工具来使用

托业考试成绩计算

考生用铅笔在电脑答题卡上作答。考试分数由答对题数决定；再将每一大类（听力类、阅读类）答对题数转换成分数，范围在5~495分。两大类加起来即为总分，范围在10~990分。答错不扣分。

托业考试内容

托业考试的设计，以职场的需要为主。考试题的内容，从全世界各地职场的英语资料中搜集而来，题材多元化，包含各种类型与情况。

一般商务	合同、谈判、营销、销售、商业企划、会议
制造业	工厂管理、生产线、品管
金融／预算	银行业务、投资、税务、会计、账单
企业发展	研究、产品研发
办公室	董事会、委员会、信件、备忘录、电话、传真、电子邮件、办公室器材与家具、办公室流程
人事	招考、雇用、退休、薪资、升迁、应征与广告
采购	比价、订货、送货、发票
技术层面	电子、科技、电脑、实验室与相关器材、技术规格
房屋／公司地产	建筑、规格、购买租赁、电力煤气服务
旅游	火车、飞机、出租车、巴士、船只、渡轮、票务、时刻表、车站、机场广播、租车、饭店、预订、延误与取消
外食	商务／非正式午餐、宴会、招待会、餐厅订位
娱乐	电影、剧场、音乐、艺术、媒体
保健	医疗保险、看医生、牙医、诊所、医院

考试重点 | Point

[听力答题技巧]

总共一百题，考试时间四十五分钟。听力测验的内容多为陈述句或疑问句。

- **Part 1 图片描述**
  - > 总共十题，选项为四选一。图片印在试卷上。
  - > 留意图片中事物的位置或状态，或人物的位置、穿着、动作、互动。
- **Part 2 回答问题**
  - > 总共三十题，选项为三选一。试卷未印选项。
  - > 留意疑问词。
- **Part 3 简短对话、Part 4 简短文章**
  - > 这两个部分各三十题，选项为四选一。题目与选项印在试卷上。
  - > 问题的前后顺序通常与该内容在对话和文章中出现的顺序一致。

[阅读答题技巧]

总共一百题，考试时间为七十五分钟。会阅读到各种题材的文章。主要测验语法、短语、单词水平。

- **Part 5 单句填空**
  - > 总共四十题，选项为四选一。
  - > 重点是易混淆单词、短语组合、词性、语法。
- **Part 6 短文填空**
  - > 总共十二题，选项为四选一。
  - > 重点是易混淆单词、短语组合、词性、语法。
- **Part 7 单篇文章理解、双篇文章理解**
  - > 单篇文章理解共二十八题，双篇文章理解共二十题，选项皆为四选一。
  - > 可先看题目再看文章，知道问题后，便可知道需留意什么信息，更容易找出答案。

[考试前须知]

确认考试通知单上的考试时间与考场，并在当天提前三十分钟到场。
需准备有效身份证件（身份证原件或其他有效证件原件）、2B 铅笔、橡皮擦。

目录 | Contents

Chapter 1 | 一般商务 General Business — 001

Unit 01 合同 Contract — 002
试题 Part1, Part4, Part7

Unit 02 谈判 Negotiation — 012
试题 Part1, Part4, Part7

Unit 03 会议 Meeting — 022
试题 Part1, Part4, Part7

Unit 04 销售 Sale — 032
试题 Part1, Part4, Part7

Unit 05 信件、电子邮件 Letters and E-mails — 042
试题 Part1, Part4, Part7

Unit 06 电话、传真 Phone and Fax — 052
试题 Part1, Part4, Part7

Chapter 2 | 办公室 Office — 063

Unit 07 办公室器材与家具 Office Equipment — 064
试题 Part1, Part3, Part7

Unit 08 面试 Interview — 074
试题 Part1, Part3, Part7

Unit 09 雇用 Employment — 084
试题 Part1, Part3, Part7

Unit 10 薪资 Wage — 094
试题 Part1, Part3, Part7

Unit 11 升迁 Promotion — 104
试题 Part1, Part4, Part7

Unit 12 退休 Retirement — 114
试题 Part1, Part4, Part7

目录 | Contents

Chapter 3 | 金融、采购、研发 Finance, Purchase and Research — 125

Unit 13 银行 Bank 126
  试题 Part1, Part4, Part7

Unit 14 会计 Accounting 136
  试题 Part1, Part3, Part7

Unit 15 仓库 Warehouse 146
  试题 Part1, Part3, Part7

Unit 16 生产线 Assembly Line 156
  试题 Part1, Part4, Part7

Unit 17 工厂 Factory 166
  试题 Part1, Part4, Part7

Unit 18 实验室 Laboratory 176
  试题 Part1, Part4, Part7

Chapter 4 | 房地产、交通 Real Estate and Traffic — 187

Unit 19 建筑 Building 188
  试题 Part1, Part4, Part7

Unit 20 购买和租赁 Purchase and Rent 198
  试题 Part1, Part4, Part7

Unit 21 机场 Airport 208
  试题 Part1, Part4, Part4

Unit 22 火车 Train 218
  试题 Part1, Part3, Part7

Unit 23 出租车 Taxi 228
  试题 Part1, Part3, Part7

Unit 24 汽车 Car 238
  试题 Part1, Part3, Part7

目录 | Contents

Chapter 5 | 餐厅 Restaurant — 249

Unit 25 订位 Reservation — 250
试题 Part1, Part3, Part4

Unit 26 正式午餐 Formal Lunch — 260
试题 Part1, Part3, Part7

Unit 27 派对 Party — 270
试题 Part1, Part3, Part7

Unit 28 餐厅点餐 Ordering — 280
试题 Part1, Part3, Part7

Unit 29 餐厅内场 Cooking Area — 290
试题 Part1, Part3, Part7

Unit 30 结账 Payment — 300
试题 Part1, Part3, Part7

Chapter 6 | 娱乐、保健 Entertainment and Health — 311

Unit 31 电影 Movies — 312
试题 Part1, Part3, Part7

Unit 32 音乐 Music — 322
试题 Part1, Part3, Part7

Unit 33 饭店 Hotel — 332
试题 Part1, Part4, Part7

Unit 34 医院 Hospital — 342
试题 Part1, Part4, Part7

Unit 35 看医生 Seeing a Doctor — 352
试题 Part1, Part3, Part7

Unit 36 药房 Pharmacy — 362
试题 Part1, Part3, Part7

Chapter 1

一般商务
General Business

Unit 01
合同 | Contract

New TOEIC

Picture 01

情境中可明确指出的单词

1. **clipboard** [ˈklɪpbɔːd] n 文件夹
2. **couch** [kaʊtʃ] n 沙发
3. **fountain pen** n 钢笔
4. **keyboard** [ˈkiːbɔːd] n 键盘
5. **mustache** [məˈstɑːʃ] n 胡子
6. **notebook** [ˈnəʊtbʊk] n 笔记本电脑，笔记本
7. **radiator** [ˈreɪdieɪtə] n 暖气片
8. **shirt** [ʃɜːt] n 衬衫

情境中可延伸记忆的单词

1. **attention** [əˈtenʃn] n 专心，注意
2. **clause** [klɔːz] n 条款
3. **content** [kənˈtent] a 满意的 [ˈkɒntent] n 内容，目录
4. **contract** [ˈkɒntrækt] n 合同 [kənˈtrækt] v 签约
5. **convince** [kənˈvɪns] v 说服
6. **couple** [ˈkʌpl] n 夫妻
7. **consensus** [kənˈsensəs] n （意见等的）一致，共识
8. **speculate** [ˈspekjuleɪt] v 沉思，思索

Unit 01 合同 | Contract

clipboard ['klɪpbɔːd] n 文件夹
Why did he put the clipboard under the table?
他为什么要把文件夹放在桌子下面？
- clipping 头等的，一流的

couch [kaʊtʃ] n 沙发
These three people are sitting on the couch and talking over the terms of the contract.
这三个人正坐在沙发上讨论合同的条款。
- couch potato 极为懒惰的人

fountain pen ph 钢笔
The lady is writing with a silver fountain pen.
这位女士正在用一支银色的钢笔写字。
- water fountain ph 饮水器

keyboard ['kiːbɔːd] n 键盘
We can only see part of the keyboard in the picture.
在照片中我们只能看到键盘的一部分。
- keyboard entry ph 键盘输入

mustache [məˈstɑːʃ] n 胡子
The man sitting on the lady's right has a mustache.
坐在女子右边的男子留有胡子。
- handlebar mustache ph 八字胡

notebook ['nəʊtbʊk] n 笔记本电脑，笔记本
These three people are sitting behind the table with a notebook and a clip board on it.
这三个人坐在放有笔记本电脑和资料夹的桌子后面。
- loose notebook ph 活页本 / take note ph 做笔记

radiator ['reɪdieɪtə] n 暖气片
There are two white radiators on the wall.
墙上有两个白色的暖气片。
- radiation n 辐射 / radiator grille ph 车辆的水箱

shirt [ʃɜːt] n 衬衫
The man wearing a black shirt is looking at the contract with a smile on his face.
穿黑色衬衫的男子面带微笑地看着合同。
- white shirt ph 白衬衫 / put one's shirt on ph 孤注一掷

003

attention [ə'tenʃn] n 专心，注意
All of them are paying attention to the contract.
他们都把注意力放在合同上。
● pay attention to 关注……

clause [klɔːz] n 条款
Looking at the picture, we can't see the clause of the contract.
从照片中我们看不出合约的条款。
● contract clause 合约条款

content [kən'tent] a 满意的 ['kɒntent] n 内容，目录
From the man's smile, we can guess that he is content with the contract.
从男子的微笑中我们可以看出，他对这份合同很满意。
● content with 对……感到满意

contract ['kɒntrækt] n 合同 [kən'trækt] v 签约
I think the man in the suit is the drafter of the contract.
我认为穿西装的那位男子是合约的起草人。
● contractor 立契约者 / parties to a contract 签约者

convince [kən'vɪns] v 说服
Before signing the paper, she must have been convinced by the drafter.
在签字之前，她一定被合同起草人说服了。
● visual convince 视觉说服

couple ['kʌpl] n 夫妻
I am guessing that the lady and the man wearing the black shirt are a couple.
我猜想那位女子和那位穿黑色衬衫的男子是夫妻。
● in couples 成对地

consensus [kən'sensəs] n （意见等的）一致，共识
Both sides of the contract have reached a consensus.
协议双方达成了一致意见。
● reach a consensus 达成共识

speculate ['spekjuleɪt] v 沉思，思索
The lady is speculating on whether the contract is reasonable.
这位女子正在思索这份合同是否合理。
● speculate on 思索，沉思

听力测验 | Part 1 图片描述题

(A) There are three men in the conference room.
(B) All of them have a pen in their hands.
(C) They reach an agreement on the contract.
(D) The woman is the assistant of the man sitting on the left.

(A) 会议室里面有三位男子。
(B) 他们手里都有一支笔。
(C) 他们就合同达成协议。
(D) 女子是左边男子的助理。

答案：(C)
从照片中我们可以看到，会议室里有两名男子、一名女子，只有一名男子手里握有笔，图片中无法确定他们的身份，但是从他们脸上的笑容可以看出他们在合同方面达成了协议，因此选 (C)。

听力测验 | Part 4 简短独白题

1. What's the most important when you plan to draw up a contract for clothing?
   (A) Taking all things into consideration.
   (B) To demand a detailed description.
   (C) To look for a good partner.
   (D) The terms of the contract.

2. What shouldn't be emphasized in the contract for both parties?
   (A) The company's name.
   (B) The penalty clause.
   (C) The breach of faith clause.
   (D) The measure to be taken.

3. What's important to the signatory?
   (A) Break even.
   (B) To make profit.
   (C) The payment.
   (D) No conflict with partner.

Many things should be considered when you are going to sign a contract for clothing. First and foremost, a detailed description should be provided. Secondly, you should consider important aspects, such as price, price terms, quality inspection, payment, and delivery time of the clothing. Last but not least, responsibilities of both parties should be emphasized. These may include a penalty clause, a breach of faith clause, and what measures would be taken upon a broken contract. In addition, you should assure your own interest. In other words, there is a good profit for you, not just cost and revenue.

Unit 01 合同 | Contract

Chapter 1 一般商务

中译

1. 签订服装合同时，什么是最重要的？
   (A) 考虑所有的事情。
   (B) 要求提供详细说明。
   (C) 寻求好的合作伙伴。
   (D) 合同条款。

2. 在合同中不必对双方强调的是什么？
   (A) 公司的名字。
   (B) 违约条款。
   (C) 违约责任。
   (D) 对违约采取的措施。

3. 对签约方来说，什么比较重要？
   (A) 不赚不赔。
   (B) 有利可图。
   (C) 支付方式。
   (D) 与合作方关系友好。

当你准备签订服装合同的时候，你要考虑很多事情。首先对方要提供商品的详细说明。其次你要考虑一些重要因素，比如：价格、价格条款、品质检查、支付方式以及服装的交货时间。最后一点，也是非常重要的一点，要强调双方应该承担的责任，包括违约条款、违约责任，以及会采取什么措施来处理违约情况。另一方面，你要确保自己的利益。换句话说就是，除掉成本和税收之外，你是有利可图的。

解析与答案

答案：1. (B) 2. (A) 3. (B)

1. 听力中提到：First and foremost, a detailed description should be provided. 其中 first and foremost 相当于 the most important，所以选择 (B)。
2. 根据听力中 responsibilities of both parties should be emphasized 可知，除了 (A) 没有提到外，其他三项都有提到，所以选 (A)。
3. 这篇听力是以签约方的立场来写的，根据最后一句 there is a good profit for you, except cost and revenue 可知，对于签约方来说，签订合约一定是有利可图的，所以选 (B)。

单词 Vocabulary

payment ['peɪmənt] n 付款，报酬，惩罚
delivery [de'liveri] n 递送，交付，分娩
penalty ['penəlti] n 罚款，处罚
breach [briːtʃ] n 违背，缺口 v 打破，违反
revenue ['revənjuː] n 税收，收益

阅读测验 | Part 7 文章理解题

NEW TOEIC

Fresh Seafood Market
William Clinton
SeafoodUS.com

Dear Mr. Clinton,

We noticed your official website last month and are interested in the seafood you sell. You may know that we are the most famous, large-scale chain store in the U.S. I want to point out that we can't guarantee order amounts at this time.

We have read the items in your online sales agreement without any objection, but we are curious about how you keep your seafood fresh for long periods of time. (For example, tropical fish, lobsters, salmons, cod, and so on.) New York Seafood Company is known for providing our customers with fresh seafood, so we must guarantee the freshness of seafood we buy. Our main pride is that we do our best, and that no other seafood company is more popular than us.

Our board of directors has decided to purchase a small amount of seafood from your company providing that you provide good quality seafood. We would like to order a small amount of every kind of seafood that you sell, to be delivered within the next ten days, so that we can decide whether to place a bulk order in the near future or not. If we are satisfied with your seafood, we will discuss details of the contract with you, and then sign a contract.

Regards,
Stefan Bush
New York Seafood Company

Unit 01 合同 | Contract

1. What is this e-mail about?

    (A) The party last night.
    (B) Complaints from customers.
    (C) Rules and regulations of the company to the employees.
    (D) Placing an order with William Clinton.

2. What may William Clinton NOT supply according to this e-mail?

    (A) Tropical fish.
    (B) Apples.
    (C) Lobster.
    (D) Salmon.

3. What is New York Seafood Company famous for?

    (A) Providing soft drinks.
    (B) Providing fresh seafood.
    (C) Providing heavy machinery.
    (D) Providing luxury clothes.

4. Before placing a bulk order, what does Stefan Bush ask William Clinton to do?

    (A) Deliver some samples for free.
    (B) Deliver a small amount of every kind of seafood.
    (C) Visiting the company of William Clinton.
    (D) Ask William Clinton to sign a contract with his assistant.

5. When may Stefan Bush receive the seafood from William Clinton according to this e-mail?

    (A) Today.
    (B) Within three days.
    (C) Within ten days.
    (D) Within a month.

新鲜海鲜市场
威廉姆·克林顿
SeafoodUS.com

尊敬的克林顿先生：

我们上个月注意到你们的官方网站，并对你们卖的海鲜感兴趣。你知道我们是美国最出名的大规模连锁店。然而，我想指出的是我们不能确保这次的订货量。

我们已经阅读了你们协定中的全部条款，并无异议，但是我们十分好奇你们是如何对海鲜进行长期保鲜的，比如说热带鱼、龙虾、鲑鱼、鳕鱼等。纽约海鲜公司以提供新鲜海鲜而著名，因此我们必须保证我们购买的海鲜的新鲜度。我们竭尽全力，因此没有其他海鲜公司比我们公司更受欢迎的，这是我们的骄傲。

老实说，我们的董事会已经决定从你们公司购买少量海鲜，前提是你们提供的是优质海鲜。我们想订购每样你们贩卖的海鲜少许，并请在十天之内递送给我们，这样我们可以决定在不久的将来是否要下大笔订单。如果我们对你们的海鲜满意，我们将会与你们签订合约，并讨论合约中的每一项细节。

此敬
敬礼！

斯忒凡·布希
纽约海鲜公司

1. 这封电子邮件是关于什么？
   (A) 昨晚的派对。
   (B) 顾客的抱怨。
   (C) 公司对员工的规章制度。
   (D) 从威廉姆·克林顿处下订单。

2. 根据这封邮件可知，威廉姆·克林顿可能不提供什么？
   (A) 热带鱼。
   (B) 苹果。
   (C) 龙虾。
   (D) 鲑鱼。

3. 纽约海鲜公司以什么而出名？
   (A) 提供汽水。
   (B) 提供新鲜海鲜。
   (C) 提供重型机器。
   (D) 提供奢侈服装。

4. 在下大宗订单之前，斯特凡·布希要威廉姆·克林顿做什么？
   (A) 免费送一些样品。
   (B) 每种海鲜都送少量。
   (C) 拜访威廉姆·克林顿的公司。
   (D) 让威廉姆·克林顿与他的助理签订合约。

5. 根据这封邮件可知，斯特凡·布希什么时候能够收到威廉姆·克林顿发送的海鲜？
   (A) 今天。
   (B) 三天之内。
   (C) 十天之内。
   (D) 一个月之内。

解析与答案

答案：1. (D) 2. (B) 3. (B) 4. (B) 5. (C)

1. 此题考阅读能力，可见邮件正文的第一段第一句 ... interested in the seafood you sell，并且后面整个邮件都是围绕海鲜订购展开的，而收件者是威廉姆·克林顿，因此选 (D)。
2. 此题考细节，可见第二段第一句 ... about how you keep your seafood fresh for long periods of time，此句提到的都是海鲜，没有水果，因此选 (B)。
3. 此题考细节，可见第二段第二句 ... New York Seafood Company is known for providing our customers with fresh seafood...，因此选 (B)。
4. 此题考阅读能力，由第三段第二句 ... We would like to order a small amount of every kind of seafood... 可知每种海鲜皆订购少许，因此选 (B)。
5. 此题考细节，通过第三段第二句 to be delivered within the next ten days... 可知寄件者希望在十天内收到海鲜，因此选 (C)。

单词 Vocabulary

seafood [ˈsiːfuːd] n 海鲜
store [stɔː] n 商店 v 储存，保管
order [ˈɔːdə] n 订单，订购，秩序
item [ˈaɪtəm] n 条款
objection [əbˈdʒekʃn] n 异议
guarantee [ˌɡærənˈtiː] v 保证
purchase [ˈpɜːtʃəs] v 购买，赢得 n 购买，购买之物
bulk [bʌlk] n 大块，体积
business [ˈbɪznəs] n 商业，职业，事务

Unit 02
谈判 | Negotiation

New TOEIC

Picture 02

情境中可明确指出的单词

1. **back** [bæk] n 椅背
2. **chin** [tʃɪn] n 下巴
3. **conference table** ph 会议桌
4. **gesture** [ˈdʒestʃə] n 手势 v 做手势
5. **blonde** [blɒnd] a 金黄色的，亚麻色的
6. **grin** [grɪn] n / v 露齿微笑
7. **outfit** [ˈaʊtfɪt] n 全套服装
8. **pad** [pæd] n 平板电脑

情境中可延伸记忆的单词

1. **collaborate** [kəˈlæbəreɪt] v 合作
2. **confidence** [ˈkɒnfɪdəns] n 自信心
3. **course** [kɔːs] n 过程，进程
4. **discussion** [dɪˈskʌʃn] n 讨论，商讨
5. **negotiation** [nɪˌɡəʊʃɪˈeɪʃn] n 协商
6. **mutual** [ˈmjuːtʃuəl] a 相互的，共有的，彼此的
7. **specifically** [spəˈsɪfɪkli] ad 明确地
8. **viewpoint** [ˈvjuːpɔɪnt] n 观点

Unit 02 谈判 | Negotiation

back [bæk] n 椅背
The client put his coat on the back of the chair.
客户把他的外套放在椅背上。
- backmost a 最后面的 / back and forth ph 来来回回地

chin [tʃɪn] n 下巴
The man is resting his chin on his thumb and forefinger.
那位男子用他的拇指和食指支撑着下巴。
- chinless a 优柔寡断的 / keep one's chin up 不气馁

conference table ph 会议桌
Give your ideas at the conference table.
在会议桌前，说出你的想法。
- press conference ph 记者招待会

gesture [ˈdʒestʃə] n 手势 v 做手势
The man was making gestures with his hands as he told his story.
这男子在说他的故事的时候不断用手做手势。
- gesticulation n 手势

blonde [blɒnd] a 金黄色的，亚麻色的
The lady sitting in the middle has blonde hair.
中间的那位女子有一头金黄色的头发。
- blond n 金发碧眼的人 / blonde bombshell 金发美人

grin [grɪn] n / v 露齿微笑
There was a big grin on his face after he saw the contract.
他看到合同后，脸上露出了满意的笑容。
- grinning n 露齿笑 / grin from ear to ear 咧嘴笑

outfit [ˈaʊtfɪt] n 全套服装
Our company uniforms consist of three, differently styled outfits.
我们公司的制服有三种不同风格的套装。
- diving outfit ph 潜水装备

pad [pæd] n 平板电脑
There is a pad computer in front of the lady in gray.
穿灰色衣服的女子前面有一台平板电脑。
- mouse pad ph 滑鼠垫

collaborate [kəˈlæbəreɪt] v 合作
It seemed that they would collaborate with each other.
他们双方似乎要进行合作。
● collaboration n 合作

---

confidence [ˈkɒnfɪdəns] n 自信心
Confidence is one of the main points in the negotiation.
自信心是谈判的要点之一。
● confident a 自信的 / confidence in ph 对……信任 / confidence trick 骗局

---

course [kɔːs] n 过程，进程
The course of the negotiation lasted for four hours.
谈判的过程持续了四个小时。
● basic course ph 基础课 / in (the) course of ph 在……过程中

---

discussion [dɪˈskʌʃn] n 讨论，商讨
The atmosphere of this discussion is pleasant.
这次讨论的氛围是愉快的。
● discussant n 商讨者 / discuss v 讨论

---

negotiation [nɪˌɡəʊʃiˈeɪʃn] n 协商
I think they will come to an agreement during the negotiation.
我认为他们会在这次谈判中达成一致意见。
● negotiator n 谈判者 / negotiate v 谈判 / enter into negotiations with sb. 开始和某人谈判

---

mutual [ˈmjuːtʃuəl] a 相互的，共有的，彼此的
They want to reach a mutual agreement in the negotiation.
他们想在这次谈判中达成一个彼此都同意的方案。
● mutual benefit ph 互惠互利

---

specifically [spəˈsɪfɪkli] ad 明确地
They specifically put forward their requirements.
他们明确提出他们的要求。
● specific a 特性 / specification n 说明书，明细单

---

viewpoint [ˈvjuːpɔɪnt] n 观点
Their viewpoints might not be in agreement at the start.
他们的观点在一开始可能会不一致。
● opposite viewpoint ph 对立观点 / perspective n 看法，观点

听力测验 | Part 1 图片描述题

题目
(A) Every man here has a beard.
(B) The negotiation is not going well.
(C) The woman has long, blonde hair.
(D) There are five pieces of paper on the desk.

中译
(A) 这里的每位男子都有胡子。
(B) 这次的谈判进展得不顺利。
(C) 这名女子留着金黄色的长发。
(D) 桌子上有五张纸。

解析与答案

答案：(C)
从照片中我们可以看出，共有四位男子、一位女子，并不是所有的男子都有胡子，而且从他们的表情可以看出，这次的谈判进行得非常顺利，可排除 (A) 和 (B)；桌上只有三张纸，排除 (D)，所以选 (C)。

听力测验 | Part 4 简短独白题

NEW TOEIC

1. What might the final result be if you don't know the cultural difference during negotiations?
   (A) You might terminate the business relationship.
   (B) You might irritate the opposite side.
   (C) There is no harm to their negotiation.
   (D) They will go on their business relationship.

2. Why does cross-cultural communication play an important role in business negotiations?
   (A) It can improve the relationship between you and your partner.
   (B) It may help you have a successful negotiation.
   (C) It will promote cultural communication.
   (D) It makes us have good manners.

3. What should you do when you are going to hold a negotiation?
   (A) You should learn more about your partner.
   (B) You should learn more about their company.
   (C) There is no mention of it.
   (D) You should study the culture of the people with whom you are going to negotiate.

Cross-cultural communication has significant impact on business negotiations. Unfortunately, it hasn't been sufficiently taken into account by people. Cross-cultural communication exerts positive or negative influence on the results of negotiations. It may bring a bright future for a business relationship, but it may also bring an end to a business connection.

Generally, we tend to be kind and distinguish business from entertainment. But our behavior and speech during negotiations may irritate the opposite side, without knowing why. Therefore, you must learn about a person's culture before you begin to negotiate with him.

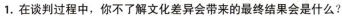

Unit 02 谈判 | Negotiation

中译

1. 在谈判过程中，你不了解文化差异会带来的最终结果会是什么？
   - (A) 中止合作关系。
   - (B) 激怒对方。
   - (C) 对谈判没有影响。
   - (D) 他们会继续合作。

2. 为什么跨文化交流在商业谈判中占有重要的地位？
   - (A) 它会改善你和合作伙伴的关系。
   - (B) 它会促进谈判的顺利完成。
   - (C) 它会促进文化交流。
   - (D) 它会让我们的行为习惯更加合乎礼仪。

3. 当准备进行谈判的时候，你应该怎么做？
   - (A) 对合作伙伴进行更多的了解。
   - (B) 对对方的公司进行更多的了解。
   - (C) 文中没有提到。
   - (D) 了解要和你进行谈判的人的文化。

跨文化交流对商业谈判有至关重要的影响，然而，这并未引起人们足够的重视。跨文化交流会对谈判结果产生正面或负面的影响。它可以让双方的业务关系良性地发展下去，也可以使双方的业务关系中止。

一般来说，我们都希望自己是友善的，并将商业和娱乐区别开，但是有时候我们在谈判中的言行举止会激怒对方，而我们还不知道原因。所以，当你决定要和某人谈判的时候，你一定要先了解对方国家的文化。

解析与答案

答案：1. (A) 2. (B) 3. (D)

1. 听力中提到文化交流会给谈判带来正面和负面的影响，不了解文化差异自然会带来负面的影响，文中提到的负面影响是 but it may also bring an end to a business connection，即中止合作关系，所以选 (A)。
2. 这个题目是在问一个总结性的问题，文化交流给谈判带来的影响要么是促进合作，要么是中止合作，答案中只有 (B) 是正确的。
3. 根据最后一句 you must learn about a person's culture before you begin to negotiate with him 可知，答案选 (D)。

单词 Vocabulary

significant [sɪɡˈnɪfɪkənt] n 象征 a 有意义的，重大的，显著的
exert [ɪɡˈzɜːt] v 运用，发挥
negotiation [nɪˌɡəʊʃɪˈeɪʃn] n 谈判，顺利地通过，转让
distinguish [dɪˈstɪŋɡwɪʃ] v 区分，辨别
irritate [ˈɪrɪteɪt] v 刺激，激怒

阅读测验 | Part 7 文章理解题

Discussion of Best Negotiation Skills and Strategies

Many of us seem to know negotiation skills and strategies, but actually just a few of us really understand them. So, let's talk about negotiation skills and strategies.

In my point of view, negotiation wisdom comes from comprehending the negotiation process and understanding what the other side needs. It requires that we be careful of the tricks that the other side plays in the negotiation process. These tricks lead us to easily believe what the other side says is right and what we think is wrong. The purpose of negotiation is to solve disputes between both sides so that an agreement can be reached in the end. It's better to figure out the tricks of the other side so that we can avoid falling into their traps.

We should prepare everything well before negotiation, including materials and information about the other side, knowing what they value and think. That is to say, "If you know the enemy and know yourself, you need not fear the result of a hundred battles." In business, it is important to know what others need and what they fear. We should grasp the key points and understand why they argue with us.

It takes the best negotiation skills to deeply understand where the contradiction lies and work it out. To begin with, we must know what the other side can compromise on and what they can't. At this time, we must consider the contradiction in their situation and make them compromise rather than give up. That is to say, we have persuaded them successfully and have grasped the point of negotiation.

1. What is the topic of the article?
   (A) Honesty in business.
   (B) Tricks and traps in negotiations.
   (C) Negotiation skills and strategies.
   (D) Cooperation rules.

2. Where does negotiation wisdom come from?
   (A) Understanding the negotiation process and what the other side needs.
   (B) Knowing what the other side does at any time.
   (C) Trying to make sure if the other side trusts us.
   (D) Winning national prizes.

3. What should we be careful of in the negotiation process?
   (A) Tricks of the other side.
   (B) Facial expressions of the other side.
   (C) Voices of the other side.
   (D) Gestures of the other side.

4. What need we not prepare before negotiation?
   (A) Food and drinks.
   (B) Information about the other side.
   (C) Materials about the other side.
   (D) Knowing what they value and think.

5. What does the proverb "If you know the enemy and know yourself, you need not fear the result of a hundred battles" mean in paragraph 3 according to the article?
   (A) If you know your enemy, you are bound to fail.
   (B) If you know your enemy better, you can succeed easier.
   (C) If you don't know your enemy, you are bound to fail without doubt.
   (D) If you don't know your enemy, you can succeed easier.

关于最佳谈判技巧与策略的讨论

我们很多人表面上都知道谈判技巧与策略,但实际上,我们中只有少数人真正地理解。现在让我们谈论一下谈判技巧与策略。

在我看来,谈判的智慧源自对谈判过程以及对方所需的理解。这需要我们留意对方在谈判过程中使用的技巧。这些技巧使我们更容易相信对方说的是正确的、我们想的是错误的。谈判的目的就是解决双方之间存在的异议,最终达成一致。在谈判中能够看出对方的技巧是比较好的,这样能让我们避免陷入他们的圈套。

在谈判之前我们应该准备好一切,包括对方的资料以及信息,知道他们看重什么、他们在想什么。也就是说,"知己知彼,百战百胜"。在商业谈判中,知道别人需要什么、害怕什么尤为重要。我们应该抓住重点,理解他们为什么要和我们争论。

最好的谈判技巧就是深入了解矛盾所在,并加以克服。首先,我们必须知道对方会妥协什么以及不会妥协什么。此时,我们应该站在他们的立场上去考虑矛盾点,并说服他们,而不是使之放弃。也就是说,我们成功地说服了他们,掌握了谈判的要点。

1. 这篇文章的主题是什么?
   (A) 商业中的诚实。
   (B) 谈判中的技巧与圈套。
   (C) 谈判技巧与策略。
   (D) 合作原则。

2. 谈判智慧源自哪里?
   (A) 理解谈判过程,理解对方所需。
   (B) 随时知道对方在做什么。
   (C) 尽量确定对方是否信任我们。
   (D) 获得国家奖项。

3. 在谈判过程中,我们应该留意什么?
   (A) 对方的技巧。
   (B) 对方的面部表情。
   (C) 对方的声音。
   (D) 对方的手势。

4. 在谈判之前,我们不必准备什么?
   (A) 食物与饮料。
   (B) 有关对方的信息。
   (C) 有关对方的资料。
   (D) 知道他们看重什么以及在想什么。

5. 根据文章可知，第三段中的谚语"If you know the enemy and know yourself, you need not fear the result of a hundred battles"是什么意思？
   (A) 了解敌人，你注定会输。
   (B) 对敌人的了解越深，获胜的概率越大。
   (C) 不了解敌人，无疑一定会输。
   (D) 不了解敌人，容易获胜。

解析与答案

答案：1. (C) 2. (A) 3. (A) 4. (A) 5. (B)

1. 这篇文章的题目即为答案 Discussion of Best Negotiation Skills and Strategies，因此选 (C)。
2. 这题在考信息提取能力，可见第二段第一句 ... negotiation wisdom comes from comprehending the negotiation process and understanding what the other side needs，直接点出谈判智慧源于理解谈判过程与对方所需，因此选 (A)。
3. 此题考信息提取能力，题目关键为 be care of，答案可见第二段第二句 It requires that we be careful of the tricks...，因此选 (A)。
4. 此题考细节，从第三段第一句 We should prepare everything well before negotiation, including materials and information about the other side, knowing what they value and think 可知答案应选 (A)。
5. 此题考推断能力，可见第三段第一句 We should prepare everything well before negotiation, including materials and information about the other side, knowing what they value and think 与第三句、第四句 In business, it is important to know what others need and what they fear. We should grasp the key points and understand why they argue with us，谚语前后都在讲述要去了解对方，因此选 (B)。

单词 Vocabulary

strategy ['strætədʒi] n 策略，计谋，战略
apparently [əˈpærəntli] ad 表面上，显然地
wisdom ['wɪzdəm] n 智慧，才智
comprehend [ˌkɒmprɪˈhend] v 理解
process ['prəʊses] n 过程，步骤
dispute [dɪˈspjuːt] n / v 争辩，争执
fear [fɪə(r)] v / n 害怕，恐惧
compromise ['kɒmprəmaɪz] v 妥协 n 妥协（方案），和解
persuade [pəˈsweɪd] v 说服
grasp [ɡrɑːsp] v 抓住，抓住机会，握紧，理解

Unit 03 会议 | Meeting

New TOEIC

Picture 03

情境中可明确指出的单词

1. **attendance** [ə'tendəns] n 出席，到场，出席人数
2. **triangle** ['traɪæŋgl] n 三角形
3. **chair** [tʃeə(r)] n 椅子
4. **diagram** ['daɪəgræm] n 图表
5. **profile** ['prəʊfaɪl] n 侧面，轮廓，外形
6. **screen** [skri:n] n 荧幕
7. **speaker** ['spi:kə(r)] n 演讲者
8. **suit** [su:t] n 套装，西装

情境中可延伸记忆的单词

1. **agree** [ə'gri:] v 同意，赞同
2. **carefully** ['keəfəli] ad 认真地，仔细地
3. **discuss** [dɪ'skʌs] v 讨论，议论，谈论
4. **explain** [ɪk'spleɪn] v 解释，讲解，说明，阐释
5. **meeting** ['mi:tɪŋ] n 会议
6. **note** [nəʊt] n 笔记，摘记，评论，注释
7. **serious** ['sɪəriəs] a 严肃的，庄重的，认真的，真诚的
8. **speech** [spi:tʃ] n 演说，演讲

attendance [əˈtendəns] n. 出席，到场，出席人数

There was a large attendance at the meeting.
有很多人参加此次会议。
- a large / (high) attendance at... 有很多人参加 / 出席…… / be absent from... 缺席……

triangle [ˈtraɪæŋgl] n. 三角形

He pointed at the triangles and said something to his colleagues.
他的手指着那些三角形，并对同事们说着什么。
- equilateral triangle 等边三角形

chair [tʃeə(r)] n. 椅子

Suddenly, the manager threw a chair at him.
突然，经理拿椅子向他扔过来。
- chairman n. 主席 / take the chair 主持会议

diagram [ˈdaɪəgræm] n. 图表

The speaker drew a diagram on the board.
那位演讲者在板上画了一个图表。
- diagrammatic a. 图解的，图表的 / sketch n. 概略，草图

profile [ˈprəʊfaɪl] n. 侧面，轮廓，外形

You could see the speaker's side profile in the picture.
在这张照片中可以看到那位演讲者的侧面轮廓。
- in profile 以侧面 / portrait n. 描写，肖像 / outline n. 轮廓，概要

screen [skriːn] n. 荧幕

It's hard to tell the exact meaning of the diagram on the screen.
很难确切地说荧幕上的那张图表有什么含义。
- screening n. 放映 / screen out 遮挡

speaker [ˈspiːkə(r)] n. 演讲者

Hearing this, the speaker began to flush with excitement.
听到这个，演讲者由于激动开始脸红。
- speakerphone n. 喇叭扩音器 / listener n. 听者

suit [suːt] n. 套装，西装

They were asked to wear black business suits at the meeting.
他们被要求开会时穿着黑色的西装。
- suiting n. 西装衣料 / suit oneself 自便（用于祈使句）

agree [ə'gri:] v 同意，赞同
I guess most of the audience will agree with the speaker.
我猜，大多数的听众都会同意那位演讲者的观点。
● agree with sb. (about / on)... 赞同 / 同意某人

carefully ['keəfəli] ad 认真地，仔细地
The audience is listening to the speaker carefully.
听众们都在认真地听那位演讲者讲解。
● plan carefully 精打细算 / careful 仔细的，小心的

discuss [dɪ'skʌs] v 讨论，议论，谈论
It's likely that they will discuss some important issues at the meeting.
他们可能要在会议上讨论一些重要事宜。
● discussant n 商讨者 / discuss with 讨论

explain [ɪk'spleɪn] v 解释，讲解，说明，阐释
The speaker explained something in detail to the audience.
那位演讲者为听众详细地解说着某件事。
● explain... (in detail) to sb. 为某人详细解说……

meeting ['mi:tɪŋ] n 会议
It seems that someone is absent from the meeting.
看起来有人缺席了此次会议。
● meeting house 教堂 / meeting place 聚会地点 / assembly n 集会 / conference n 会议

note [nəʊt] n 笔记，摘记，评论，注释 v 做笔记
There is no need to take notes of everything the speaker says.
不必把那位演讲者所说的每个字都记录下来。
● take notes of... = note... down 记录……

serious ['sɪəriəs] a 严肃的，庄重的，认真的，真诚的
Please be serious at the meeting.
参加此次会议时请保持严肃的态度。
● seriously ad 严肃地，认真地

speech [spi:tʃ] n 演说，演讲
I wonder who will deliver a speech later at the meeting.
我想知道，稍后谁将在此次会议上发言。
● deliver / make / give a speech 发言

听力测验 | Part 1 图片描述题

(A) There is a small attendance at the meeting.
(B) The speaker is a young lady with long golden hair.
(C) A high percentage of the audience is female.
(D) The speaker is facing his audience.

(A) 只有少数人参加此次会议。
(B) 那位演讲者是一位有着金色长发的年轻女子。
(C) 听众大多都是女性。
(D) 那位演讲者面朝听众。

答案：(D)
从照片中我们可以看到，有很多人参加此次会议，演讲者是一位男子，听众以男子居多，依次排除选项 (A)、(B)、(C)，因此选 (D)。

听力测验 | Part 4 简短独白题

1. What does the speaker talk about at the beginning of the staff meeting?
   (A) His proposal.
   (B) News from a reliable source.
   (C) The competition with other companies for the contract.
   (D) Attendance at the meeting.

2. According to the speaker, what should they give their full attention on?
   (A) The release of the new messaging software.
   (B) How to find a useful source of information.
   (C) Their declining profits.
   (D) The agenda of the staff meeting.

3. Why will they have another meeting in three days?
   (A) To reinvent the messaging software.
   (B) To discuss the falling sales.
   (C) To decide what they should do.
   (D) To decide against the competition.

Good morning, everyone. To start the staff meeting, I'd like to address our competition with other companies for the contract. According to news from a reliable source, we are losing more and more ground to our competitors' latest software programs. Consequently, it's high time that we address the forthcoming release of the new messaging software. We need to come up with a good idea for new messaging software. We may even need to reinvent the software in order to make it more competitive on the market. There will be another meeting to decide what we should do in three days. Now let me explain my proposal in detail to you.

1. 此次员工会议开始时,那位演讲者谈论的是什么事宜?
(A) 他的提案。
(B) 来源可靠的消息。
(C) 为了争取这份合同而与其他家公司竞争。
(D) 参加此次会议的人数。

2. 在那位演讲者看来,他们应该全神贯注地做什么?
(A) 新通信软件的发行。
(B) 如何找到有用来源的信息。
(C) 下滑的利润。
(D) 此次员工会议的议程。

3. 三天后,他们为什么要另行召开会议?
(A) 为了重新研发新通信软件。
(B) 为了商讨下跌的销售额。
(C) 为了决定他们应该做些什么。
(D) 为了决定放弃此次竞争。

大家早安。此次员工会议,首先我想谈谈为了争取这份合同,我们与其他公司的竞争。据可靠来源的消息可知,因为那些最新开发的程序,我们正在失去越来越多的市场占比。因此,是时候集中精力来着手准备即将发行的新通信软件了。我们最好努力想出好主意来研发这款新通信软件。为了使这款软件在市场上更具竞争力,也许,我们甚至需要重新研发这款软件。三天后,将另行召开会议,以便决定我们应该做些什么。现在,我将为你们详细解说我的提案。

答案: 1. (C) 2. (A) 3. (C)

1. 独白开头就直接提到 To start the staff meeting, I'd like to address our competition with other companies for the contract,因此选 (C)。

2. 题目中的 give their full attention to…,意为"全神贯注于……",结合独白中的 … it's high time that we address the forthcoming release of the new messaging software(其中的 address… 意为"集中精力于……,致力于……")可知,应该选 (A)。

3. 演讲中明确提到 There will be another meeting to decide what we should do in three days,因此选 (C)。

单词 Vocabulary

address [ə'dres] v 提出,集中精力,致力于 n 地址
several ['sevrəl] a / pron 几个,一些
according [ə'kɔːdɪŋ] a 相符的,一致的,相应的 ad 按照,根据
reliable [rɪ'laɪəbl] a 可靠的,可信赖的
source [sɔːs] n 来源,出处,发源地
program ['prəʊɡræm] n 程序,编码指令 v 用程序指令
consequently ['kɒnsɪkwəntli] ad 因此,结果
software ['sɒftweə(r)] n 软件

阅读测验 | Part 7 文章理解题

Attention please, all customer service department employees. As you may know, there was an internal meeting to discuss the return and exchange policy in our department yesterday. The detailed memorandum of the meeting is as follows. You are required to review it carefully, in order to have a clear idea of the policy.

As a general rule, customers are required to return or exchange items within ten calendar days of the purchase, providing that they are discontented with our product. They can exchange the product or get a full refund, as long as the product remains unopened and is in the original packaging. However, if the product has been opened, there will be a deduction of 15 percent from the purchase price. In that case, customers will receive the refund after the deduction via store credit, rather than the original method of their payment.

The following products are not permitted to be returned or exchanged:

1. Customized or personalized products
2. Gift cards or gift packaging
3. Any kind of technical support

If customers want to return or exchange a certain defective product, please lead them to the manager's office. There will be special policies on proceeding with such a course of action.

1. Which of the following words is closest in meaning to the word "memorandum" in the first paragraph?

    (A) Memo.

    (B) Memory.

    (C) Agreement.

    (D) Declaration.

2. When should customers return or exchange a certain product?

    (A) Within ten calendar days of the purchase.

    (B) As soon as they receive the product.

    (C) There was no mention in the passage.

    (D) Within two weeks after the receipt of the product.

3. Which one of the following statements is false?

    (A) There was a meeting in the customer service department yesterday.

    (B) Customers can choose to exchange the unopened product or get a full refund.

    (C) Customers can claim a full refund for any purchase of the products.

    (D) A 15 percent fee will be deducted, if the product has been opened.

4. Which of the following products cannot be returned or exchanged?

    (A) Defective products.

    (B) Customized products.

    (C) Unopened products.

    (D) The latest products.

5. When might the customer get a full refund?

    (A) If the product is in its original package.

    (B) If customers are discontented with their products.

    (C) Within twenty calendar days of the purchase.

    (D) There is no mention of it.

客服部的所有员工请注意。也许你们都知道，我们部门昨天召开了一次内部会议，商讨产品退换的政策。此次会议的详细记录公示如下。请仔细审阅，以便清楚地了解这项政策。

通常，顾客购买某件产品十天之内，如果对产品有所不满，可以要求退换。如果这件产品依然是原有包装，并未拆封，顾客可以更换产品或是得到全额退款。然而，如果这件产品已经拆封，则从购买价格中扣除15%。如果是这样的话，扣除费用之后的退款额，顾客只能得到相应的店内抵用券，而不是以原付款方式获得退款额。

此外，以下产品不得退换：

1. 订制的或个性化的产品

2. 礼品卡或礼品包装

3. 任何形式的技术支援

如果顾客想要退换某件不合格产品，请带他们去经理办公室。特殊的状况将有特殊的解决方式。

1. 下列哪个单词与第一段中的单词 memorandum 意义最为相近？
   (A) 备忘录。
   (B) 记忆。
   (C) 协议。
   (D) 声明。

2. 顾客应该在什么时候退换某件产品？
   (A) 购买后的十天之内。
   (B) 一收到产品的时候。
   (C) 短文中并没有提及。
   (D) 收到产品后的两周之内。

3. 下列陈述哪一项是错误的？
   (A) 客服部昨天召开了一次会议。
   (B) 顾客可以选择更换尚未拆封的产品或是得到全额退款。
   (C) 顾客购买的所有产品都可以要求全额退款。
   (D) 如果产品已经拆封，将被扣除 15% 的费用。

4. 下列哪件产品不能退换？
   (A) 不合格的产品。
   (B) 订制的产品。
   (C) 未拆封的产品。
   (D) 最新的产品。

5. 顾客什么时候可以得到全额退款？
   (A) 产品依然是原有包装的时候。
   (B) 顾客对购买商品不满意的时候。
   (C) 购买商品后二十天之内。
   (D) 文中没有提到。

> 答案：1. (A) 2. (A) 3. (C) 4. (B) 5. (A)
>
> 1. 托业考试中常考同义词，此题便是考 memorandum 的同义词。可数名词 memorandum 意为"记录，备忘录"，其复数形式为 memorandums 或是 memoranda；memo 为其缩写形式，通常用于非正式语境中，其复数形式为 memos。因此选 (A)。
> 2. 此题考细节，可见第二段第一句中 ... customers are required to return or exchange items within ten calendar days of the purchase...，因此选 (A)。
> 3. 此题考正误判断，选项 (A) 可见第一段第二句，选项 (B) 可在第二段第二句，选项 (D) 则在第二段第三句，这三个选项都可以在文中找到相关陈述，只有选项 (C)，与第二段第三句、倒数第二段内容不符，因此选 (C)。
> 4. 此题同样是考细节，短文中有明确表述 ... The following products are not permitted to be returned or exchanged...，随即列举不能退换的三类产品，只有选项 (B) 符合文中信息，因此选 (B)。
> 5. 此题考细节，短文中明确表示 They can exchange the product or get a full refund, ... , in the original packaging，因此选 (A)。

单词 Vocabulary

attention [ə'tenʃn] n. 注意
internal [ɪn'tɜːnl] a. 内部的，国内的
return [rɪ'tɜːn] v./n. 归还，带回，返回
policy ['pɒləsi] n. 政策，方针
calendar ['kælɪndə(r)] n. 日历
providing [prə'vaɪdɪŋ] conj. 假如，倘若，在……条件下
discontented [ˌdɪskən'tentɪd] a. 不满意的，感到不满的
original [ə'rɪdʒənl] a. 原来的，最初的，原始的，新颖的
packaging ['pækɪdʒɪŋ] n. 包装，包装方式
deduction [dɪ'dʌkʃn] n. 扣除，减除，推理，演绎

Unit 04
销售 | Sale

New TOEIC

Picture 04

情境中可明确指出的单词

1. **bleach blonde** [ph] 淡金色头发
2. **blind** [blaɪnd] [n] 百叶窗
3. **business suit** [ph] 西装
4. **marker** [ˈmɑːkə(r)] [n] 白板笔
5. **opposite** [ˈɒpəzɪt] [p] 在……对面
6. **pillar** [ˈpɪlə(r)] [n] 柱子，圆柱
7. **pencil** [ˈpensl] [n] 铅笔
8. **watch** [wɒtʃ] [n] 手表

情境中可延伸记忆的单词

1. **assistant** [əˈsɪstənt] [n] 助手
2. **Caucasian** [kɔːˈkeɪziən] [n] 白种人
3. **explain** [ɪkˈspleɪn] [v] 解说
4. **expression** [ɪkˈspreʃn] [n] 表情，表达
5. **form** [fɔːm] [n] 表格
6. **lighting** [ˈlaɪtɪŋ] [n] 采光，照明
7. **performance** [pəˈfɔːməns] [n] 业绩
8. **proposal** [prəˈpəʊzl] [n] 提案

bleach blonde [ph] 淡金色头发
The lady who is standing before the board has bleach blonde hair.
站在白板前的女子有一头淡金色的头发。
- bleacher [n] 漂白剂

blind [blaɪnd] [n] 百叶窗
The blinds in the conference room are big.
会议室的百叶窗很大。
- blindness [n] 失明 / blind as a bat [ph] 看不清的，不易看清的

business suit [ph] 西装
The man wearing a business suit is making a gesture.
穿西装的男子正在做手势。
- business philosophy [ph] 经营理念 / business class [ph] 商务舱

marker ['mɑːkə(r)] [n] 白板笔
The lady is pointing at the chart on the board with a marker.
女子用一支白板笔指着白板上的图表。
- marker gene [ph] 标志基因 / eraser [n] 板擦

opposite ['ɒpəzɪt] [p] 在……对面
We don't know how many people are sitting opposite the male.
我们不知道这位男性的对面坐了几个人。
- oppositive [a] 反对的 / opposite number [ph] 职务或地位相当的人

pillar ['pɪlə(r)] [n] 柱子，圆柱
The saleswoman stood behind the pillar supporting the roof.
那个女售货员站在支撑屋顶的柱子的后边。
- pillared [a] 成柱状的 / pillar box [ph] 邮筒

pencil ['pensl] [n] 铅笔
The man is holding a yellow pencil in his left hand.
男子的左手拿着一支黄色的铅笔。
- stationery [n] 文具

watch [wɒtʃ] [n] 手表
The salesgirl is accustomed to wearing a watch on her wrist.
那位女售货员习惯在手腕上戴一块手表。
- watchful [a] 注意的 / watch for [ph] 等待

assistant [əˈsɪstənt] n 助手
I asked my assistant to take over when I was on business.
我让助手在我出差的时候接管我的工作。
🔗 assistance n 援助

Caucasian [kɔːˈkeɪziən] n 白种人
From the skin complexion, we can know that the person in the picture is Caucasian.
我们从肤色可以知道照片中的人是白种人。
🔗 Caucasian male phr 白人男子

---

explain [ɪkˈspleɪn] v 解说
Now, explain the data on the white board to us.
现在，向我们解释一下白板上的资料。
🔗 explanation n 说明 / explain oneself phr 解释自己的行为

---

expression [ɪkˈspreʃn] n 表达，表情
His bright clothing is an expression of his personality.
他明亮的衣着是他的个性的展现。
🔗 expressionism n 表现主义 / beyond expression phr 无法表达

---

form [fɔːm] n 表格
Please fill out the form with your information.
请在表格中填写你的信息。
🔗 former n 模型 / true to form phr 一如往常

---

lighting [ˈlaɪtɪŋ] n 采光，照明
The office has a big French window, so the natural lighting must be very good.
办公室有一个大落地窗，所以自然采光一定很好。
🔗 lightsome a 轻盈的

---

performance [pəˈfɔːməns] n 业绩
The sales performance of this team is very good this year.
这个团队今年的销售业绩很好。
🔗 performance evaluation phr 性能评估

---

proposal [prəˈpəʊzl] n 提案
He put forward a good proposal in this meeting.
他在这次会议上提出了一个不错的提案。
🔗 proponent n 支持者 / propose v 提议 / proposer n 提议人

听力测验 | Part 1 图片描述题

(A) One woman is pointing at the computer screen.
(B) One man is wearing a pair of glasses.
(C) There is a cup near the right hand of the man.
(D) Everyone has a notebook and pen in hand.

(A) 一位女子在指着电脑荧屏。
(B) 有一名男子戴着眼镜。
(C) 男子的右手边有一个杯子。
(D) 每个人手中都有一本笔记本和一支笔。

答案：(B)
从图片中我们可以看到有两名女子、两名男子，其中一名男子戴着眼镜，还有一名男子指着电脑荧屏；并不是所有人手中都有一本笔记本和笔，而杯子都是在男子的左手边，所以选 (B)。

听力测验 | Part 4 简短独白题

NEW TOEIC

1. Which of the following is not the reason why people are discontented with laundry powders?
   (A) Laundry powders can't clean properly.
   (B) They will make clothing faded.
   (C) They will make clothing worn.
   (D) They will hurt hands.

2. What's the main difference between Marina Deluxe and other laundry powders?
   (A) Ingredients.
   (B) Fragrance.
   (C) Environmentally friendly.
   (D) Easy-to-get.

3. Where can you get Marina Deluxe Laundry Powder?
   (A) Only online.
   (B) All grocery stores.
   (C) All supermarkets.
   (D) B and C.

Washing clothing with laundry powder perplexes many people because they think clothing can't be cleaned completely and laundry powder will make clothing faded or worn sometimes. But you will never be worried about that after trying Marina Deluxe Laundry Powder!

There are special ingredients in Marina Deluxe Laundry Powder which are a great help in cleaning clothing. Your clothing will be bright after washing, and you will smell a gentle fragrance. What's more, environmentally friendly Marina Deluxe is different from other laundry powders. So, it won't do harm to the environment.

Marina Deluxe is the best choice for your family. You can find it in all grocery stores and supermarkets.

中译

1. 下列不是人们对洗衣粉感到不满的原因是哪个？
   (A) 洗得不够干净。
   (B) 会使衣服褪色。
   (C) 会使衣服容易破损。
   (D) 伤手。

2. Marina Deluxe 和其他洗衣粉之间最主要的区别是什么？
   (A) 成分。
   (B) 香味。
   (C) 环保的。
   (D) 容易买到。

3. 你在哪里可以买到 Marina Deluxe 洗衣粉？
   (A) 只能在网上买到。
   (B) 所有的杂货店。
   (C) 所有的超市。
   (D) B 选项和 C 选项。

用洗衣粉洗衣服让很多人感到很困扰，因为人们认为洗衣粉洗不干净衣服，而且有时用洗衣粉洗衣服会使衣服褪色或破损。但是，你试过 Marina Deluxe 洗衣粉之后就不会担心这些问题了！

Marina Deluxe 洗衣粉中含有特殊的成分，这些成分可以将衣服洗得更干净。洗完后的衣服会特别干净亮丽，而且还有一股淡淡的香味。更重要的是，Marina Deluxe 洗衣粉与其他的洗衣粉不同，Marina Deluxe 是一种环保型的洗衣粉，所以，它不会对环境造成污染。

Marina Deluxe 洗衣粉是家人最好的选择，而且你可以在所有的杂货店和超市买到。

解析与答案

答案：1.(D) 2.(C) 3.(D)

1. 根据 they think clothing can't be cleaned and laundry powder will make clothing faded or worn sometimes 可知，(A)、(B)、(C) 是正确的，所以选 (D)。
2. 根据独白中 What's more, environmentally friendly Marina Deluxe is different from other laundry powders 可知，最主要的区别是 Marina Deluxe 洗衣粉是环保型的，所以选 (C)。
3. 根据最后一句 You can find it in all grocery stores and supermarkets 可知正确答案是 (D)。

单词 Vocabulary

perplex [pə'pleks] v 使困惑，使复杂化
laundry ['lɔːndri] n 洗衣房，要洗的衣服，洗好的衣服
ingredient [ɪn'griːdiənt] n 成分，原料
gentle ['dʒentl] a 文雅的，温和的 v 使温和
fragrance ['freɪɡrəns] n 芬芳，香味
environmentally [ɪnˌvaɪrən'mentəli] ad 在环境方面
grocery ['ɡrəʊsəri] n 杂货店

阅读测验 | Part 7 文章理解题

Attention: Purchasers for Skincare Products

We are Vanilla Skincare Product Co., Ltd. Our main products are facial cleanser, toner, sun cream, bath cream, shampoo, etc. We are located in the second block of the business center, which is really busy. We have more than ten retail outlets scattered in the city. If you are interested, you can come to us!

It is worth mentioning that we see the business opportunities for sales of our products on the Internet, because there is a huge increase in the Internet trade. We will develop our company on the Internet gradually. But for now, our products are just available to walk-in customers. Our shopping guides have a good command of English, German, Spanish and French, so foreigners are also welcome!

If you purchase our products, you can enjoy the follwing services:

a. You can buy products at a ten percentage discount.

b. We can teach you how to use our products properly.

c. If you bring us a customer, you will be given a bottle of toner for free.

d. Upon purchases of over five hundred dollars, an additional 50 dollars of products will be given for free.

If you show interest in our products, you can contact us at 555-6633 or vanillaskincare.@gmail.com. If you have any problems, please feel free to contact us. We will try our best to help you.

What are you hesitating for? We look forward to your coming!

1. What are the products of Vanilla Co., Ltd?
    (A) Skincare products.
    (B) Household appliances.
    (C) Furniture.
    (D) Classes.

2. What does the company think of business on the Internet?
    (A) They regard it as rubbish.
    (B) They see nothing.
    (C) They have no idea about it.
    (D) They see business opportunities and will develop their business on the Internet.

3. How much would a customer pay if they bought one hundred dollars worth of products?
    (A) Eighty dollars.
    (B) Ninety dollars.
    (C) One hundred dollars.
    (D) One hundred and ten dollars.

4. What can the customer get if they buy more than five hundred dollars worth of products?
    (A) A bottle of toner for free.
    (B) Fifty dollars.
    (C) Fifty dollars worth of products for free.
    (D) Nothing.

5. Which of the following is false?
    (A) The shopping guides understand English, Germany, Spanish and French.
    (B) The customer buys products at a discount.
    (C) The company has developed on the Internet.
    (D) The customers can consult with them at 555-6633.

注意：护肤产品购买者

我们是香草护肤产品有限公司。我们的主要产品是洗面乳、化妆水、防晒乳、沐浴乳、洗发水等。我们位于繁忙的商业中心的第二条街区。同时，在这座城市中，我们有十名家零售店。如果你感兴趣，就来找我们吧！

值得一提的是，我们看到了网络上销售我们产品的商机，因为网络交易巨幅上升。我们将逐渐在网上发展我们的公司。但是到目前为止，我们的产品只针对来店顾客。我们的导购员有良好的英语、德语、西班牙语以及法语表达能力，因此我们也欢迎外国客户！

若购买我们的产品，您可以享受如下服务：

一、购买商品可以享受九折优惠。

二、我们可以教您如何正确使用产品。

三、如果您给我们带来一位顾客，将免费赠送您一瓶化妆水。

四、消费高于五百美元，可以免费赠送您五十美元的产品。

如果您对我们的产品感兴趣，可以拨打电话555-6633，或者发邮件至vanillaskincare@gmail.com联系我们。如果您有任何问题，请随时联系我们。我们竭尽全力帮您解决。

您还在犹豫什么？期待您的光临！

1. 香草有限公司的产品是什么？
   (A) 护肤产品。
   (B) 家用电器。
   (C) 家具。
   (D) 课程。

2. 这家公司认为电子商务怎么样？
   (A) 他们将其视为垃圾。
   (B) 他们什么都看不到。
   (C) 他们没有想法。
   (D) 他们看到商机，并将在网络上做生意。

3. 如果顾客买一件价值一百美元的商品，应付多少钱？
   (A) 八十美元。
   (B) 九十美元。
   (C) 一百美元。
   (D) 一百一十美元。

4. 如果消费五百美元以上，顾客能得到什么？
   (A) 一瓶免费化妆水。
   (B) 五十美元。
   (C) 免费获得价值五十美元的产品。
   (D) 没有任何东西。

5. 下列哪一项说法是错误的？
   (A) 导购员精通英语、德语、西班牙语以及法语。
   (B) 顾客购买产品可以打折。
   (C) 公司已经在网上发展。
   (D) 顾客可以拨打 555-6633 咨询。

答案：1. (A) 2. (D) 3. (B) 4. (C) 5. (C)

1. 此题答案十分明显，可见标题 Purchasers for Skincare Products 或正文第一段第一句、第二句 We are Vanilla Skincare Product Co., Ltd. Our main products are facial cleanser, toner, sun cream, bath cream, shampoo, etc.，因此选 (A)。

2. 此题考信息提取能力，答案可见第二段第一句 ... we see the business opportunities for sales of our products on the Internet...，因此选 (D)。

3. 此题考思维转换能力，可见第二段罗列服务中的第一条 ... You can buy products at a ten percentage discount...，商品打九折，一百美元的九折是九十美元，因此选 (B)。

4. 此题考信息提取能力，答案在第二段的最后一句 Upon purchases of over five hundred dollars, an additional 50 dollars of products will be given for free，因此选 (C)。注意，化妆水是介绍顾客来店的人才能得到。

5. 此题考细节，第二段提到"将在"网络上发展，再看第二段第三句 But for now, our products are just available to walk-in customers，因此选 (C)。

单词 Vocabulary

purchaser ['pɜːtʃəsə(r)] n 购买者
skincare ['skɪnkeə(r)] a 护肤的
facial ['feɪʃl] a 面部的，表面的
mention ['menʃn] v 提到，说起 n 提及，提名表扬
opportunity [ˌɒpə'tjuːnəti] n 机会
Internet ['ɪntənet] n 网络
command [kə'mɑːnd] v 掌握，命令，指挥 n 运用能力
foreigner ['fɒrənə(r)] n 外国人
discount ['dɪskaʊnt] n 打折

Unit 05
信件、电子邮件
Letters and E-mails

New TOEIC

Picture 05

情境中可明确指出的单词

1. **bookcase** ['bʊkkeɪs] n 书柜
2. **corner** ['kɔːnə(r)] n 墙角
3. **doorframe** ['dɔːfreɪm] n 门框
4. **brown** [braʊn] n 棕色 a 棕色的
5. **fax machine** ph 传真机
6. **shadow** ['ʃædəʊ] n 影子
7. **smile** [smaɪl] n / v 微笑
8. **woodwork** ['wʊdwɜːk] n 木制品

情境中可延伸记忆的单词

1. **address** [ə'dres] n 地址
2. **affirm** [ə'fɜːm] v 确认，证实
3. **letter-size** ['letə saɪz] a 信纸规格的
4. **patient** ['peɪʃnt] a 有耐心的
5. **receptionist** [rɪ'sepʃənɪst] n 接待人员
6. **refer** [rɪ'fɜː(r)] v 使求助于，查询
7. **E-mail** ['iːmeɪl] n 电子邮件（= electronic mail）
8. **secret** ['siːkrət] n 秘密

Unit 05 信件、电子邮件 | Letters and E-mails

bookcase ['bʊkkeɪs] n 书柜
Many papers are crammed into the **bookcase**.
书柜里被塞进了许多纸张。
- **bookcase drier** 书柜式干燥器 / **bookend** n 书挡

---

corner ['kɔːnə(r)] n 墙角
I saw the **corner** of the envelope sticking out from under the carpet.
我看到毯子下露出了信封的一角。
- **cornered** a 有角的 / **corner the market** ph 垄断市场

---

doorframe ['dɔːfreɪm] n 门框
We can only see a part of the **doorframe** in the picture.
从照片中我们只能看见门框的一部分。
- **doorframe wall** ph 门框墙

---

brown [braʊn] n 棕色 a 棕色的
The postman with **brown** hair used to be a cook.
那个棕色头发的邮差以前是厨师。
- **browning** n 棕色着色剂 / **brown bagging** ph 自备午餐

---

fax machine ph 传真机
You can send your letter to your friends by the **fax machine**.
你可以通过传真机把信件传给你的朋友。
- **fax** n 传真 / **receive** v 接收（传真）

---

shadow ['ʃædəʊ] n 影子
The postman's **shadow** fell on the wall.
邮差的影子倒映在墙上。
- **shadowy** a 朦胧的 / **be afraid of one's own shadow** ph 非常胆怯

---

smile [smaɪl] n / v 微笑
Kate **smiled** when she received her boyfriend's letter.
收到男朋友的信件时，凯特笑了。
- **smiley** a 微笑的 / **smile at** ph 向……微笑 / **all smiles** ph 微笑

---

woodwork ['wʊdwɜːk] n 木制品
It's clear that the bookcase is **woodwork**.
很显然，这个书柜是木制品。
- **woodworker** n 木工 / **woodworking** n 木工艺 / **metalwork** n 金属制品

address [ə'dres] n. 地址

You must write the detailed address on the envelope.
你必须在信封上写上详细的地址。
- addressee n. 收件人 / sender n. 寄件人 / address book n. 通信录

---

affirm [ə'fɜːm] v. 确认，证实

I would like to affirm our commitment to peace between our countries.
我想要确认我们国家之间和平的承诺。
- affirmable a. 可断言的 / affirmance n. 断言

---

letter-size ['letə saɪz] a. 信纸规格的

I guess the letter-size paper in the bookcase is used for writing letters.
我猜书柜上信纸大小的纸张是用来写信的。
- letter-size paper n. 信纸大小的纸 / letter box n. 邮筒，信箱

---

patient ['peɪʃnt] a. 有耐心的

Be patient when the postman doesn't deliver your letter on time.
当邮差没有准时送信给你时，要有耐心。
- patience n. 耐性 / patient of n. 能忍受 / patient with n. 对……有耐心

---

receptionist [rɪ'sepʃənɪst] n. 接待人员

The man in black is a receptionist in the office.
这位穿黑色衣服的男子是这间办公室的接待人员。
- reception room n. 接待室

---

refer [rɪ'fɜː(r)] v. 使求助于，查询

She is going on vacation, so she will refer the case to her coworker.
她要去度假，所以她将向同事求助做这项工作。
- reference n. 参考 / refer to n. 提及，参考

E-mail ['iːmeɪl] n. 电子邮件 (= electronic mail)

Excuse me, can you tell me how to send E-mails?
打扰了，你能告诉我怎样发送电子邮件吗？
- E-mail address n. 电子邮箱地址

---

secret ['siːkrət] n. 秘密

The contents of the E-mail remain a secret.
这封电子邮件的内容是个秘密。
- secretive a. 秘密的 / secret ballot n. 无记名投票 / secret agent n. 间谍

听力测验 | Part 1 图片描述题

(A) The woman is sitting on a chair.
(B) The woman is reading a book.
(C) There is a cup in her left hand.
(D) There is a desktop computer on her desk.

(A) 这位女子坐在椅子上。
(B) 这位女子在看一本书。
(C) 她的左手拿着一个杯子。
(D) 她的桌子上有一台台式电脑。

答案：(C)

从图片上可以看出，这位女子是坐在桌子的一角，左手拿着一个杯子，右手拿着一片纸，她正在看这片纸，桌子上有一个笔记本电脑，所以排除 (A)、(B)、(D)，选 (C)。

听力测验 | Part 4 简短独白题

1. Why will Christine have a busy schedule?
   (A) She will attend an important occasion.
   (B) She will organize the company's Annual General Meeting.
   (C) She will go to visit her friend.
   (D) She will do a favor for her friend.

2. Who will attend the company's Annual General Meeting?
   (A) Investment fund managers.
   (B) Small shareholders.
   (C) Top executives.
   (D) All of the above.

3. Why does the speaker mention Cater Gourmet?
   (A) The speaker wants to invite Christine to have dinner there.
   (B) This is a catering service which the speaker wants to recommend to Christine for the meeting.
   (C) The speaker is an employee of Cater Gourmet.
   (D) The speaker wants Christine to have a look at their flyer.

Hello, Christine!

I have learned that you are the organizer of the company's Annual General Meeting which will be held next week. Considering this momentous occasion, I know you are busy preparing for the meeting. If there is a need, I can help at anytime.

First, I'd like to tell you something important from my experience. There will be many people at the meeting, including investment fund managers, top executives, and small shareholders. So, you should make sure that the food will agree with them. Given that, you should sample the food yourself first.

Have you heard of Cater Gourmet? It's a new catering service. I think the food they provide won't disappoint you or anyone else. You can have a look at their flyer.

Unit 05 信件、电子邮件 | Letters and E-mails

中译

1. 克丽斯汀为什么行程繁忙？
   (A) 她要出席一个重大的场合。
   (B) 她要负责公司的年度大会。
   (C) 她要去拜访她的朋友。
   (D) 她要去帮助她的朋友。

2. 谁会出席公司的年度大会？
   (A) 投资基金经理。
   (B) 小股东。
   (C) 最高行政官。
   (D) 以上所有人。

3. 说话者为什么提到 Cater Gourmet？
   (A) 说话者想邀请克丽斯汀去那里吃饭。
   (B) 这是说话者为克丽斯汀举办年度大会推荐的宴会服务。
   (C) 说话者是 Cater Gourmet 的一名员工。
   (D) 说话者想让克丽斯汀看看他们的宣传单。

克丽斯汀，你好！

我得知你是下周举办公司年度大会的组织者。考虑到那是个非常重要的场合，所以我想你接下来会很忙。如果有需要的话，我可以随时过来帮忙。

首先，根据我的经验，我想告诉你一些重要的事情。年度大会会有很多人，包括投资基金经理、最高行政官和小股东等人。所以，你要确保提供的食物会合他们的胃口。鉴于这一点，你可以事先品尝一下。

你听说过 Cater Gourmet 吗？这是一家新的宴会服务公司。我认为他们提供的食物一定不会让你或其他人失望。你可以看看他们的宣传单。

解析与答案

答案：1. (B) 2. (D) 3. (B)

1. 独白的开头就提到克丽斯汀是这次年度大会的负责人，所以她接下来会很忙，答案选 (B)。
2. 根据听力中 There will be many people at the meeting, including investment fund managers, top executives and small shareholders 可知，(A)、(B)、(C) 选项都包括，所以选 (D)。
3. 说话者知道克丽斯汀要为年度大会准备食物，因为她认为这家宴会提供的食物会让人很满意，所以将其推荐给克丽斯汀，答案选 (B)。(D) 虽然也有提到，但并非说话者提到 Cater Gourmet 的主因。

单词 Vocabulary

occasion [əˈkeɪʒn] n 场合，时机，理由 v 引起
momentous [məˈmentəs] a 重大的，重要的
investment [ɪnˈvestmənt] n 投资，封锁
shareholder [ˈʃeəhəʊldə(r)] n 股东（美式为 stockholder）
catering [ˈkeɪtərɪŋ] n 承办酒席，给养
disappoint [ˌdɪsəˈpɔɪnt] v 使失望

阅读测验 | Part 7 文章理解题

NEW TOEIC

To: Sheldon Green

From: Oliver Queen

Subject: The problem discussed at the meeting

Dear Mr. Green,

Thank you for sharing your idea with us yesterday at the meeting. All of the people in our group thought it a meaningful meeting. For now, all of us understand the program better, and I think we can update our software to help you with your program.

You know that the primary functions of our software fit your program well, so we are trying to work out a way to make it suit various kinds of needs and make it more adaptable and competitive in the market. This will be more costly, which I mentioned yesterday at the meeting, but we will try to lower cost, and we will present you all of the details in an e-mail. As soon as we work out the plan, we will let you know.

The other reason I am writing to you is that I'd like to tell you that our professional, John, will provide you with the related materials within a week before our group begins to offer his services to you. John himself, will contact you to discuss this problem because you two have cooperated with each other before.

Lastly, I'd like to invite you to attend the next meeting in the conference center, next Tuesday so that we can have a further discussion on these matters in detail. If there is no objection, we will sign the contract. If you have any questions, please let me know.

Regards,

Oliver Queen

Unit 05 信件、电子邮件 | Letters and E-mails

1. **Why did Oliver Queen send e-mail to Sheldon Green?**
   (A) To invite Sheldon Green to attend a ball.
   (B) To discuss a program.
   (C) To have dinner together.
   (D) To borrow his car.

2. **When was the last meeting held?**
   (A) Last week.
   (B) The day before yesterday.
   (C) Yesterday.
   (D) This afternoon.

3. **According to this e-mail, who will provide Sheldon Green with the related materials?**
   (A) Oliver.
   (B) John.
   (C) Oliver's assistant.
   (D) Oliver's manager

4. **Where will the next meeting be held?**
   (A) In Sheldon's department.
   (B) In Sheldon's office.
   (C) In the conference center.
   (D) Not mentioned in the e-mail.

5. **What kind of features does Oliver not want the software to have?**
   (A) Competitiveness.
   (B) Adaptation.
   (C) High-efficiency.
   (D) Low-efficiency.

收件人：谢尔敦·格林
寄件者：奥利弗·奎恩
主题：会议上讨论的问题

尊敬的格林先生：

十分感谢您在昨天的会议上与我们分享您的想法。我们团队所有人都认为那场会议十分有意义。现在我们都更加理解这项计划，我认为我们可以更新软件帮助您完成计划。

您知道我们软件的基本功能十分适合您的计划，所以我们正在努力找出让它适应不同需要的方法，使之在市场上具有更强的适应性与竞争力。但是这样会产生更多的费用，这点我在昨天的会议上提到了，我们会尽量降低费用，我们将在电子邮件中向您呈现一切细节。我们一做出计划，就会通知您。

我写信给您的另一个原因是想告诉您，在我们团队开始向您提供服务之前，我们的专业人员约翰将会在一周之内向您提供相关资料。当然，是约翰他自己，而不是我，与您联系讨论这个问题，因为你们两个之前合作过。

最后，我想邀请您来参加下一次在会议中心举办的会议（下周二），我们会对接下来的事情进行进一步的详细讨论。如果没有异议，我们将会签订合约。如果有问题，请让我知道。

　　此致
敬礼！

奥利弗·奎恩

1. 奥利弗·奎恩为什么寄邮件给谢尔敦·格林？
   (A) 邀请谢尔敦·格林参加舞会。
   (B) 讨论专案。
   (C) 一起吃晚餐。
   (D) 借车。

2. 上次会议什么时候举行？
   (A) 上周。
   (B) 前天。
   (C) 昨天。
   (D) 今天下午。

3. 根据这封邮件可知，谁将提供相关资料给谢尔敦·格林？
   (A) 奥利弗。
   (B) 约翰。
   (C) 奥利弗的助理。
   (D) 奥利弗的经理。

Unit 05 信件、电子邮件 | Letters and E-mails

4. 下次会议将在哪里举行？
   (A) 谢尔敦的公寓。
   (B) 谢尔敦的办公室。
   (C) 会议中心。
   (D) 邮件中并未提及。

5. 奥利弗不想让软件有什么特点？
   (A) 竞争性。
   (B) 适应性。
   (C) 高效性。
   (D) 低效性。

解析与答案

答案：1. (B) 2. (C) 3. (B) 4. (C) 5. (D)

1. 此题考细节，在邮件的第三句开始 ... understand the program better and I think we can update our software to help you with your program... 寄件者就提出专案的问题，因此选 (B)。
2. 此题同样是考细节，可见第一段第一句中 ... yesterday at the meeting（上次会议是昨天开的），因此选 (C)。
3. 此题考分辨能力，可见邮件的第七句 ... our professional, John, will provide you with the related materials within a week...，因此选 (B)。
4. 此题考阅读能力，在邮件正文的倒数第三句提到下次会议的相关信息 ... the next meeting in the conference center...，因此选 (C)。
5. 此题考阅读分析能力，在邮件正文的第四句与第五句 ... make it more adaptable and competitive in the market. This will be more costly, which... we will try to lower cost...，因故选 (D)。

单词 Vocabulary

meaningful [ˈmiːnɪŋfl] a 有意义的
program [ˈprəʊɡræm] n 专案，程序，节目
software [ˈsɒftweə(r)] n 软件
primary [ˈpraɪməri] a 主要的，最初的，基本的
suit [suːt] v 适合，相配
adaptable [əˈdæptəbl] a 能适应的
professional [prəˈfeʃnl] n 专业人员 a 职业上的
material [məˈtɪəriəl] n 材料，原料 a 物质的，身体上的
conference [ˈkɒnfərəns] n 会议，讨论
objection [əbˈdʒekʃn] n 异议，反对（的理由），缺点

Unit 06
电话、传真 | Phone and Fax

New TOEIC

Picture 06

情境中可明确指出的单词

1. **blouse** [blaʊz] n. 女式衬衫
2. **desk** [desk] n. 办公桌
3. **desktop** [ˈdesktɒp] n. 台式电脑
4. **display** [dɪˈspleɪ] n. 荧幕
5. **frame** [freɪm] n. 相框
6. **handset** [ˈhændset] n. 电话听筒
7. **notebook** [ˈnəʊtbʊk] n. 笔记本
8. **phone** [fəʊn] n. 电话

情境中可延伸记忆的单词

1. **communicate** [kəˈmjuːnɪkeɪt] v. 沟通
2. **customer** [ˈkʌstəmə(r)] n. 客户
3. **inquire** [ɪnˈkwaɪə] v. 质疑，询问
4. **manipulate** [məˈnɪpjuleɪt] v. 掌控，操作
5. **record** [ˈrekɔːd] n. 记录
    [rɪˈkɔːd] v. 记录
6. **reply** [rɪˈplaɪ] n./v. 回应，答复
7. **service** [ˈsɜːvɪs] n. 服务
8. **tone** [təʊn] n. 语气 v. 用某种语调说

Unit 06 电话、传真 | Phone and Fax

blouse [blaʊz] n. 女式衬衫
All of the employees are dressed in light blouses.
所有的雇员都穿着浅色衬衫。
- sweater blouse 毛线衫上衣

desk [desk] n. 办公桌
The manager put all his client materials on the desk.
经理把他所有客户的资料都放在桌子上。
- desk lamp 台灯 / desk job 办公室工作 / desk jockey 坐办公室的人

desktop ['desktɒp] n. 台式电脑
Our office desktops were all attacked by a hacker.
我们的台式电脑都被黑客攻击了。
- desktop search 桌面搜索 / desk man 坐办公室的人 / desk job 办公室工作

display [dɪ'spleɪ] n. 显示器
Can't you see the forms on the visual display unit?
你难道看不见显示器上的表格吗?
- display system 显示系统 / on display 展览,展出

frame [freɪm] n. 相框
He put a picture frame on the wall to decorate his office.
他在墙上挂一幅图片相框来装饰他的办公室。
- framing n. 框架 / frame of reference 准则

handset ['hændset] n. 电话听筒
The lady clamped the handset to her ear.
这位女子把电话听筒贴在她耳边。
- megaphone 话筒,扩音器

notebook ['nəʊtbʊk] n. 笔记本
Take your notebook to the meeting this afternoon.
今天下午开会的时候带你的笔记本。
- notepaper n. 信纸 / note n. 笔记 v. 记下 / noted a. 有名的

phone [fəʊn] n. 电话
The client complained about their service on the phone.
客户打电话抱怨他们的服务。
- pay phone 公用电话 / phone booth 公用电话亭

communicate [kəˈmjuːnɪkeɪt] v 沟通

Leaders are supposed to communicate with employees at all times.
领导者应该时常与员工交流。
- communicant n 传达消息的 / communication n 沟通

customer [ˈkʌstəmə(r)] n 客户

The lady is answering a telephone call from a customer.
这位女子正在接客户打来的电话。
- customer first 客户至上 / customer satisfaction 顾客满意度

inquire [ɪnˈkwaɪə] v 质疑，询问

The customer calls the lady to inquire something about the production.
客户打电话给女子询问有关产品的事。
- inquirer n 调查者 / inquire for 求见 / inquire into 调查

manipulate [məˈnɪpjuleɪt] v 掌控，操作

This job requires you to manipulate the computer.
这份工作需要你操作电脑。
- manipulation n 操纵

record [ˈrekɔːd] n 记录 [rɪˈkɔːd] v 记录

The lady is taking records over the phone.
女子通过打电话做记录。
- recorder n 答录机 / recordable a 可记录的 / record-breaking a 破纪录的

reply [rɪˈplaɪ] n / v 回应，答复

The lady will reply to the customer in a short time.
这位女子会在短时间内回复顾客。
- reply for 代表……作答 / in reply 作为答复 / answer v 回答 / respond v 回应

service [ˈsɜːvɪs] n 服务

The lady is a service provider.
这位女子是一位客服人员。
- servicing n 维修 / service charge 服务费 / service industry n 服务业

tone [təʊn] n 语气 v 用某种语调说

The lady is talking with her manager in a respectable tone.
女子用敬重的语气与经理谈话。
- toneless a 沉闷的 / tone in with 与……相配

听力测验 | Part 1 图片描述题

 (A) The man is dressed in a black suit.
(B) The man is on the phone.
(C) The man is wearing a pair of glasses.
(D) The man is looking at the computer.

 (A) 男子穿着黑色的西装。
(B) 男子正在打电话。
(C) 男子戴着一副眼镜。
(D) 男子在看电脑。

答案：(B)
从图片中可以看出，这名男子穿着衬衫，正在接或是打电话，眼睛看着他左手中的一片纸，而他没有戴眼镜，所以选 (B)。

听力测验 | Part 4 简短独白题

1. Where will the talker go for his business trip?
   (A) France.
   (B) Canada.
   (C) Canada and France.
   (D) France and Magana.

2. When will he arrive in Chicago?
   (A) On Sep. 18th.
   (B) On Sep. 8th.
   (C) On Oct. 18th.
   (D) On Oct. 8th.

3. How long will he stay in Chicago?
   (A) Ten days.
   (B) Two days.
   (C) Twelve days.
   (D) Eighteen days.

I'm going to Canada and France for a business trip, and I want to know if you can make contact with someone who has the same position as you at their plant site, EMA Canada. I'll meet you and look at the operations of your plant when I arrive in Chicago, in the morning on Sep. 18th. I will leave for Toronto on Sep. 20th. I want to see first hand how they operate on that day, if they are free. Moreover, our president will visit the plant in Toronto On Oct. 8th with the Singapore president during his trip.

Unit 06 电话、传真 | Phone and Fax

1. 讲话者要去哪里出差？
(A) 法国。
(B) 加拿大。
(C) 加拿大和法国。
(D) 法国和马迦纳。

2. 他什么时候到达芝加哥？
(A) 九月十八日。
(B) 九月八日。
(C) 十月十八日。
(D) 十月八日。

3. 他会在芝加哥待多久？
(A) 十天。
(B) 两天。
(C) 十二天。
(D) 十八天。

我要去加拿大和法国出差，我想知道你能否和加拿大 EMA 的相关人员取得联系。我会在九月十八日早上到达芝加哥，然后和你见面，以及查看你们工厂的运转情况。我会在九月二十日飞往多伦多。如果他们有时间的话，我希望在当天直接看到他们的运作情况。此外，十月八日我们的董事长会和新加坡董事长一起在旅行过程中参观多伦多的工厂。

答案：1. (C) 2. (A) 3. (B)

1. 根据第一句 I'm going to Canada and France for a business trip 可知，作者是要去加拿大和法国出差，所以选 (C)。
2. 根据 I arrive in Chicago in the morning on Sep. 18th 可知，正确答案选 (A)。
3. 从独白中得知讲话者是九月十八日到达芝加哥，九月二十日前往多伦多，所以他停留在芝加哥的时间为两天，所以选 (B)。

单词 Vocabulary

contact [kən'tækt] v 联系，使接触 ['kɒntækt] n 联系，接触，交往
position [pə'zɪʃn] n 位置，工作 v 安置，把……放在适当位置
plant [plɑ:nt] n 车间，植物 v 种植 n 工厂
operation [ˌɒpə'reɪʃn] n 操作，手术，经营
operate ['ɒpəreɪt] v 经营，运转，动手术
president ['prezɪdənt] n 总统，校长，董事长

Dear Mrs. King,

We saw your information on the Internet. The reason that we want to contact you is that we need a conference room for our meeting the day after tomorrow. There will be many foreign manufacturers, suppliers, clients and partners from all over the world attending the meeting, so we wonder whether you can provide us with interpreters, too.

We are sending you our requirements by fax and hope you can let us know what kind of services you provide and what prices you charge, especially the price for renting a conference room. I would like a conference room that can hold more than four hundred people. We were not able to get enough information from your website, so would like to request detailed information by fax as soon as possible. We also want to make sure what kind of conference room is available.

The last thing I almost forgot to say is that we need twenty accomodation rooms for our superiors and these rooms should be fully equipped and have the best views. We can pay extra for the twenty superiors if necessary providing that you offer them the best services. For now, I have no other requirements. I will let you know if there are other demands.

I hope you will reply as soon as possible. I look forward to your reply.

Regards,

Robert Schwimmer

Manager

Europe International Trade Limited Company

RobertSchwimmer@gmail.com

1. Where did Robert see Mrs. King's information?

    (A) In the journal.

    (B) In the newspaper.

    (C) On the Internet.

    (D) In the book.

2. What does Robert want to know from Mrs. King?

    (A) Services and Charges.

    (B) Her position.

    (C) News.

    (D) Her cooperation experience with other companies.

3. What are the requirements of the living rooms for the twenty supervisors?

    (A) They should be economical.

    (B) They should be fully equipped.

    (C) They should be served with meals.

    (D) They should be on the second floor.

4. When will the meeting be held?

    (A) Today.

    (B) Tomorrow.

    (C) The day after tomorrow.

    (D) Next weekend.

5. Which of the following is false according to the fax?

    (A) Robert needs to arrange a meeting.

    (B) Mrs. King can provide services for Robert.

    (C) Mrs. King charges a high price from Robert.

    (D) Robert needs interpreters for the meeting, too.

尊敬的金夫人：

　　我们在网上看到您的信息。我们联系您，是因为我们需要一间后天开会的会议厅。因为有许多来自世界各地的厂商、供应商、客户以及合作伙伴来参加本次会议，因此我们想知道您是否也能为我们提供口译人员。

　　我们传真我们的要求给您，希望您能让我们知道您提供什么样的服务以及报价，尤其是租用会议室的价格。我希望会议室能容纳四百人以上。我们在网站上无法得到足够的信息，因此请您尽快传真详细信息给我们。我们也想确定一下可预订的会议室类型。

　　最后一点，我差点忘记说，我们需要为主管准备二十间住宿房，这些房间应配备齐全并有最好的视野。如果需要的话，我们可以为这二十名主管支付额外的费用，前提是你们给他们提供最好的服务。现在我没有其他要求，如果有其他要求我会让您知道的。

　　希望您能尽快回复，我期待您的回复。

　　此致
敬礼！

罗伯特·修蒙
经理
欧洲国际贸易有限公司
RobertSchwimmer@gmail.com

1. 罗伯特在哪里看到金夫人的信息？
   (A) 杂志。
   (B) 报纸。
   (C) 网络。
   (D) 书上。

2. 罗伯特想从金夫人那里知道些什么？
   (A) 服务与费用。
   (B) 她的职位。
   (C) 新闻。
   (D) 她与其他公司的合作经历。

3. 对于二十位主管的居住房间，有什么要求？
   (A) 经济划算。
   (B) 配备齐全。
   (C) 提供膳食。
   (D) 处于二楼。

4. 会议什么时候举行？
   (A) 今天。
   (B) 明天。
   (C) 后天。
   (D) 下周。

5. 根据传真，下列哪一项错误？
   (A) 罗伯特需要安排一场会议。
   (B) 金夫人可以为罗伯特提供服务。
   (C) 金夫人向罗伯特要高价。
   (D) 罗伯特也需要为会议准备口译人员。

解析与答案

答案：1. (C) 2. (A) 3. (B) 4. (C) 5. (C)

1. 此题考细节，可见正文第一段第一句 We saw your information on the Internet，因此选 (C)。
2. 此题考信息提取能力，答案在第二段第一句 ... hope you can let us know what kind of services you provide and what prices you charge...，因此选 (A)。
3. 此题考信息提取能力，从第三段第一句 ... we need twenty accomodation rooms for our superiors and these rooms should be fully equipped... 可知答案要选 (B)。
4. 此题考细节，可见第一段第二句 ... a conference room for our meeting the day after tomorrow，因此选 (C)。
5. 此题考判断能力，选项 (A) 可见第一段第二句 ... we need a conference room for our meeting... 以及关于会议的问题贯穿全文；选项 (B)，文中第二段第一句 ... let us know what kind of services you provide...；选项 (D)，可见第一段最后一句 ... we wonder whether you can provide us with interpreters, too；但是文中并没有提到关于服务价格高低的问题，因此选 (C)。

单词 Vocabulary

foreign ['fɒrən] a 外国的，陌生的
manufacturer [ˌmænjuˈfæktʃərə(r)] n 厂商，制造业者
supplier [səˈplaɪə(r)] n 供应商
client [ˈklaɪənt] n 客户
interpreter [ɪnˈtɜːprɪtə(r)] n 口译人员
requirement [rɪˈkwaɪəmənt] n 要求，必要条件，需要
rent [rent] v 租用 n 租金
forget [fəˈget] v 忘记，忽视
superior [suːˈpɪərɪə(r)] n 上级，领导 a 较高（大、多）的
demand [dɪˈmɑːnd] n / v 要求，请求，需要

学习重点

| 页 数 | 笔记内容 |

NEW TOEIC

办公室 Office

Chapter 2

Unit 07
办公室器材与家具 | Office Equipment

New TOEIC

Picture 07

情境中可明确指出的单词

1. **clamp** [klæmp] n. 夹子
2. **clip** [klɪp] n. 回纹针
3. **cell phone** ph. 手机
4. **earphone** [ˈɪəfəʊn] n. 耳机
5. **key** [kiː] n. 钥匙 v. 锁上
6. **loose-leaf** [luːs liːf] a. 活页式的
7. **post-it** [pəʊst ɪt] n. 便利贴
8. **stapler** [ˈsteɪplə(r)] n. 订书机

情境中可延伸记忆的单词

1. **accountant** [əˈkaʊntənt] n. 会计
2. **arrange** [əˈreɪndʒ] v. 摆设
3. **calculate** [ˈkælkjuleɪt] v. 计算
4. **female** [ˈfiːmeɪl] n. 女性
5. **multiplication** [ˌmʌltɪplɪˈkeɪʃn] n. 乘法
6. **office stationery** ph. 办公文具
7. **organized** [ˈɔːɡənaɪzd] a. 井然有序的
8. **profession** [prəˈfeʃn] n. 职业

clamp [klæmp] n 夹子

To tidy her desk, she put clamps on every document.
为了整理桌子，她给每一份文件都夹上夹子。
- clamp down ph 关紧，取缔

clip [klɪp] n 回纹针

The assistant was asked to put a clip on the papers.
助理被要求在文件上夹一枚回纹针。
- clipping n 剪裁 / clip sb.'s wings ph 限制某人的权力

cell phone ph 手机

The salesman was rewarded with a cell phone for his excellent performance.
那名销售人员表现优秀，获得了一部手机作为鼓励。
- office phone ph 办公电话 / phone number ph 电话号码

earphone ['ɪəfəʊn] n 耳机

If you want to listen to music, you had better put on your earphones.
如果你想听音乐，最好戴上耳机。
- wear earphone ph 戴耳机

key [kiː] n 钥匙 v 锁上

I found a bunch of keys in the office.
我在办公室发现一串钥匙。
- keyer n 调制器 / key in ph 用键盘输入 / key part ph 关键部分 / key punch ph 打孔机

loose-leaf [luːs liːf] a 活页式的

He takes notes in the loose-leaf notebook at the meeting in case he needs it.
在会议上，他在活页本上做了记录，以防不时之需。
- loose-leaf diary ph 活页日记本

post-it [pəust it] n 便利贴

The assistant always keeps post-its in her bag.
助理在包里总是备有便利贴。
- kick post-it ph 便携即时贴 / post off ph 匆忙出发 / post office ph 邮局

stapler ['steɪplə(r)] n 订书机

The red stapler is put between the post-its and clamps.
红色订书机被放在便利贴和夹子之间。
- staple a 主要的 n 订书针

accountant [əˈkaʊntənt] n. 会计

I guess the owner of these things is an accountant.
我猜这些物品的主人是一位会计。
accountancy n. 会计工作 / accounting n. 会计（学）

arrange [əˈreɪndʒ] v. 摆设

The man was supposed to arrange this meeting.
那位男子应该来安排这次会议。
arrangement n. 安排 / arrange for ph. 为……安排 / settle v. 安排，确定

calculate [ˈkælkjuleɪt] v. 计算

You can use the calculator to calculate the simple accounts.
你可以用计算机计算简单的账目。
calculation n. 计算 / calculate on ph. 指望 / calculate upon ph. 指望

female [ˈfiːmeɪl] n. 女性

She is the only female employee in this company.
她是这家公司唯一的女性雇员。
male n. 男性 / gender n. 性别 / feminine a. 女性的

multiplication [ˌmʌltɪplɪˈkeɪʃn] n. 乘法

With the calculator, you can work out the multiplication quickly.
借助计算机，你可以很快地计算出乘法。
multiplication table ph. 乘法表

office stationery ph. 办公文具

The purchasing agent was asked to purchase some office stationery.
采购员被要求采购一些办公文具。
office block ph. （英）办公大楼

organized [ˈɔːɡənaɪzd] a. 井然有序的

The things on the table are organized.
桌上的物品井然有序。
organizational a. 组织的 / orderly a. 有条理的 / neat a. 整洁的

profession [prəˈfeʃn] n. 职业

The woman is well known in the accounting profession.
这女子在会计界很出名。
professional a. 专业的 / professional foul ph. （球赛）故意犯规

听力测验 | Part 1 图片描述题

题目
(A) A high percentage of the workers are male.
(B) All women's hair is black.
(C) Everyone is making a phone call.
(D) There are three men and five women.

中译
(A) 大部分工作者都是男性。
(B) 所有女子头发都是黑色。
(C) 每个人都在打电话。
(D) 这里一共有三位男子和五位女子。

解析与答案

答案：(D)
从图片中可以看出，共有八个人，三位男子和五位女子，其中有一位女子的头发不是黑色，只有两个人在打电话，所以选 (D)。

听力测验 | Part 3 简短对话题

1. Where are the speakers?
   (A) In a supermarket.
   (B) In a furniture shop.
   (C) In an office.
   (D) In a conference room.

2. What does the man want to know before he moves furniture?
   (A) Where the conference room is.
   (B) If all of the furniture should be moved out.
   (C) If he needs to sweep the carpet.
   (D) How long it will last.

3. Why should all of the furniture be moved out?
   (A) Because all offices will be redecorated.
   (B) Because the carpet will be replaced.
   (C) Because the working place has been changed.
   (D) Because all furniture will be renewed.

Martin: Excuse me. I reported to the manager just now and I have learned that all of the furniture should be moved out of the offices.

Lisa: You are Martin, right? We are badly in need of an assistant. All of the furniture in this office should be moved into the conference room, including desks, tables and chairs.

Martin: OK. But I have never been there, so would you mind telling me where the conference room is? By the way, do you want to refurnish all these offices?

Lisa: No, but we're going to replace the carpet, so everything in these offices should be moved out.

Unit 07 办公室器材与家具 | Office Equipment

中译

1. 说话者在什么地方？
   (A) 超市。
   (B) 家具店。
   (C) 办公室。
   (D) 会议室。

2. 男子在搬家具之前想知道什么？
   (A) 会议室在哪里。
   (B) 是不是所有的家具都要搬出去。
   (C) 他是否需要打扫地毯。
   (D) 搬家具需要多长时间。

3. 为什么所有的家具都要搬出去？
   (A) 因为所有的办公室都要重新装修。
   (B) 因为要换新地毯。
   (C) 因为工作地点改变了。
   (D) 因为要换新家具。

马丁：打扰了，我刚刚向经理报告，得知办公室里的所有家具都要搬出去。
丽莎：你是马丁，对吧？我们现在急需一名帮手。这个办公室里的家具，包括书桌、工作台和椅子都要搬到会议室。
马丁：好的。但是我之前没有去过那里，所以你可以告诉我会议室在哪里吗？顺便再问一下，你是想重新装修所有的办公室吗？
丽莎：不是的。但是我们想要换地毯，所以办公室里所有的东西都要搬出去。

解析与答案

答案：1. (C) 2. (A) 3. (B)

1. 从听力中 All furniture in this office... 可知，他们的对话发生在办公室里，所以选 (C)。
2. 女子说所有家具要搬到会议室，但是从 ... would you mind telling me where the conference is 可知，男子不知道会议室的位置，所以他在搬家具之前会问会议室在哪里，答案是 (A)。
3. 根据最后一句 we're going to replace the carpet, so everything in these offices should be moved out 可知，所有家具都要搬出去是因为要换地毯，答案选 (B)。

单词 Vocabulary

report [rɪˈpɔːt] n 报告，成绩单，报道 v 报告
furniture [ˈfɜːnɪtʃə(r)] n 家具，设备
assistant [əˈsɪstənt] n 助手 a 辅助的
conference [ˈkɒnfərəns] n 会议，协商
refurnish [ˌriːˈfɜːnɪʃ] v 重新装备
replace [rɪˈpleɪs] v 取代，替换，偿还
carpet [ˈkɑːpɪt] n 地毯 v 在……上铺地毯

阅读测验 | Part 7 文章理解题

To: All the employees

From: Henry Wood

Hello everyone,

I would like to announce the good news that the manufacturer, Bill High and New Tech. Co., Ltd., will provide us several computers for free. They specialize in technology research and electronic product production. I think there will be a great increase in our working efficiency with their computers. We have made an agreement with them. If we think their computers are great, we can purchase their computers with a five percent discount later.

Their company produces not only computers, but printers, air-conditioners, smart phones and so on. If we need their products, we can also get them at a discount.

There is an increasing demand on functions of modern electronic products, so more and more companies are concentrating on the electronic market. They are investing more funds in developing electronic products with new functions. The competition among these companies will push the development of the electronic industry. In the future, I think computers will be installed with better video and audio quality, and office software. We all know that it is Bill High and New Tech. Co., Ltd. that is responsible for these improvements.

The CEO of Bill High and New Tech. Co., Ltd. says that they will certainly make a difference in the near future based on their experience.

In the future, I believe our office will be equipped with more advanced equipment and working efficiency will be improved greatly.

Regards,

Henry Wood

Dec. 1st, 2015

Unit 07 办公室器材与家具 | Office Equipment

1. What is the good news to the employees?
   (A) They will be provided with smart phones for free.
   (B) They will be provided with computers for free.
   (C) They will be provided with air-conditioners for free.
   (D) They will be provided with printers for free.

2. Which of the following is NOT a product of Bill High and New Tech. Co., Ltd.?
   (A) Computer.
   (B) Car.
   (C) Phone.
   (D) Printer.

3. What is a demand on modern electronic products?
   (A) Prices.
   (B) Appearance.
   (C) Functions.
   (D) Life.

4. What is Bill High and New Tech. Co., Ltd. responsible for?
   (A) Improvements.
   (B) Decline.
   (C) Recession.
   (D) Bankruptcy.

5. What does Henry say last?
   (A) They will invest in the electronic industry.
   (B) They will make much more profit than any other company.
   (C) Their working efficiency will certainly be improved.
   (D) Their office will not be equipped with more advanced equipment.

收件人：全体雇员
寄件者：亨利·伍德

大家好！

  我将宣布一条好消息，厂商——比尔高新技术有限公司，将向我们免费提供几台电脑。他们专注于技术研发与电子产品生产。我认为，有了他们的电脑，我们的工作效率将会大幅提高。我们已经和他们签署协议。如果我们觉得他们的电脑不错，我们未来可以以九五折购买他们的电脑。

  他们的公司不仅生产电脑，还生产打印机、冷气机、智能手机等。如果我们需要他们的产品，购买他们的产品可以享受打折优惠。

  人们对现代电子产品功能的要求越来越高，因此越来越多的公司把精力集中在电子产品市场。他们正在电子产品新功能研发方面投入更多资金。这些公司之间的竞争将会推动电子行业的发展。我认为，将来电脑会安装高质视频与音频以及办公室软件。我们都知道是比尔高新技术有限公司负责改善这方面。

  比尔高新技术有限公司的首席执行官说基于他们的经验，将来他们一定会有所作为。

  我相信，将来我们办公室会配备更加先进的设备。公司效率会大幅提高。

  此致
敬礼！

亨利·伍德
2015 年 12 月 1 日

1. 对于员工来说，好消息是什么？
   (A) 他们会得到免费的智能手机。
   (B) 他们会得到免费的电脑。
   (C) 他们会得到免费的冷气机。
   (D) 他们会得到免费的印表机。

2. 下列哪一项不是比尔高新技术有限公司的产品？
   (A) 电脑。
   (B) 汽车。
   (C) 手机。
   (D) 印表机。

3. 在现代电子产品上有什么要求？
   (A) 价格。
   (B) 外观。
   (C) 功能。
   (D) 寿命。

4. 比尔高新技术有限公司会对什么进行负责？
   (A) 改善。
   (B) 下降。
   (C) 衰落。
   (D) 破产。

5. 亨利最后说了什么？
   (A) 他们将会投资电子行业。
   (B) 他们会比其他公司创造更多的利润。
   (C) 他们的工作效率一定会提高。
   (D) 他们的办公室不会配备更先进的设备。

答案：1. (B) 2. (B) 3. (C) 4. (A) 5. (C)

1. 此题考细节，答案在第一段第一句 ... good news that the manufacturer, Bill High an New Tech. Co., Ltd., will provide us several computers for free，选 (B)。
2. 此题考分辨能力，从第二段第一句 Their company produces not only computers but printers, air-conditioners, smart phones... 可知，公司生产电脑、打印机、冷气机、手机，没有生产汽车，答案选 (B)。
3. 此题考细节，可见第三段第一句 ... increasing demand on functions of modern electronic products...，关键词是"function"，此题要选 (C)。
4. 此题考细节，可见第三段最后一句 ... it is Bill High and New Tech. Co., Ltd. that is responsible for these improvements，因此选 (A)。
5. 此题考细节，答案在最后一段 ... working efficiency will be improved greatly，因此选 (C)。

单词 Vocabulary

electronic [ɪˌlekˈtrɒnɪk] a 电子的
efficiency [ɪˈfɪʃnsi] n 效率
printer [ˈprɪntə(r)] n 打印机
function [ˈfʌŋkʃn] n 功能，功用 v 起作用，运行
modern [ˈmɒdn] a 现代的 n 现代人
concentrate [ˈkɒnsntreɪt] v 集中，聚集，全神贯注
competition [ˌkɒmpəˈtɪʃn] n 竞争，比赛，角逐
video [ˈvɪdiəʊ] n 影视，录影带（机）a 电视的，录影的
audio [ˈɔːdiəʊ] a 音频的
experience [ɪkˈspɪəriəns] n 经验，经历 v 体验，感受

Unit 08
面试 | Interview

New TOEIC

Picture 08

情境中可明确指出的单词

1. **alfresco** [æl'freskəʊ] a 户外的，露天的
2. **document** ['dɒkjumənt] n 文件，公文
3. **gray** [greɪ] n 灰色 a 灰色的
4. **interviewee** [ˌɪntəvjuː'iː] n 面试者，被面试的人
5. **notebook** ['nəʊtbʊk] n 笔记本电脑，笔记本
6. **opposite** ['ɒpəzɪt] p 在……对面
7. **shank** [ʃæŋk] n 小腿
8. **tie** [taɪ] n 领带

情境中可延伸记忆的单词

1. **dispassionate** [dɪs'pæʃənət] a 冷静的，公平的
2. **enroll** [ɪn'rəʊl] v 录取
3. **experience** [ɪk'spɪərɪəns] n 经历
4. **hairstyle** ['heəstaɪl] n 发型
5. **interview** ['ɪntəvjuː] n / v 面试
6. **oneself** [wʌn'self] pr 自己，本人
7. **strenuous** ['strenjuəs] a 艰苦的，繁重的，费力的
8. **talk** [tɔːk] n 交谈 v 讨论

Unit 08 面试 | Interview

alfresco [æl'freskəʊ] a 户外的，露天的
They will have an **alfresco** conference tomorrow.
明天，他们将开一场户外会议。
● alfresco dining 户外就餐

---

document ['dɒkjumənt] n 文件，公文
Submit the **documents** before you leave.
你离开之前，要提交文件。
● document ['dɑkjə,mɛnt] v 用文件证明 / documentation n 文件

---

gray [greɪ] n 灰色 a 灰色的
The interviewee gets dressed in a **gray** dress.
面试者着灰色裙装。
● grayish a 浅灰色的 / gray area 灰色地区

---

interviewee [,ɪntəvjuː'iː] n 面试者，被面试的人
The **interviewee** was first asked to give an introduction about himself.
要求面试者先做一个自我介绍。
● interviewer n 面试官 / recruit v 招募（新兵），雇用 / applicant n 申请者

---

notebook ['nəʊtbʊk] n 笔记本电脑，笔记本
She recorded everything in her **notebook**.
她把所有事情都记录在她的笔记本上。
● notepaper n 信纸

---

opposite ['ɒpəzɪt] p 在……对面
Three interviewers are sitting **opposite** to the interviewee.
三位面试官坐在面试者的对面。
● oppositive a 反对的 / opposite sex 异性

---

shank [ʃæŋk] n 小腿
The woman is really slim with long thin **shanks**.
那位女子腿细长，真苗条。
● straight shank 直柄 / thigh 大腿 / ankle 脚踝

---

tie [taɪ] n 领带
Men are supposed to wear **ties** on formal occasions.
在正式场合，男士应该打领带。
● tying 结 / tie down 束缚 / tie in 相配

dispassionate [dɪsˈpæʃənət] a. 冷静的，公平的
The interviewer has a dispassionate look on his face.
面试官的表情冷静。
● dispassion n. 冷静 / calm a. 镇静的，沉着的

enroll [ɪnˈrəʊl] v. 录取
We don't know if the interviewee is enrolled.
我们不知道面试者是否被录取了。
● enrollment n. 登记 / admission rate n. 录取率

experience [ɪkˈspɪəriəns] n. 经历
The interviewee must be asked to introduce her work experience.
面试者一定会被要求介绍自己的工作经历。
● experiential a. 经验的 / experienced a. 有经验的

hairstyle [ˈheəstaɪl] n. 发型
The interviewee needs to notice her hairstyle.
面试者需要注意自己的发型。
● bad hairstyle n. 糟糕的发型 / hairstylist n. 发型师

interview [ˈɪntəvjuː] n. / v. 面试
He did well in the interview.
在面试中，他表现很好。
● job interview n. 求职面试 / interrogate v. 审问

oneself [wʌnˈself] pr. 自己，本人
I think it is very important to educate oneself.
我觉得培养自己很重要。
● above oneself 自命不凡 / by oneself 单独地 / for oneself 为自己

strenuous [ˈstrenjuəs] a. 艰苦的，繁重的，费力的
A daily routine of strenuous exercise has kept him in good shape.
每天规律地进行高强度锻炼塑造了他的好身材。
● strenuosity n. 费力 / strenuously ad. 奋力地

talk [tɔːk] n. 交谈 v. 讨论
The interviewers learned something about the interviewee by talking with him.
通过这次谈话，面试官初步了解了面试者。
● talk about 谈论某事 / talk around 说服 / talk away 不断地说

听力测验 | Part 1 图片描述题

(A) There is a telephone on the desk.
(B) They are not satisfied with the interviewee.
(C) There are many interviewees.
(D) There are two interviewers and they are male.

(A) 桌子上有一部电话。
(B) 他们对面试者感到不满意。
(C) 有很多的面试者。
(D) 有两名面试官，而且都是男性。

答案：(A)

从图片可以看出，一共有三个人，一个面试者、两个面试官，面试官分别是一男一女，从他们的微笑表情可以看出他们对面试者感到满意，女子的旁边有一台电话，所以选 (A)。

听力测验 | Part 3 简短对话题

1. Why has the interviewee been to America for half a year?
   (A) He went to America as an exchange student.
   (B) He went to travel.
   (C) He went to America for a business trip.
   (D) He went to visit his friends.

2. What is the interviewee's attitude to overtime work?
   (A) Rejective.
   (B) Not exclusive.
   (C) Neutral.
   (D) Satisfied.

3. When will the interviewee receive notification if he has been hired?
   (A) Within a week.
   (B) After a week.
   (C) After one day.
   (D) WIthIn a day.

Interviewer: Do you think you are proficient in English?

Interviewee: Yes, I'm an English major and I have been to America for half a year as an exchange student.

Interviewer: Good. This job requires a lot of travel. What do you think about that?

Interviewee: No problem. I love traveling very much.

Interviewer: What's your opinion on overtime work?

Interviewee: I don't object to working overtime, but I don't want to work overtime every day.

Interviewer: What's are your salary expectations?

Interviewee: I think it depends on my responsibilities in the company.

Interviewer: When will you be available to work?

Interviewee: At anytime, because I have resigned from my old job.

Interviewer: OK. We will inform you within one week if you are hired.

Interviewee: OK. Thank you!

Unit 08 面试 | Interview

中译

1. 面试者为什么在美国待了半年？
   (A) 作为交换学生去美国。
   (B) 去旅游。
   (C) 因为出差去了美国。
   (D) 去拜访他的朋友。

2. 应聘者对加班的态度是什么？
   (A) 拒绝的。
   (B) 不排斥的。
   (C) 中立的。
   (D) 满意的。

3. 如果被录用，应聘者多久会收到通知？
   (A) 一周之内。
   (B) 一周之后。
   (C) 一天之后。
   (D) 一天之内。

面试官：你认为你精通英语吗？
应聘者：是的，我学的是英语专业，而且曾作为交换学生在美国待了半年。
面试官：好的。这份工作需要你经常出差。对于这一点你怎么看？
应聘者：没有问题。我非常喜欢旅行。
面试官：你对加班有什么看法？
应聘者：我不排斥加班，但是我希望不是每天都要加班。
面试官：你期望的薪资是多少？
应聘者：我认为这要取决于我在公司所承担的责任。
面试官：你什么时候可以上班？
应聘者：随时都可以，因为我已经辞掉了上一份工作。
面试官：好的。如果你被录用了，我们会在一周之内通知你的。
应聘者：好。谢谢！

解析与答案

答案：1. (A) 2. (B) 3. (A)

1. 由 I have been to America for half a year as an exchange student 可知，面试者是作为交换学生才去美国，并且在那里待了半年，所以选 (A)。
2. 根据 I don't object to work overtime, but I don't want to work overtime every day 可知，面试者对加班的态度是不排斥的，但是不希望每天都加班，所以选 (B)。
3. 根据 We will inform you within one week if you are hired 可知，如果被录用，面试者会在一周内收到通知，所以选 (A)。

单词 Vocabulary

proficient [prə'fɪʃnt] n 专家 a 熟练的
require [rɪ'kwaɪə(r)] v 要求，需要
overtime ['əʊvətaɪm] n 加班时间 a 超时的 ad 加班地 [əʊvə'taɪm] v 使延长时间
object ['ɒbdʒɪkt] n 目标，客体 [əb'dʒekt] v 反对
available [ə'veɪləbl] a 可获得的，有空的
inform [ɪn'fɔːm] v 通知，告发

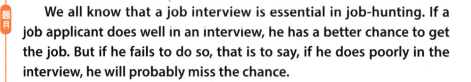

We all know that a job interview is essential in job-hunting. If a job applicant does well in an interview, he has a better chance to get the job. But if he fails to do so, that is to say, if he does poorly in the interview, he will probably miss the chance.

When walking into the interview room, the applicant should shake hands with the interviewer with a smile on his face. The first question is usually to ask him to give an introduction about himself. But he is not supposed to make a long speech. So, just make the speech concise and to the point.

To succeed in a job interview, the job applicant should show his personality and professional knowledge. First, he should pay attention to appearance and politeness. He shouldn't attend the interview if he doesn't look good.

Secondly, he should show his knowledge and ability, especially his professional knowledge and the abilities required for the post he is applying for. This is the most important part of the interview. He should talk about the achievements he has made.

Finally, he should appear to be confident and positive; he should have a good attitude about the job. If the applicant is successful in showing these qualities and characteristics in the interview, the interviewer may decide to employ him in the interview. Last but not least, when finishing the interview, the applicant should express his appreciation to the interviewer.

Unit 08 面试 | Interview

1. What does the text mainly talk about?
   (A) A job interview.
   (B) Appearance of a job applicant.
   (C) Experience of a job applicant.
   (D) The past of a job applicant.

2. What is usually the first question in the interview?
   (A) To do an introduction.
   (B) To talk about achievements.
   (C) To talk about future.
   (D) To comment on himself.

3. What should an applicant pay attention to first according to the third paragraph?
   (A) Appearance and politeness.
   (B) The interviewer.
   (C) The way he talks.
   (D) The time to start the interview.

4. What is the most important part for an applicant in the interview?
   (A) Giving a moving speech.
   (B) Praising the interviewer.
   (C) Showing his knowledge and ability.
   (D) Showing how confident he is.

5. Which of the following is NOT right?
   (A) The applicant should show his ability.
   (B) The applicant will be more likely to seize the opportunity if he does well in the interview.
   (C) The applicant should be polite.
   (D) The applicant can say what he wants to say.

我们都知道,面试是找工作过程中不可缺少的。如果工作申请者能够在面试中有优秀表现,他更有机会得到这份工作。但是如果不是这样,也就是说,他在面试中表现不好,他很可能会失去机会。

走进面试房间时,申请者应面带微笑,与面试官握手。第一个问题通常是请他做自我介绍。但是不应讲过长。言简意赅即可。

为了能在面试中胜出,工作申请者应该展现个性以及专业知识。首先,他应该注意外表与礼貌。如果看起来状态不佳,就不应参加面试。

其次,应该展现知识与能力,尤其是申请职位所需的专业知识与能力。这是面试中最重要的部分。应该谈论已经取得的成绩。

最后,应该表现自信、积极;对待工作应该有一个良好的态度。如果申请者在面试中成功地展示了这些品质、特性,面试官可能在面试中就决定雇用他。最后同样重要的是,面试结束时,申请者最好向面试官表达谢意。

1. 文章主要讨论的是什么?
    (A) 工作面试。
    (B) 工作申请者的外表。
    (C) 工作申请者的经验。
    (D) 工作申请者的过去。

2. 面试过程中第一个问题通常是什么?
    (A) 做自我介绍。
    (B) 谈论成就。
    (C) 谈论将来。
    (D) 评价自己。

3. 根据第三段,申请者首先应该多注意什么?
    (A) 外表与礼貌。
    (B) 面试官。
    (C) 说话的方式。
    (D) 开始面试的时间。

4. 对于申请者，面试中最重要的部分是什么？
   (A) 做一场感人的演讲。
   (B) 赞美面试官。
   (C) 展示知识与能力。
   (D) 展示自信。

5. 下列哪一项是不正确的？
   (A) 申请者应该展现他的能力。
   (B) 申请者如果在面试中表现良好，将会更有可能抓住机会。
   (C) 申请者应该礼貌。
   (D) 申请者可以畅所欲言。

解析与答案

答案：1. (A) 2. (A) 3. (A) 4. (C) 5. (D)

1. 从第一段第一句 All we know that a job interview is essential in the job-hunting，可判断选 (A)。
2. 此题可见第二段第二句 The first question is usually to ask him to give an introduction about himself，因此选 (A)。
3. 此题可见第三段第二句 First, he should pay attention to appearance and politeness，因此选 (A)。
4. 此题可见第四段第一句、第二句 ... he should show his knowledge and ability... This is the most important part in the interview，文中特别强调这是最重要的部分，因此选 (C)。
5. 文中并未提及申请者可以畅所欲言，因此选 (D)。

单词 Vocabulary

essential [ɪˈsenʃl] a 重要的，必要的 n 要素
applicant [ˈæplɪkənt] n 申请者
performance [pəˈfɔːməns] n 表现，演出
poor [pɔː(r)] a 贫穷的，不好的
interview [ˈɪntəvjuː] n / v 面试
suppose [səˈpəʊz] v 应该，猜想，期望，假设
personality [ˌpɜːsəˈnæləti] n 个性，人格
appearance [əˈpɪərəns] n 外表，外观，出现，显露
post [pəʊst] n 职位，邮件 v 寄送邮件
successful [səkˈsesfl] a 成功的

Unit 09
雇用 | Employment

New TOEIC

Picture 09

情境中可明确指出的单词

1. **bar graph** ph 长条图
2. **curve** [kɜːv] n 曲线图 v 使成曲线
3. **glass** [glɑːs] n 杯子,玻璃杯
4. **glasses** [ˈglɑːsɪz] n 眼镜
5. **shake** [ʃeɪk] v 握手
6. **office** [ˈɒfɪs] n 办公室
7. **pie chart** ph 圆饼图
8. **whiteboard** [ˈwaɪtbɔːd] n 白板

情境中可延伸记忆的单词

1. **competent** [ˈkɒmpɪtənt] a 胜任的
2. **hire** [ˈhaɪə(r)] n / v 雇用
3. **positive** [ˈpɒzətɪv] a 确定的,确实的,积极的
4. **presentation** [ˌpreznˈteɪʃn] n 表现
5. **probation** [prəˈbeɪʃn] n 试用期
6. **solution** [səˈluːʃn] n 解答,解释
7. **tense** [tens] a 紧绷的 v 使紧张
8. **training** [ˈtreɪnɪŋ] n 培训,训练

Unit 09 雇用 | Employment

bar graph [n] 长条图
The man was explaining the bar graphs to all the staff.
男子正在向全体员工解释长条图。
- line graph [n] 折线图

curve [kɜ:v] [n] 曲线图 [v] 使成曲线
The curve on the graph demonstrates the increase in our operating expenses for this year.
根据曲线图，我们可以知道今年的营运费用的增加。
- curvature [n] 弯曲 / curvy [a] 弯曲的

glass [glɑ:s] [n] 杯子，玻璃杯
I didn't mean to break the glasses.
我不是有意打破玻璃杯的。
- glassy 像玻璃的 / glass ceiling [n] 指女性在工作升迁时碰到的无形障碍

glasses ['glɑ:sɪz] [n] 眼镜
He takes off his glasses and walks away.
他摘掉眼镜并走开。
- a pair of glasses [n] 一副眼镜 / telescope [n] 望远镜 / nearsightedness [n] 近视

shake [ʃeɪk] [v] 握手
Before leaving, she shook hands with the client.
离开之前，她和客户握手。
- handshake [n] 握手 / shake hands [n] 握手 / shake it up [n] 赶快

office ['ɒfɪs] [n] 办公室
Nobody is allowed to leave the office during working hours.
谁都不允许在上班时间离开办公室。
- officer [n] 军官 / office hours [n] 办公时间

pie chart [n] 圆饼图
You should analyze the pie chart for us as soon as possible.
你应该尽快为我们分析圆饼图。
- pie in the sky [n] 不可及的梦想

whiteboard ['waɪtbɔ:d] [n] 白板
The manager drew a chart on the whiteboard.
经理在白板上画了一个图表。
- whiteboard pens [n] 白板笔

competent ['kɒmpɪtənt] a 称职的，胜任的
This lady must be competent at work.
这位女子一定能够胜任这份工作。
- competence n 能力 / competitive advantage n 竞争优势

hire ['haɪə(r)] n / v 雇用
I am happy to tell you that you are hired.
很高兴告诉你，你被雇用了。
- hireling n 雇员 / hirer n 雇主 / employ v 雇用 / engage v 聘，雇，订婚

positive ['pɒzətɪv] a 确定的，确实的
The man gave a positive response to the lady.
那位男子给女子一个确切的答复。
- positive energy n 正能量 / negative a 否定的，反面的

presentation [ˌprezn'teɪʃn] n 表现
The lady must have a good presentation at the meeting.
这位女子在会议上一定有好的表现。
- presentment n 描写 / present to n 出现在

probation [prə'beɪʃn] n 试用期
The probation period of new employees does not usually exceed three months.
新员工的试用期一般不超过三个月。
- probationary a 试用的 / on probation n 在试用期的

solution [sə'luːʃn] n 解答，解释
We need to find a solution to the problem.
我们必须找到这个问题的答案。
- resolution n 解答 / dilemma n 困境，两难推理

tense [tens] a 紧绷的 v 使紧张
The woman was very tense as she listened to the news report.
听新闻报道的时候，这位女子很紧张。
- tensional a 紧张的 / tense up n 紧张

training ['treɪnɪŋ] n 培训，训练
The company will provide the pre-employment training for the new employees.
公司会为新员工提供入职前培训。
- trainee n 练习生 / training school n 职业学校

听力测验 | Part 1 图片描述题

(A) They are dressed in white shirts.
(B) The hair of both men is black.
(C) The woman has long hair.
(D) Both of the men are dressed in black suits.

(A) 他们都穿着白色的衬衫。
(B) 两位男子的头发都是黑色的。
(C) 女子留着长头发。
(D) 两位男子都穿着黑色的西装。

答案：(C)
从图片可以看出，一共有三个人，一位留着长发的女子和两位男子，其中一位黑色头发的男子穿着蓝色衬衫和黑色西装，另一位有白头发的男子穿着白色衬衫和灰白色西装，所以答案选 (C)。

听力测验 | Part 3 简短对话题

1. What's the good news for the woman?
    (A) She has a chance to go abroad for a business trip.
    (B) She was invited to attend the company's annual meeting.
    (C) She was employed by the company.
    (D) She was promoted to be the manager of the company.

2. What does the woman want to do when she comes to the company first?
    (A) She wants to make a self-introduction to her workmates.
    (B) She wants to know what her position is.
    (C) She wants to know her colleagues.
    (D) She wants to know her responsibilities here.

3. What's Jack's position in the company?
    (A) General manager.
    (B) Assistant manager.
    (C) Personnel manager.
    (D) Director.

Jack: Hi, I'm Jack, the assistant manager of the company. You have been employed by our company. Welcome!

Zoe: I'm glad to work here. I appreciate you giving me this opportunity.

Jack: Not at all. You performed well in the interview. We're impressed with you.

Zoe: Thank you! May I make a self-introduction to our colleagues? And by the way, would you mind introducing our workmates to me? I hope we can get along well.

Jack: OK. But you should learn your responsibilities here and what your position is first.

Zoe: Yes. I will.

Jack: OK. I hope you are happy here. You are welcome to ask me if you have any problems.

♪ 088

Unit 09 雇用 | Employment

中译

1. 女子收到的好消息是什么？
   (A) 她有机会去国外出差。
   (B) 她被邀请参加公司的年度大会。
   (C) 她被公司录用了。
   (D) 她被提升为公司经理。

2. 女子来到公司后想先做什么？
   (A) 她想向同事做自我介绍。
   (B) 她想知道她的任务。
   (C) 她想认识这里的同事。
   (D) 她想知道自己在公司的职责。

3. 杰克在公司的职位是什么？
   (A) 总经理。
   (B) 副经理。
   (C) 人事经理。
   (D) 总监。

杰克：你好，我是杰克，公司的副经理，你被我们公司录用了，欢迎你的加入！
佐伊：我非常开心能在这里工作。感谢您能给我提供这个机会。
杰克：不客气，你在面试的时候表现得很好，你给我们留下了深刻的印象。
佐伊：谢谢！我能向同事们做个自我介绍吗？顺便问一下，您可不可以帮我介绍一下同事？我希望今后我们都能愉快地相处。
杰克：没问题，但是你要先了解你在这里的责任和任务。
佐伊：好的，我会的。
杰克：好，希望你在这里工作愉快。如果有什么问题，你可以来找我。

解析与答案

答案：1. (C) 2. (A) 3. (B)
1. 根据第一句话可知，佐伊收到的好消息是被公司录用了，所以选 (C)。
2. 根据听力可知，女子问的第一个问题就是她能否向同事做个自我介绍，所以选 (A)。
3. 根据 I'm Jack, the assistant manager of the company 可知，杰克是公司的副经理，所以选 (B)。

单词 Vocabulary

employ [ɪm'plɔɪ] n 雇用 v 雇用，使从事于
appreciate [ə'priːʃɪeɪt] v 感激，欣赏，增值
perform [pə'fɔːm] v 执行，表演
impress ['ɪmpres] n 印象 [ɪm'pres] v 给某人留下深刻印象
colleague ['kɒliːg] n 同事 [kɒ'liːg] v 联合

089

Good morning, Linda. I'm Sara. Welcome to our company! We expect you to adapt yourself as soon as possible. If you have any problems, we can all lend you a hand. For now, you are assigned to a group with Jack whose seat is right beside you and has worked here for five years, to help you with your adaptation and work.

Our manager of the sales department is Steven. He is very aggressive and brilliant. After work, we will hold a party to celebrate your joining our company and then you can get acquainted with our colleagues.

Next, I will tell you the rules and regulations of our company. It is clear what you mustn't do and what you must do according to the rules and regulations.

   a. Nobody is allowed to be late for work and leave earlier than scheduled for no reason or he / she will be punished. If a person violates this rule four times in one month, he / she will be dismissed immediately.

   b. Nobody is allowed to reveal confidential information about our company or he / she will definitely be fired.

   c. If you want to ask for leave, you need to get permission from the manager ahead of time.

   d. If you want to quit the job, you need to let the manager know thirty days in advance.

From now on, you should try your best to do your job. If you are outstanding, you will be promoted. Come on!

1. Where may this memo be seen?
    (A) At home.
    (B) In the gym.
    (C) In the museum.
    (D) In the office.

2. Who is assigned to a group with Linda to help with her adaption and work?
    (A) Sara.
    (B) Steven.
    (C) Jack.
    (D) Someone else.

3. What will they hold a party for after work?
    (A) To celebrate Linda's joining the company.
    (B) To celebrate the New Year.
    (C) To celebrate the Christmas.
    (D) To celebrate the promotion of Jack.

4. What will happen to an employee if he/she is late four times in one month?
    (A) He/She will be punished to work overtime.
    (B) He/She will be fired immediately.
    (C) He/She will be promoted.
    (D) He/She will be demoted.

5. Which of the following is NOT true?
    (A) Nobody is allowed to be late for work for no reason.
    (B) Nobody is allowed to reveal confidential information about our company.
    (C) If the employee wants to ask for leave, he / she should get permission from Jack.
    (D) Sara encourages Linda to work hard.

早安,琳达。我是莎拉。欢迎加入我们公司!我们期望你能够尽快适应。如果你有任何问题,我们都可以帮助你。现在我们将你与杰克分配到一组,他的位置在你旁边,他在这里工作已经五年了,可以帮助你适应以及帮助你工作。

我们销售部门的经理是史蒂芬。他积极进取、才能卓越。下班后,我们将会为你举行一场派对,来欢迎你加入我们公司,然后你就可以很快熟悉我们的同事了。

接下来,我要告诉你一些我们公司的规章制度。根据规章制度,必须去做的事情以及一定不能做的事情就一目了然了。

一、任何人不允许无故迟到、早退,否则会予以处罚;若在一个月内违规四次,将会被立即开除。

二、任何人不允许泄露我们公司的机密,否则绝对予以开除。

三、若要请假,则需要提前取得经理同意方能离开。

四、若要辞职,则需要提前三十天告知经理。

从现在起,你应该竭尽全力做好工作。若表现优秀,则给予升职。加油!

1. 这则备忘录可能在哪里看到?
   (A) 家。
   (B) 健身房。
   (C) 博物馆。
   (D) 办公室。

2. 为了帮助琳达适应工作,她与谁分配到了一组?
   (A) 莎拉。
   (B) 史蒂芬。
   (C) 杰克。
   (D) 另有他人。

3. 下班后,他们为什么举行派对?
   (A) 庆祝琳达加入公司。
   (B) 庆祝新年。
   (C) 庆祝圣诞节。
   (D) 庆祝杰克升职。

4. 若员工一个月迟到四次，会如何处置？
   (A) 处罚要加班。
   (B) 立即开除。
   (C) 升职。
   (D) 降职。

5. 下列哪一项说法是不正确的？
   (A) 任何人不允许无故上班迟到。
   (B) 任何人不允许泄露公司机密。
   (C) 若雇员要请假，应该征得杰克同意。
   (D) 莎拉鼓励琳达努力工作。

答案：1. (D) 2. (C) 3. (A) 4. (B) 5. (C)

1. 此题考获取信息的能力，可见第一段第二句 Welcome to join our company，因此选 (D)。
2. 此题考细节，答案在第一段最后一句 you are assigned to a group with Jack... to help you with your adaptation and work，所以选 (C)。
3. 此题考细节，可见第二段最后一句 After work, we will hold a party to celebrating you joining our company...，因此选 (A)。
4. 此题考信息提取能力，见第三段的第一条 if violates this four times in one month, he / she will be dismissed immediately，选 (B) 立即开除。
5. 此题考细节，可见第三段的第三条 if you want to ask for leave, you need to get permission from the manager ahead of time，需要获得经理（史蒂芬）的同意，而不是杰克，因此选 (C)。

单词 Vocabulary

expect [ɪk'spekt] v 期望，预计，期待
possible ['pɒsəbl] a 可能的，合理的 n 可能性
lend [lend] v 把……借给，贷款（borrow 是"向……借"）
adaptation [,ædæp'teɪʃn] n 适应
introduce [,ɪntrə'djuːs] v 介绍，引荐，提出
department [dɪ'pɑːtmənt] n 部门
colleague ['kɒliːg] n 同事
regulation [,regjʊ'leɪʃn] n 规则，规定 a 标准的
outstanding [aʊt'stændɪŋ] a 杰出的
promote [prə'məʊt] v 升职，晋升，促进

Unit 10
薪资 | Wage

New TOEIC

Picture 10

情境中可明确指出的单词

1. **account book** ph 账本
2. **ambidextrous** [ˌæmbɪˈdekstrəs] a 双手灵巧的，双手都善用的
3. **cabinet** [ˈkæbɪnət] n 柜子
4. **calculator** [ˈkælkjuleɪtə(r)] n 计算器
5. **denomination** [dɪˌnɒmɪˈneɪʃn] n （货币等的）面额
6. **dossier** [ˈdɒsieɪ] n 档案
7. **greenback** [ˈɡriːnbæk] n 美钞
8. **pony tail** ph 马尾

情境中可延伸记忆的单词

1. **accounting** [əˈkaʊntɪŋ] n 会计，结账
2. **bonus** [ˈbəʊnəs] n 奖金
3. **cubicle** [ˈkjuːbɪkl] n 小隔间
4. **delighted** [dɪˈlaɪtɪd] a 快乐的，高兴的
5. **department** [dɪˈpɑːtmənt] n 部门
6. **finance** [ˈfaɪnæns] n 财政
7. **painstaking** [ˈpeɪnzteɪkɪŋ] a 仔细的，勤勉的
8. **salary** [ˈsæləri] n 薪资 v 给……薪水

account book ph 账本

The accountant is checking the account books for last month.
会计正在核对上一个月的账本。
- accountable a 有责任的 / account n 账目

ambidextrous [ˌæmbɪˈdekstrəs] a 双手灵巧的，双手都善用的

The woman is ambidextrous and can use either hand to write with.
这个双手灵巧的女子可以用任何一只手写字。
- ambidexterity n 怀二心

cabinet [ˈkæbɪnət] n 柜子

They often put documents back in the cabinet before leaving the office.
离开办公室之前，他们通常都会把档案放回柜子。
- filing cabinet ph 档案橱柜

calculator [ˈkælkjuleɪtə(r)] n 计算器

To avoid mistakes, you had better use the calculator.
为了避免错误，你最好用计算器。
- calculation n 计算 / calculate v 计算 / calculate on ph 指望

denomination [dɪˌnɒmɪˈneɪʃn] n （货币等的）面额

We don't accept the lowest denomination.
我们不接受最低面额。
- denominational a 教派的

dossier [ˈdɒsɪeɪ] n 档案

I want his complete dossier before he comes.
在他来之前，我需要他的全部档案。
- secret dossier ph 绝密档案 / archive n 档案，文件 / document n 文件

greenback [ˈɡriːnbæk] n 美钞

The woman is counting the greenbacks with a smile.
女子正面带微笑地数美钞。
- United States note ph 美钞 / dollar n 美元

pony tail ph 马尾

The woman with the pony tail is really outstanding.
绑着马尾辫的那位女子真的十分优秀。
- braid n 辫子 / hair piece ph 假发

accounting [ə'kaʊntɪŋ] n. 会计，结账

The woman is a member of the accounting department.
这位女子是会计部的一员。
- accountable a. 有责任的 / accounting earnings n. 会计盈余

---

bonus ['bəʊnəs] n. 奖金

In addition to their salary, outstanding employees have a bonus.
除了薪水，优秀的员工还会有奖金。
- annual bonus n. 年终分红 / bonus shares n. 奖金分配 / penalty n. 罚款

---

cubicle ['kju:bɪkl] n. 小隔间

He went into the cubicle and never came out.
他走进小隔间，再也没出来。
- control cubicle n. 操纵室

---

delighted [dɪ'laɪtɪd] a. 快乐的，高兴的

The employees will be delighted on pay day.
员工在发薪水的那一天会很高兴。
- delightful a. 可爱的 / delight in n. 以……为乐 / contented a. 满意的，知足的

---

department [dɪ'pɑ:tmənt] n. 部门

He makes the highest pay in the sales department.
在销售部门，他拿的薪水最高。
- departmental a. 部门的 / department store n. 百货公司

---

finance ['faɪnæns] n. 财政

The boss is in charge of the company's finances.
老板掌握着公司的财政大权。
- financier n. 金融家 / financial a. 财政的，金融的 / cost n. 成本 / profit n. 利润

---

painstaking ['peɪnzteɪkɪŋ] a. 仔细的，勤勉的

The woman is counting the money with painstaking attention.
这位女子正在仔细地数钱。
- painstakingly ad. 煞费苦心地

---

salary ['sæləri] n. 薪资 v. 给……薪水

The woman has a good salary.
这位女子有一份不错的薪水。
- salaried a. 有薪水的 / salary cap n. 薪水上限 / wage n. 薪水，工资

听力测验 | Part 1 图片描述题

题目
(A) They have the same haircut.
(B) Both of them are counting money.
(C) Both of them have beards.
(D) They are keeping accounts.

中译
(A) 他们留着同样的发型。
(B) 他们都在数钱。
(C) 他们都留有胡须。
(D) 他们都在记账。

解析与答案

答案：(B)
从图片可以看出来，这两位男子都在数钱，他们的发型不一样；另外，一个有胡须，另一个没有胡须，所以选 (B)。

听力测验 | Part 3 简短对话题

NEW TOEIC

1. Why does the employee choose this company?
   (A) Because he just wants to get some experience.
   (B) Because he can earn a lot of money.
   (C) Because he can get extra commissions.
   (D) Because he is interested in being an assistant.

2. When could the employee start to work?
   (A) Tomorrow.
   (B) The day after tomorrow.
   (C) After tomorrow.
   (D) After the day after tomorrow.

3. What can we learn about the employee from this conversation?
   (A) He is confident.
   (B) He is selfish.
   (C) He is self-contemptuous.
   (D) He is decisive.

Interviewer: Hello! We have seen your resume. We want to know why you chose our company?

Interviewee: Because I'm interested in the assistant position.

Interviewer: I know you have plenty of experience in this field. So, let's talk about your wage.

Interviewee: OK.

Interviewer: What's your salary expectations?

Interviewee: I hope it won't be lower than someone with my qualifications.

Interviewer: You won't, but you will have a trial period with just a basic salary.

Interviewee: It's OK. Would you mind telling me more about salary in our company?

Interviewer: Wages rise with working-age, and you can get extra commissions.

Interviewee: Thank you! When should I start to work?

Interviewer: You can work tomorrow.

Unit 10 薪资 | Wage

中译

1. 面试者为什么要选择这家公司？
   (A) 因为他只是想获得一些经验。
   (B) 因为他可以赚很多的钱。
   (C) 因为他能得到额外的提成。
   (D) 因为他对助理这个职位感兴趣。

2. 面试者什么时候可以开始工作？
   (A) 明天。
   (B) 后天。
   (C) 明天之后。
   (D) 后天之后。

3. 从这段对话中我们可以推断出面试者是个什么样的人？
   (A) 自信的。
   (B) 自私的。
   (C) 自卑的。
   (D) 果断的。

面试官：你好！我们已经看过你的简历。你为什么会选择我们公司？
面试者：因为我对助理这个职位很感兴趣。
面试官：我知道你在这方面有丰富的经验，所以，我们来谈谈你的薪资吧。
面试者：好的。
面试官：你的期望薪资是多少？
面试者：我希望不要低于和我有同等条件的人。
面试官：这一点你可以放心，但是试用期间你只能拿到基本工资。
面试者：没问题。你能告诉我更多有关薪资方面的事情吗？
面试官：薪资会随着工作资历增长，而且还会有额外的提成。
面试者：谢谢！我什么时候可以开始工作呢？
面试官：你明天就可以工作了。

解析与答案

答案：1. (D) 2. (A) 3. (A)

1. 听力开始面试官就问到这个问题，面试者的回答是 Because I'm interested in the assistant position，所以选 (D)。
2. 从听力最后一句 You can work tomorrow 可知，面试者明天就可以上班了，所以选 (A)。
3. 一开始面试官就提到面试者有丰富的经验，在谈到薪水的时候，面试者说希望不要低于和他有同等条件的人，从中可以感觉到他是非常自信的，所以选 (A)。

单词 Vocabulary

resume ['rezju:m] n 简历 [rɪ'zju:m] v 继续，重新开始
plenty ['plenti] n 大量，丰富 a 足够的，很多的
qualification [ˌkwɒlɪfɪ'keɪʃn] n 条件，资格
period ['pɪəriəd] n 期间，（一堂）课，句号 a 某一时代的
commission [kə'mɪʃn] n 委员会，佣金 v 委任

阅读测验 | Part 7 文章理解题

To: All Staff

From: Jack Queen

Subject: Rules and regulations on salary

Hello everyone,

Good afternoon, everyone. This is Jack Queen. This e-mail is for all the staff in our company. There are changes in salary that you need to know. Please read carefully.

We have made a new salary. There is a little alteration of compensation and benefits for the full-time and part-time staff. Some employees came up with a proposal last month. After an intense discussion, the board of directors passed a ruling that the salary shall be paid on the basis of performance and achievements, not the length of service. Here are the details of the proposal:

a. The salary of full-time staff consists of basic salary and commission. All full-time staff will have one-week of paid sick leave and one-week paid annual leave. Long-term disability compensation shall be half of the basic wage. There is no change in the pension plan.

b. Part-time staff will get only commission without basic salary and pension.

The changes will be posted on the door of the administration building. All staff can see this there.

Most of the directors think it preferable to carry out the proposal from next season, so we decided to carry it out next season. If there is any objection about the rules and regulations on salary, contact the Administrative Department at 666-8888, please.

Regards, Jack Queen

Nov. 18th, 2015

1. What is the e-mail about?
   (A) Holidays.
   (B) Travel.
   (C) Business.
   (D) Salary.

2. When was this proposal raised by the employees?
   (A) Last year.
   (B) Last month.
   (C) Last week.
   (D) Yesterday.

3. What does the salary of full-time staff consist of?
   (A) Only basic salary.
   (B) Only commission.
   (C) Basic salary, commission and bonus.
   (D) Basic salary and commission.

4. What can the part-time staff get?
   (A) Only basic salary.
   (B) Only pension.
   (C) Only commission.
   (D) Only basic salary and commission.

5. What can the staff do if they have problems about the changes of salary according to this e-mail?
   (A) To consult the Administrative Department at 666-8888.
   (B) To ask the board of directors directly.
   (C) To call the announcer.
   (D) To go on a strike.

收件人：全体员工
寄件者：杰克·奎恩
主题：有关薪水的规章制度

大家好！

大家下午好。我是杰克·奎恩。这封邮件是针对我们公司全体员工的。在薪水上有些许变化，请认真阅读。

我们制定出一项有关薪水的新政策。对于全职人员以及兼职人员的薪资福利有些许变动。上个月，一些员工提出了一项提议。经过激烈的讨论后，董事会将其通过，薪水应该按照表现情况以及取得的业绩发放，而非按照资历长短。这里是提议的详细内容：

一、全职人员的薪水由基本薪资与提成组成；全职人员有一周的带薪病假和一周的带薪年假。长期伤残补助为基本薪资的一半。关于公积金这方面，没有变动。

二、兼职人员只有提成，没有基本薪资与津贴。

这些变动内容将会贴在行政大楼的门上。所有员工可以在那里看到这些内容。

大部分董事认为下一季度实施本提议较恰当，因此我们决定下一季度实施。对于薪水的规章制度，若有异议，请拨打 666-8888 联系行政部门。

此致

敬礼！

杰克·奎恩
2015 年 11 月 18 日

1. 这封邮件是关于什么的？
   (A) 假期。
   (B) 旅行。
   (C) 贸易。
   (D) 薪资。

2. 这项提议是员工什么时候提出来的？
   (A) 去年。
   (B) 上个月。
   (C) 上周。
   (D) 昨天。

3. 全职人员的薪水包括什么？
   (A) 只有基本薪资。
   (B) 只有提成。
   (C) 基本薪资加上提成和红利。
   (D) 基本薪资加上提成。

Unit 10 薪资 | Wage

4. 兼职员工可以得到什么？
   (A) 只有基本薪资。
   (B) 只有津贴。
   (C) 只有提成。
   (D) 只有基本薪资和提成。

5. 根据邮件可知，如果员工对薪水的调整有任何疑问的话，他们可以做什么？
   (A) 拨打 666-8888 向行政部门进行咨询。
   (B) 直接问董事会人员。
   (C) 打电话给宣布这个消息的人。
   (D) 举行罢工。

答案：1. (D) 2. (B) 3. (D) 4. (C) 5. (A)

1. 此题考细节，邮件的主题点明此题答案，文中不断出现关键词"salary"，因此选 (D)。
2. 此题考阅读能力，答案在邮件正文第二段的第三句 Some employees came up with a proposal last month，选 (B)。
3. 此题考细节，可见第二段的第六句 the salary of full-time staff consists of basic salary and commission，因此选 (D)。
4. 此题同样是考细节，见第二段的第十句 Part-time staff will get only commission without basic salary or pension，选 (C)。
5. 此题考阅读能力，可见邮件正文的最后一句，因此选 (A)。

单词 Vocabulary

regulation [ˌrɛɡjʊˈleɪʃn] n 规则 a 标准的
staff [stɑːf] n 职员，全体工作人员
policy [ˈpɒləsɪ] n 政策
compensation [ˌkɒmpenˈseɪʃn] n 补偿，报酬
discussion [dɪˈskʌʃn] n 讨论
director [dəˈrektə(r)] n 主管
consist [kənˈsɪst] v 组成
leave [liːv] n 请假 v 离开
administration [ədˌmɪnɪˈstreɪʃn] n 行政
department [dɪˈpɑːtmənt] n 部门

Unit 11
升迁 | Promotion

New TOEIC

Picture 11

情境中可明确指出的单词

1. **dark blue** ph 深蓝色
2. **clap** [klæp] n 拍手喝彩 v 为……鼓掌
3. **co-worker** ['kəʊˌwɜːkə] n 同事
4. **office chair** ph 办公椅
5. **lattice** ['lætɪs] n 格子窗
6. **medium length hair** ph 中长发
7. **open** ['əʊpən] v 打开 a 打开的
8. **portfolio** [pɔːt'fəʊliəʊ] n 文件夹，卷宗夹

情境中可延伸记忆的单词

1. **congratulate** [kən'grætʃuleɪt] v 祝贺，庆贺
2. **happy** ['hæpi] a （感到）高兴的
3. **development** [dɪ'veləpmənt] n 发展
4. **feedback** ['fiːdbæk] n 回馈
5. **pride** [praɪd] n 骄傲，自豪
6. **promotion** [prə'məʊʃn] n 升迁
7. **roomy** ['ruːmi] a 宽敞的
8. **strength** [streŋθ] n 实力，优点

Unit 11 升迁 | Promotion

dark blue [ph] 深蓝色
The first man from the left is wearing a dark blue tie.
从左边数第一位男子戴了一条深蓝色的领带。
※ blue print [ph] 蓝图 / light [a] 浅色的

clap [klæp] [n] 拍手喝彩 [v] 为……鼓掌
The three people are clapping for the man wearing a dark blue tie.
三个人向戴着深蓝色领带的那位男子鼓掌。
※ clapping [n] 掌声 / clap on [ph] 急速穿上

co-worker [ˈkəʊˌwɜːkə] [n] 同事
He always helps his co-workers when they are in trouble.
同事有困难时，他总是会帮助他们。
※ colleague [n] 同事 / superior [n] 上司，主管

office chair [ph] 办公椅
He took a break in the office chair at noon.
中午的时候，他坐在办公椅上休息。
※ comfortable office chair [ph] 舒服的办公椅 / swivel chair [ph] 旋转椅

lattice [ˈlætɪs] [n] 格子窗
The balcony outside of our office has a lattice fence.
我们办公室外面的阳台有格子围栏。
※ latticed [a] 装有格子的

medium length hair [ph] 中长发
The man points to the lady with medium length hair.
男子指着留有中长发的女子。
※ breadth [n] 宽度 / depth [n] 深度

open [ˈəʊpən] [v] 打开 [a] 打开的
Please open the door; I need some fresh air.
请把门打开；我需要新鲜空气。
※ openness [n] 公开 / open bid [ph] 公开投标 / close [v] 关闭

portfolio [pɔːtˈfəʊlɪəʊ] [n] 文件夹，卷宗夹
Could you please bring me the portfolio?
请把文件夹拿给我，好吗？
※ asset portfolio [ph] 资产组合 / portfolio management [ph] 卷宗管理

congratulate [kənˈgrætʃuleɪt] v 祝贺，庆贺
The colleagues are congratulating the man.
同事们在祝贺这位男子。
⊕ congratulation n 祝贺 / congratulate sb. on sth. phr 为某事向某人祝贺

happy [ˈhæpi] a （感到）高兴的
They are happy for the man's promotion.
他们都替男子的升迁感到高兴。
⊕ happiness n 幸福 / happily ad 幸福地

development [dɪˈveləpmənt] n 发展
The man, who was promoted to manager, contributes a lot to the development of company.
那位升迁为经理的男子，对公司的发展做出了很大贡献。
⊕ developmental a 发展的 / development area phr （英）开发地区

feedback [ˈfiːdbæk] n 回馈
This promotion is the feedback to the man's efforts.
这次晋升是对这位男子努力的回报。
⊕ information feedback phr 信息回馈 / feedback mechanism phr 回馈机制

pride [praɪd] n 骄傲，自豪
The man must take immense pride in his achievements.
这位男子一定为自己的成就感到自豪。
⊕ prideful a 高傲的 / Pride goes before a fall. 骄者必败。

promotion [prəˈməʊʃn] n 升迁
The man's promotion means a higher salary.
这位男子的晋升意味着他薪资的提高。
⊕ promote v 晋升 / promotive a 奖励的 / promotion worker phr 推销员

roomy [ˈruːmi] a 宽敞的
We need an office as roomy as theirs.
我们需要一间和他们一样宽敞明亮的办公室。
⊕ roominess n 广阔 / spacious a 宽敞的 / narrow a 狭窄的

strength [streŋθ] n 实力，优点
His promotion is attributed to his strength of mind and will.
他的升职归功于他精神强大、意志坚强。
⊕ strengthen v 加强 / on the strength of phr 基于，根据

听力测验 | Part 1 图片描述题

题目
(A) Both of the men are black men.
(B) All the women left their hair loose.
(C) All the women have their hair tied up.
(D) One of the women has her hair loose.

中译
(A) 两位男子都是黑人。
(B) 所有的女子都披着头发。
(C) 所有的女子都将头发扎了起来。
(D) 有一位女子披着头发。

解析与答案
答案：(D)
从图片中可以看出，有三位女子、两位男子，其中两位女子扎着头发，一位女子披着头发，一位男子是白人，另一位男子是黑人，所以选 (D)。

听力测验 | Part 4 简短独白题

1. What could people get if they apply for this position?
    (A) They will get more money.
    (B) They will get promoted.
    (C) They will recruit more people.
    (D) They will take on more responsibilities.

2. What must be handed in when the program ends?
    (A) A report.
    (B) An essay.
    (C) A market research.
    (D) An application form.

3. Which duty of the following is not necessary for the applicants?
    (A) They should fill out a form.
    (B) They should write a report.
    (C) They should write an essay.
    (D) They should invite more people.

The middle manager's position is vacant now. The chance for middle managers is to participate in a program which is related to international exchange. This program will last for six months. You will learn the best practice principles with counterparts in the respective country in the head office. The domestic branches market is so complicated that you should spend a lot of time there. During that time, you should pay particular attention to market research in domestic consumers' preferences. Then, you are supposed to write a report based on research results.

If you are satisfied with this position, you must fill out an application. You must include an essay about what benefits you can provide for the program. The deadline for applying is September 21st.

Unit 11 升迁 | Promotion

中译

1. 如果人们申请该职位,他们会获得什么?
   (A) 他们会获得更多的金钱。
   (B) 他们的职位会得到提升。
   (C) 他们会招募更多的人。
   (D) 他们会承担更多的责任。

2. 专案结束的时候,必须提交什么?
   (A) 一份报告。
   (B) 一篇论文。
   (C) 一份市场调查。
   (D) 一张申请表。

3. 下列职责中,申请者不必要做哪一项?
   (A) 他们需要填写一份申请表。
   (B) 他们要写一份报告。
   (C) 他们要写一篇文章。
   (D) 他们要邀请更多的人。

现在中层管理者的位置还有空缺。中层管理者有机会参加有关国际汇兑的专案,这项专案将会历时六个月。你会和各国的相应人员在总部学习最佳操作规则。国内分支的消费市场非常复杂,你需要花费大量的时间在这上面。在这期间,你要特别注意国内消费者偏好的市场调查。然后,你要基于调查结果上交一份报告。

如果你对这个职位感到满意,你需要填写一份申请,而且,你要写一篇你可以为这项专案带来什么利益的文章。申请的截止日期是九月二十一日。

解析与答案

答案:1. (B) 2. (A) 3. (D)

1. 从全文可判断这是一则关于公司内部职位升迁申请的公告,所以申请者最终会获得的是职位的提升,答案选 (B)。
2. 根据 you are supposed to write a report based on research results 可知,专案结束后,申请人要写一份报告,所以选 (A)。
3. 根据听力可知,申请人在申请该职位的时候需要填写一份申请表,一篇可以为这项专案带来什么好处的文章,专案结束时要提交一份报告,只有 (D) 没有提到,所以选 (D)。

单词 Vocabulary

vacant ['veɪkənt] a (职位)空缺的,心不在焉的,空闲的
participate [pɑː'tɪsɪpeɪt] v 参与,分担
counterpart ['kaʊntəpɑːt] n 相似的人或物,副本
respective [rɪ'spektɪv] a 各自的,分担的
domestic [də'mestɪk] a 国内的,家庭的 n 佣人,国货
application [ˌæplɪ'keɪʃn] n 申请,应用
deadline ['dedlaɪn] n 截止日期

To: Roy Harper

From: Tommy Merlyn

Subject: Promotion of Robert Queen

Dear Mr. Harper,

I am happy to announce that Robert Queen has been promoted to leading trader of the Europe Currency Bureau, which will take effect on Oct. 23rd, 2015.

Robert Queen has earned an MBA at Harvard University and has ten years of experience in Europe's currency markets. He has contributed a lot to our company, and made great profits with his knowledge and experience in currency markets. We can see his outstanding skills and ability to deal with all kinds of unexpected situations.

In sum, Robert is a talented trader with great potential and enormous experiences and will be promoted in our company. He has shown his ability to make profits while taking certain risks, and he seized opportunities as they arose. He is able to take chances and avoid risks.

Robert has shown us his ability to prove academics and professionals wrong about the problems and difficulties in the business. Although his strategies are sometimes against business philosophies, he has made huge profits for our company. As European markets are now free, we still expect an increasing presence with excellent leaders like Robert to direct the way.

In general, Robert Queen has no limits to his strategies providing that the base rules and regulations of our company are not violated.

We welcome you to congratulate Robert on his promotion.

Regards,

Tommy Merlyn

Unit 11 升迁 | Promotion

1. What is the e-mail about?
   (A) Promotion of Roy Harper.
   (B) Promotion of Robert Queen.
   (C) Promotion of Barry Allen.
   (D) Promotion of Tommy Merlyn.

2. When will the promotion take effect?
   (A) From Oct. 23rd, 2015.
   (B) From Oct. 24th, 2015.
   (C) From Oct. 25th, 2015.
   (D) From Oct. 26th, 2015.

3. Where did Robert graduate from?
   (A) University of Cambridge.
   (B) Harvard University.
   (C) Yale University.
   (D) MIT.

4. What kind of person does Tommy think Robert is?
   (A) Stupid.
   (B) Talented.
   (C) Timid.
   (D) Dishonest.

5. Which of the following is not true?
   (A) Robert always takes chances and avoids risks.
   (B) Robert has contributed a lot to our company.
   (C) No one is allowed to violate the base rules and regulations of the company.
   (D) Roy will not celebrate Robert on his promotion.

收件人：罗伊·哈珀
寄件者：汤米·梅林
主题：罗伯特·奎恩升迁

尊敬的哈珀先生：

　　我很高兴宣布罗伯特·奎恩已经升为欧洲货币办公室的领导交易者，这将于2015年10月23日生效。

　　罗伯特·奎恩持有哈佛大学工商管理学硕士学位，并有十年的欧洲货币市场经验。他对我们公司奉献了许多，凭着他的货币市场知识与经验为公司获取了巨额利润。我们能看到他那出众的技巧与处理各种突发情况的能力。

　　总之，罗伯特是一位优秀的商人，拥有巨大潜力、丰富经验，在我们公司能够升迁。他显示了能冒一定风险、赚取利润的能力，在机遇到来时能够抓住。他总是能抓住机会，避免风险。

　　罗伯特向我们展示了他的能力，用商业中遇到的问题与困难解释纯理论学术与专业是错误的。尽管他的策略有时违背商业哲学，但是他还是为我们公司创造了巨额利润。欧洲市场继续开放，在像罗伯特如此优秀的领导的指引下，我们仍然期待一个上升的表现。

　　总之，罗伯特·奎恩的策略在没有违背我们公司的基本规则的情况下，不受到任何限制。

　　欢迎你来庆贺罗伯特的升迁。

　　此致

敬礼！

汤米·梅林

1. 这封邮件是关于什么？
   (A) 罗伊·哈珀的升迁。
   (B) 罗伯特·奎恩的升迁。
   (C) 巴里·艾伦的升迁。
   (D) 汤米·梅林的升迁。

2. 升迁从什么时候生效？
   (A) 2015年10月23日。
   (B) 2015年10月24日。
   (C) 2015年10月25日。
   (D) 2015年10月26日。

3. 罗伯特毕业于哪里？
   (A) 剑桥大学。
   (B) 哈佛大学。
   (C) 耶鲁大学。
   (D) 麻省理工。

4. 汤米认为罗伯特是什么样的人？
   (A) 愚蠢的。
   (B) 优秀的。
   (C) 胆小的。
   (D) 不忠诚的。

5. 下列哪项说法不正确？
   (A) 罗伯特总是能抓住机遇，回避风险。
   (B) 罗伯特对公司奉献很多。
   (C) 任何人不允许违反公司的基本规章制度。
   (D) 罗伊不会为罗伯特庆祝升迁。

解析与答案

答案：1. (B) 2. (A) 3. (B) 4. (B) 5. (D)

1. 此题可见邮件主题 Subject: Promotion of Robert Queen，因此选 (B)。
2. 此题答案在第一段第一句 ... Robert Queen has been promoted to leading trader of Europe Currency Bureau, which will take effective on Oct. 23rd, 2015，选 (A)。
3. 从第二段第一句 Robert Queen has an MBA of Harvard University... 可知此题答案要选 (B)。
4. 此题可见第三段第一句 ... Robert is a talented trader...，关键词是 talented，因此选 (B)。
5. 整封邮件中并未提及罗伊对罗伯特升迁事件的态度，因此选 (D)。

单词 Vocabulary

leading ['li:dɪŋ] a 领导的 n 领导
currency ['kʌrənsi] n 货币
market ['mɑrkɪt] n 市场 v 销售
knowledge ['nɒlɪdʒ] n 知识
sum [sʌm] n 全部，总和 v 总计
potential [pə'tenʃl] n 潜力，可能性 a 可能的
enormous [ɪ'nɔːməs] a 无数的
academic [ækə'demɪk] n 学术，教授 a 大学的，学术的
reason ['riːzn] n 理由，理性 v 推论
violate ['vaɪəleɪt] v 违反，侵犯

Unit 12
退休 | Retirement

New TOEIC

Picture 12

情境中可明确指出的单词

1. **balloon** [bə'luːn] n 气球
2. **bottle** ['bɒtl] n 瓶
3. **celebrate** ['selɪbreɪt] v 庆祝
4. **champagne** [ʃæm'peɪn] n 香槟
5. **colleague** ['kɒliːg] n 同事
6. **goblet** ['gɒblət] n 高脚杯
7. **black** [blæk] n 黑人,黑种人
8. **slogan** ['sləʊgən] n 口号,标语

情境中可延伸记忆的单词

1. **cheers** [tʃɪəz] n 欢呼声
2. **diligent** ['dɪlɪdʒənt] a 勤勉的,勤奋的
3. **fatigued** [fə'tiːgd] a 疲劳的
4. **hail** [heɪl] v 向……欢呼,为……喝彩
5. **livelihood** ['laɪvlihʊd] n 生活,生计
6. **pension** ['penʃn] n 退休金
7. **provision** [prə'vɪʒn] n 准备,规定
8. **retirement** [rɪ'taɪəmənt] n 退休,退职

Unit 12 退休 | Retirement

balloon [bə'luːn] n 气球
The ladies are holding colored **balloons** in their hands.
女子们手里拿着彩色的气球。
- ballooning n 充气 / balloonfish n 河豚

bottle ['bɒtl] n 瓶
The man standing between the two ladies is holding a **bottle** in his hand.
站在两位女子中间的那位男子手里拿着一个瓶子。
- bottleful n 一瓶的容量 / bottled a 瓶装的 / bottle cap opener n 开瓶器

celebrate ['selɪbreɪt] v 庆祝
The colleagues are **celebrating** this senior colleague's retirement.
同事们正在庆祝年长同事的退休。
- celebration n 庆典 / celebrated a 著名的

champagne [ʃæm'peɪn] n 香槟
They prepared a lot of **champagne** for the celebration.
他们为这次庆祝准备了很多香槟。
- champagne cork n 香槟酒的瓶塞

colleague ['kɒliːg] n 同事
All of our **colleagues** will attend the party to celebrate his retirement.
所有的同事都会参加派对，庆祝他的退休。
- comrade n 同事

goblet ['gɒblət] n 高脚杯
They raised their **goblets** in a toast to the king.
他们举起高脚杯向国王致敬。
- goblet cells n 杯状细胞 / wineglass n 高脚玻璃杯，葡萄酒杯

black [blæk] n 黑人，黑种人
The **black** man over there is an incredible singer.
在那里的那位黑人是很棒的歌手。
- Black singer n 黑人歌手 / black case work 暗箱操作

slogan ['sləʊgən] n 口号，标语
The colored **slogan** says, "Happy retirement."
彩色的横幅上写着"退休快乐"。
- sloganeer v 使用标语口号 / sloganize v 形成标语 / banner n 旗帜，横幅

cheers [tʃɪəz] n. 欢呼声
I can hear the cheers of the party.
我能听见派对的欢呼声。
- cheerful a. 欢乐的 / cheer on v. 鼓励 / cheer up v. 使高兴

diligent ['dɪlɪdʒənt] a. 勤勉的，勤奋的
He is a diligent worker.
他是个勤勉的工人。
- diligence n. 勤奋 / diligently ad. 勤勉地 / industrious a. 勤勉的

fatigued [fə'tiːgd] a. 疲劳的
After working all day, I am feeling a little fatigued.
在工作一整天后，我感到有点疲惫。
- fatigued driving n. 疲劳驾驶

hail [heɪl] v. 向……欢呼，为……喝彩
The man was hailed by his colleagues.
这名男子得到了同事们的称赞。
- hail from v. 来自 / cheer v. （向……）欢呼 / greet v. 招呼

livelihood ['laɪvlihʊd] n. 生活，生计
The elderly man is not worried about his livelihood after retirement.
这位年长者不担心他退休后的生计问题。
- liven v. 快活起来 / bread and butter n. 生计，谋生之道

pension ['penʃn] n. 退休金
The company grants retired people a pension.
公司将给退休人员发放退休金。
- pensionable a. 有资格领退休金的

provision [prə'vɪʒn] n. 准备，规定
The elderly man has made provisions for his retirement.
这位年长者已经为他的退休做好了准备。
- provisional a. 临时的 / provisionally ad. 暂时地

retirement [rɪ'taɪəmənt] n. 退休，退职
After retirement, he will have more time to accompany his family.
退休后，他将有更多的时间陪伴家人。
- retirement pay n. 退休金 / retirement plan n. 退休计划 / retiree n. 退休人员

听力测验 | Part 1 图片描述题

题目
(A) Everyone has a cup in his or her hand.
(B) Everyone is dressed in a suit.
(C) The women are blond.
(D) Everyone has a bottle of beer in his or her hand.

中译
(A) 每个人手中都有一个杯子。
(B) 每个人都穿着套装。
(C) 女子的头发是金色的。
(D) 每个人手中都有一瓶啤酒。

解析与答案

答案：(B)
从图片可以看出，每个人都穿着套装，大部分人手中拿着一个杯子，有的人拿两个，有的人则没有拿，他们手中一共只有一瓶香槟，两位女子当中有一位的头发是黑色的，所以答案选 (B)。

听力测验 | Part 4 简短独白题

1. What's Steven's position in this company?
   (A) General manager.
   (B) Human Resources general manager.
   (C) Representative.
   (D) Group leader.

2. Which of the following is not Steven's contribution?
   (A) He reduced the staff turnover.
   (B) He changed the way they handle human resources.
   (C) He cultivated many great employees.
   (D) A and C.

3. When will the farewell party be held?
   (A) At 8 p.m. on this weekend.
   (B) At 8 p.m. on next weekend.
   (C) At 8 a.m. on this weekend.
   (D) At 8 a.m. on next weekend.

Steven has been an excellent general manager of Human Resources. He is going to be retiring from his position at the end of next week. Steven was a representative in charge of market planning at first, but he was soon transferred to Human Resources because of his excellent interpersonal communication skills. Then, he was promoted to General Manager in his own right. Staff turnover has been reduced while he was General Manager, and he cultivated many great employees in his 20 years here. Now, the method in which we handle human resources has changed. So, he thinks it's time for him to retire. We are going to hold a farewell party for him at 8 p.m. this weekend. I hope everyone is available for this party.

Unit 12 退休 | Retirement

1. 史蒂芬在公司的职位是什么？
   (A) 总经理。
   (B) 人力资源部总经理。
   (C) 代表。
   (D) 组长。

2. 下列不属于史蒂芬的贡献的是哪一个？
   (A) 减少了人员的流动率。
   (B) 改变了人力资源的运行方式。
   (C) 培养了优秀的员工。
   (D) A 选项和 C 选项。

3. 欢送会什么时候举办？
   (A) 这个周末晚上八点。
   (B) 下个周末晚上八点。
   (C) 这个周末上午八点。
   (D) 下个周末上午八点。

史蒂芬是一位优秀的人力资源部经理。他下周将要退休。史蒂芬刚开始的时候只是一名市场策划的代表，但是他出色的人际交往能力使他在极短的时间内就被调到了人力资源部。接着，他又凭借自己的能力被提升为总经理。他在职的二十年间，员工流动率降低了，他还培养了许多优秀的员工。现在，人力资源的运作方式发生了改变。他觉得自己也该退休了。我们计划这个周末晚上八点为他举办一个欢送会，希望每个人都可以来参加。

解析与答案

答案：1. (B) 2. (B) 3. (A)

1. 听力第一句就讲到 general manager，别急着选 (A)，把整句听完，由 Steven has been an excellent general manager of Human Resources 可知，史蒂芬是公司人力资源部的经理，所以选 (B)。
2. 根据 The staff turnover has been reduced... 可知，(A)、(C) 选项听力中都有提及，(B) 选项中的人力资源运行方式虽然改变了，但并没有说是史蒂芬改变的，所以选 (B)。
3. 根据 We are going to hold a farewell party for him at 8 p.m. this weekend 可知，正确答案选 (A)。

单词 Vocabulary

representative [ˌreprɪˈzentətɪv] n 代表，众议员 a 有代表性的
transfer [trænsˈfɜː(r)] v 转让，转移 [ˈtrænsfɜː(r)] n 转移，传递
interpersonal [ˌɪntəˈpɜːsənl] a 人际的
turnover [ˈtɜːnəʊvə(r)] n 营业额，流通量 a 可翻转的
cultivate [ˈkʌltɪveɪt] v 培养，耕作，陶冶
handle [ˈhændl] v 处理，操作 n 把手，口实
farewell [ˌfeəˈwel] n 告别，再见 a 告别的

To: All Staff

From: Slade WIlson, Manager of Human Resources

Subject: Retirement of Malcolm Merlyn

Hello everyone,

I have something to announce. Malcolm Merlyn, our assistant manager of Human Resources, is going to retire from our company this week. Let's look back his work experience and contribution to our company.

Malcolm was a market researcher in the Marketing Department of our company in the beginning, but was transferred to Human Resources due to his outstanding communication skills. He worked very hard. He was so good that he was appointed to Vice Manager within two months. Nobody had ever been promoted so quickly before. He made a big contribution to reducing of personnel turnover; everyone was satisfied with him during his occupancy.

These days, there has been an increasing use of innovative technology in the way we deal with Human Resources and he has found it difficult to learn this new technology. So, Malcolm thinks he should move on in his life and enjoy his twilight years. At the same time, he can avoid many problems by retiring earlier than expected. He has contributed most of his life to our company, so I appreciate him.

This evening, there will be a farewell party for him at six in the office. I hope all staff will be present at the party and give him a farewell. Thank you so much!

Regards,

Slade Wilson

Unit 12 退休 | Retirement

1. Who will retire from the company?
   (A) All staff.
   (B) Slade Wilson.
   (C) Malcolm Merlyn.
   (D) Not mentioned in the e-mail.

2. What did Malcolm do in the beginning in the company?
   (A) Vice manager of Human Resources.
   (B) A market researcher.
   (C) Manager of Human Resources.
   (D) Salesman.

3. Why was Malcolm transferred to Human Resources?
   (A) For his outstanding communication skills.
   (B) For his incompetence.
   (C) For his excellent writing skills.
   (D) For his experience.

4. Why did Malcolm decide to retire ahead of time?
   (A) Because he is ill.
   (B) Because he wants to avoid technology problems and enjoy his twilight years.
   (C) Because he hates the company.
   (D) Because he has a bad performance in his position.

5. Who is invited to attend the farewell party?
   (A) Board of directors.
   (B) All the staff.
   (C) All the managers of the company.
   (D) Nobody.

收件人：全体职员
寄件者：斯莱德·威尔森，人力资源部经理
主题：麦克·梅林退休

大家好！

我有事情要通知。麦克·梅林，我们人力资源部的副经理，本周要从我们公司退休。让我们回顾一下他在我们公司的工作经历与贡献。

麦克起初是我们公司市场部门的市场调查人员，然而由于他杰出的沟通技巧被调到人力资源部门。他工作十分努力，表现十分优秀，两个月内被任命为副经理，之前没人这么快就能晋升。他对降低人员变动率做出了巨大贡献；他在职期间，每个人都很喜欢他。

这些日子以来，我们处理人力资源的方式有着越来越大的科技革新；他发现很难学习新科技。因此，麦克认为他应该继续他的生活，安享晚年。同时，提前退休，能避免很多问题。他将他大部分人生都奉献在了我们公司，我对此十分感激。

今晚我们在公司将会为他开一场欢送派对。我希望全体职员都能出席，为他送别。十分感谢！

此致

敬礼！

斯莱德·威尔森

1. 谁将从公司退休？
(A) 全体员工。
(B) 斯莱德·威尔森。
(C) 麦克·梅林。
(D) 邮件中未提及。

2. 麦克最初在公司做什么？
(A) 人力资源副经理。
(B) 市场调查员。
(C) 人力资源经理。
(D) 销售员。

3. 麦克为什么会调到人力资源部门？
(A) 由于他出色的沟通技巧。
(B) 由于他能力不足。
(C) 由于他优秀的写作技巧。
(D) 由于他的经验。

Unit 12 退休 | Retirement

4. 麦克为什么决定提前退休？
   (A) 因为他生病了。
   (B) 因为他想避免科技难题，并享受晚年。
   (C) 因为他讨厌公司。
   (D) 因为他在职表现不好。

5. 谁被邀请参加欢送会？
   (A) 董事会。
   (B) 全体职员。
   (C) 公司所有经理。
   (D) 没人。

解析与答案

答案：1. (C) 2. (B) 3. (A) 4. (B) 5. (B)

1. 此题可见邮件主题 Subject: Retirement of Malcolm Merlyn，是麦克·梅林要退休了，因此选 (C)。

2. 第二段讲述麦克在公司的经历，从第一句 Malcolm was a market researcher in the marketing department of our company in the beginning... 即可找到答案，因此选 (B)。

3. 此题可见第二段第一句 ...he was transferred to Human Resources due to his outstanding communication skills，选 (A)。

4. 第三段讲述了退休相关的事情。从第二句 So, Malcolm thinks he should move on in his life and enjoy his twilight years. At the same time, he can avoid many problems by retiring earlier than expected，得知答案应选 (B)。

5. 此题可见最后一段第二句 I hope all staff will be present at the party...，因此选 (B)。

单词 Vocabulary

resource [rɪˈsɔːrs] n 资源，办法
retirement [rɪˈtaɪərmənt] n 退休，退休生活
assistant [əˈsɪstənt] a 助理的，辅助的
researcher [rɪˈsɜːtʃə(r)] n 调查员
communication [kəˌmjuːnɪˈkeɪʃn] n 交流，沟通，信息
appoint [əˈpɔɪnt] v 任命，指派
duration [djuˈreɪʃn] n 持续时间
twilight [ˈtwaɪlaɪt] n 黄昏，衰退期 a 昏暗的，晚期的

学习重点

页 数	笔记内容

NEW TOEIC

金融、采购、研发

Finance, Purchase and Research

Chapter 3

Unit 13
银行 | Bank

New TOEIC

Picture 13

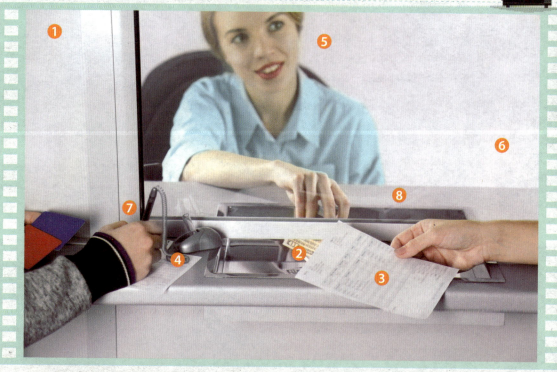

情境中可明确指出的单词

1. **bank** [bæŋk] n 银行
2. **banknote** ['bæŋknəʊt] n 纸币，钞票
3. **bank statement** ph 银行对账单
4. **strap** [stræp] v 用（绳子）捆绑
5. **teller** ['telə(r)] n （银行）出纳员
6. **tempered glass** ph 强化玻璃
7. **write** [raɪt] v 写
8. **wicket** ['wɪkɪt] n 窗口

情境中可延伸记忆的单词

1. **bankbook** ['bæŋkbʊk] n 银行存折
2. **deposit** [dɪ'pɒzɪt] n 存款，押金 v 把（钱）储存
3. **document** ['dɒkjumənt] n 证件，单据 ['dɒkju'ment] v 用文件证明
4. **queue** [kjuː] n / v 排队
5. **remit** [riː'mɪt] v 汇款
6. **sign** [saɪn] v 签名，签约雇用
7. **service charge** ph 手续费
8. **withdrawal** [wɪð'drɔːəl] n 提款

♪ 126

Unit 13 银行 | Bank

bank [bæŋk] n 银行
He went to the bank to open an account.
他去银行开一个账户。
- banker n 银行家

banknote ['bæŋknəʊt] n 纸币，钞票
I want to change the banknotes into coins.
我想将纸钞换成硬币。
- banknote paper ph 钞票纸 / bill n 钞票 / coin n 硬币 / currency n 货币

bank statement ph 银行对账单
Could you show the bank statement to me?
你能向我出示银行对账单吗？
- statement n 银行的报告单 / bank on ph 指望，依赖

strap [stræp] v 用（绳子）捆绑
The pen that is strapped to the counter is not allowed to be taken away.
绑有线圈的笔不允许带走。
- strapless a 无带的 / bind v 捆，绑 / wrap v 包，裹

teller ['telə(r)] n （银行）出纳（员）
A teller sits behind the tempered glass.
一位银行出纳坐在钢化玻璃后面。
- cashier n 出纳（员）/ tellership n 出纳职务 / telling a 有效的，生动的

tempered glass ph 强化玻璃
Tempered glass divides tellers from clients.
一块强化玻璃把出纳和客户隔开。
- temper n （钢的）韧度，（皮革的）质地，情绪 / glass reinforce ph 强化玻璃

write [raɪt] v 写
You need to write your name on the sheet.
你需要把你的名字写在单子上。
- written a 书面的 / scribe v 抄写 / write down ph 把……写下 / write down as ph 把……描写成

wicket ['wɪkɪt] n 窗口
The teller does business at this wicket.
出纳在这个窗口办理业务。
- window n 窗户，橱窗，电脑视窗 / wicket keeper ph 板球的守门员

127

bankbook [ˈbæŋkbʊk] n. 银行存折

Bankbooks are not frequently used at present.
现在，银行存折已经不常用了。
- deposit book n. 存折 / banking n. 银行业 / bankcard n. 银行信用卡

---

deposit [dɪˈpɒzɪt] n. 存款，押金 v. 把（钱）储存

Some people would like to **deposit** money in the bank.
有些人喜欢把钱存在银行。
- store v. 贮存 / depositor n. 存款人 / deposit slip n. 存款单 / pledge n. 抵押（品）

---

document [ˈdɒkjumənt] n. 证件，单据 [ˈdɒkjumənt] v. 用文件证明

Bring the **documents** here next time.
下次带你的文件。
- documentary a. 记录的 / certificate n. 证明书 / 证明 / archive n. 档案

---

queue [kjuː] n. / v. 排队

He was asked to leave because he jumped the **queue**.
因为插队，他被要求离开。
- queue up v. 排队等候 / line up 排队 / cut in (a line / a queue) 插队

---

remit [riːˈmɪt] v. 汇款

People **remit** money at the bank.
人们在银行汇钱。
- remittance n. 汇款 / remittee n. 汇款的收款人 / remitter n. 汇款人

---

sign [saɪn] v. 签名，签约雇用

The client needs to **sign** his name on the statement.
客户需要在对账单上签上自己的名字。
- sign for 签收 / sign in 签到 / endorse v. 签名背书 / signal n. 信号

---

service charge ph. 手续费

The client has to pay a **service charge** for banking business.
办理银行业务，客户需要支付手续费。
- service industry 服务业 / commission n. 佣金

---

withdrawal [wɪðˈdrɔːəl] n. 提款

People also can make the **withdrawal** at the machine.
人们也可以在这台机器上提款。
- withdraw v. 撤退，取回 / automatic teller machine (ATM) 自助提款机

听力测验 | Part 1 图片描述题

题目

(A) This bank is tiny.
(B) There are many people in this bank.
(C) There are a few people in this bank.
(D) All the people here are dressed in black.

中译

(A) 这个银行很小。
(B) 银行里有很多人。
(C) 银行里的人很少。
(D) 每个人都穿着黑色的衣服。

解析与答案

答案：(C)
从图片可以看出，这个银行非常大，但是人很少，每个人的衣服都是不一样的颜色，所以选 (C)。

听力测验 | Part 4 简短独白题

NEW TOEIC

1. Which bank is not mentioned?
   (A) Barclays Bank.
   (B) Royal Bank of Scotland.
   (C) Halifax Bank of England.
   (D) Lloyds TSB Group.

2. How much does the interest rate of Barclays Bank decrease?
   (A) A tenth of a percentage point.
   (B) Two-tenths of a percentage point.
   (C) Two-fifth of a percentage point.
   (D) There is no mention of it.

3. Which bank's reduction rates are not mentioned?
   (A) Barclays Bank's.
   (B) Royal Bank of Scotland's.
   (C) Halifax Bank of England's.
   (D) Bank of England's.

It's said that the mortgage rates of some England's largest banks will be decreased. Barclays Bank will decrease its rates by two-tenths of a percentage point. At the same time, the rates of the Royal Bank of Scotland will be decreased by the same margin. On the other hand, the fixed-rate mortgages for five-year terms and longer of the Bank of England will decreased by two-tenths of a percentage point. Finally, Halifax Bank of Scotland has also announced that they will decrease their rates. No one knows the exact numbers, but some insiders have speculated that they will decrease rates by the same margin.

Unit 13 银行 | Bank

1. 哪个银行没有被提到？
 (A) 巴克莱银行。
 (B) 皇家苏格兰银行。
 (C) 英格兰哈利法克斯银行。
 (D) 劳埃德 TSB 集团。

2. 巴克莱银行的利率会下调多少？
 (A) 0.1%。
 (B) 0.2%。
 (C) 五分之二个百分点。
 (D) 文中没有提到。

3. 下列哪个银行的下调利率没有被提到？
 (A) 巴克莱银行。
 (B) 皇家苏格兰银行。
 (C) 英格兰哈利法克斯银行。
 (D) 英格兰银行。

据说英国一些大银行将会降低抵押贷款利率。巴克莱银行的利率会下降 0.2%，与此同时，皇家苏格兰银行也会下调同样的利率。另一方面，英格兰银行五年或五年以上的固定利率抵押也会下降 0.2%。最后，英格兰哈利法克斯银行也宣布将下调利率，但是没有人知道具体的下调力度。然而一些内部人员猜测英格兰哈利法克斯银行下调的利率会和其他银行一样。

答案：1. (D) 2. (B) 3. (C)

1. 由听力可知，文中共提到四个银行，分别是 Barclays Bank、Royal Bank of Scotland、Bank of England 和 Halifax Bank of Scotland，所以答案选 (D)。
2. 根据 Barclays Bank will decrease its rate by two-tenths of a percentage point 可知答案选 (B)。
3. 听力最后提到英格兰哈利法克斯银行也宣布要下调利率，但是没有人知道具体的数字，所以此题答案选 (C)。

单词 Vocabulary

mortgage ['mɔːgɪdʒ] v 抵押，把……做担保 n 抵押，抵押借款
percentage [pə'sentɪdʒ] n 百分比，百分数，比例
margin ['mɑːdʒɪn] n 利润，边缘 v 加旁注于
insider [ɪn'saɪdə(r)] n 内部人员，会员
speculate ['spekjuleɪt] v 推断，投机，思索

阅读测验 | Part 7 文章理解题

Our bank has kept our customers' personal data safe for years. Customers realize that personal information sometimes needs to be uploaded. For instance, when information is needed for customer service or when it comes to legal requests. The cases in which the customers' account information should be available are as follows:

Due to the latest tax laws passed by the state government, the state government shall have the right to check the customer's account information when they need it. Additionally, rules and regulations of the bank demand that we employ an auditing company, which is independent from us, to check if all the accounts and our electronic fund transfer procedures are as safe and accurate as customers expect them to be. We certainly can't be responsible for all services. Some services are handled by other companies in the name of our bank, such as automatic banking machines. It is very common to see these subcontracting services nowadays, and leaves us to focus on other services as well as saving money.

We want to emphasize that we have never revealed any customer's account information and no company which cooperates with us has ever done such things either. If you have any question, please feel free to contact us at 567-6868. We will help you to solve your question as soon as possible.

1. Whom is this announcement for?
   (A) Customers.
   (B) The chairman of the bank.
   (C) Staff at the bank.
   (D) Businessmen.

2. When does the customer's information need to be uploaded?
   (A) When the chairman of the bank wants to see it.
   (B) When it needs to check for customer service or when it comes to legal requests.
   (C) When anyone wants to see.
   (D) When the staff of the bank want to see.

3. Who has the right to check the customer's account information?
   (A) The chairman of the bank.
   (B) The state government.
   (C) Everyone.
   (D) Nobody.

4. Who operates the automatic banking machines?
   (A) The bank.
   (B) Other companies which cooperate with the bank.
   (C) The state government.
   (D) Not mentioned in the announcement.

5. Which of the following is false?
   (A) The bank and other companies cooperating with the bank have never revealed customer information.
   (B) All services are operated by only the bank.
   (C) Customer account information needs to be passed on in some cases.
   (D) Customers can contact the bank at 567-6868.

这些年来我们银行一直都在保护客户私人信息的安全。然而客户意识到在某些情况下需要上传客户信息。例如，核查客户服务，甚至涉及法律时，需要上传客户信息。需要上传客户信息的情况如下：

根据州政府最新通过的法律，需要时，州政府有权核查客户账户信息。而且，银行法规要求雇用一家独立的审计公司核查所有的账户信息是否正确无误、我们的电子资金转账程序是否像人们认为的那样安全并且正确无误。当然，我们不会对所有的服务负责。一些程序是由其他以我们银行的名义的公司处理的，例如自助提款机的自助服务。现在这些分包服务十分常见，这让我们可以专注于其他服务，同时也能节约钱财。

我们想强调的是我们从不泄露任何客户的账户信息，与我们合作的公司也未做过这样的事情。如果您有任何问题，请拨打 567-6868 联系我们。我们会尽快帮助您解决问题。

1. 这则公告是写给谁的？
   (A) 客户。
   (B) 行长。
   (C) 银行职员。
   (D) 商人。

2. 客户信息什么时候需要上传？
   (A) 银行行长想看的时候。
   (B) 需要核查客户服务，甚至涉及法律的时候。
   (C) 任何人想看的时候。
   (D) 银行职员想看的时候。

3. 谁有权核查客户账户信息？
   (A) 银行行长。
   (B) 州政府。
   (C) 每个人。
   (D) 没有人。

4. 自助提款机的自助服务是由谁操作的？
   (A) 银行。
   (B) 与银行合作的其他公司。
   (C) 州政府。
   (D) 公告中未提及。

5. 下列哪一项说法错误？
   (A) 银行以及与银行合作的其他公司从未泄露客户信息。
   (B) 所有的服务都只是由银行操作的。
   (C) 客户账户信息在某些情况下需要上传。
   (D) 客户可以拨打 567-6868 联系银行。

> **解析与答案**
>
> 答案：1. (A) 2. (B) 3. (B) 4. (B) 5. (B)
>
> 1. 此题考信息提取能力，整篇公告都在叙述客户信息安全的问题，从最后一段倒数第二句可知对象是客户，If you have any question, please feel free to contact us at 567-6868 揭晓了此题答案，因此选 (A)。
> 2. 此题可见第一段第三句 For instance, when information is needed for customer service or when it comes to legal requests，可知答案选 (B)。
> 3. 从第二段第一句 ... the state government shall have the right to check the customers' account information... 得知州政府有权查看账户，因此选 (B)。
> 4. 此题先找关键词 automatic banking machines，可见第二段倒数第二句 Some services are handled by other companies in the name of our bank, such as automatic banking machines，因此选 (B)。
> 5. 此题可见第二段第三句 We certainly can't be responsible for all the services，因此选 (B)。

单词 Vocabulary

personal ['pɜːsənl] a 个人的，本人的 n 人称代词
realize ['riːəlaɪz] v 意识，了解
law [lɔː] n 法律，法学，司法界
account [ə'kaʊnt] n 账户，账目，利益，解释 v 报账，解释
latest ['leɪtɪst] a 最新的，最近的 ad 最近地 n 最新的事物
government ['gʌvənmənt] n 政府，政体，政治，治理，管理
electronic [ɪˌlek'trɒnɪk] a 电子的
automatic [ˌɔːtə'mætɪk] a 自动的，必然的 n 自动机械，汽车
subcontract [ˌsʌbkən'trækt] v 分包，外包 [ˌsʌb'kɒntrækt] n 分包契约
cooperate [kəʊ'ɒpəreɪt] v 合作，协作

Unit 14
会计 | Accounting

New TOEIC

Picture 14

情境中可明确指出的单词

1. **data** [ˈdeɪtə] n 资料
2. **calculator** [ˈkælkjuleɪtə(r)] n 计算器
3. **earring** [ˈɪərɪŋ] n 耳环
4. **file cabinet** ph 档案柜
5. **forehead** [ˈfɔːhed] n 额头
6. **nail polish** ph 指甲油
7. **pencil** [ˈpensl] n 铅笔
8. **accumulate** [əˈkjuːmjəleɪt] v 累积,积成堆

情境中可延伸记忆的单词

1. **stack** [stæk] n (整齐的)一堆,一叠
2. **burnout** [ˈbɜːnaʊt] n 精疲力竭
3. **code** [kəʊd] n 代码
4. **concentrate** [ˈkɒnsntreɪt] v 专心于……,集中于
5. **financial year** ph 会计年度,财政年度
6. **ledger** [ˈledʒə(r)] n 会计总账
7. **statistic** [stəˈtɪstɪk] n 统计数据
8. **troubled** [ˈtrʌbld] a 为难的,忧虑的

Unit 14 会计 | Accounting

data ['deɪtə] n 资料
The **data** indicates that our marketing strategies have worked.
资料表明，我们的营销策略起作用了。
🔸 data analysis ph 资料分析

---

calculator ['kælkjuleɪtə(r)] n 计算器
There must be something wrong with the **calculator**.
这台计算器一定有毛病。
🔸 calculation n 计算 / calculating machine ph 计算机 / calculate v 计算

---

earring ['ɪərɪŋ] n 耳环
Men are not allowed to wear **earrings** in the company.
在公司不允许男子佩戴耳环。
🔸 pearl earring ph 珍珠耳环 / ear n 耳朵 / be all ears 全神贯注地听

---

file cabinet ph 档案柜
You can find it in the **file cabinet**.
你可以在档案柜里找到它。
🔸 file n 文件 / on file ph 存档 / file attach ph 信件附件 / file for ph 提起诉讼

---

forehead ['fɔːhed] n 额头
The woman placed her right hand on her own **forehead**.
这位女子把右手放在自己的额头上。
🔸 forehanded a 深谋远虑的，预先做的 / brow n 额头

---

nail polish ph 指甲油
The woman's nails are coated with light **nail polish**.
这位女子的指甲上涂有浅色的指甲油。
🔸 nail scissors ph 指甲剪 / polished a 擦亮的

---

pencil ['pensl] n 铅笔
I can't find my **pencil** and notebook anywhere.
我在哪里都找不到我的铅笔和笔记本。
🔸 penciled a 用铅笔写的 / pencil skirt ph 直筒长裙 / fountain pen ph 钢笔

---

accumulate [əˈkjuːmjəleɪt] v 累积，积成堆
The woman's work has **accumulated**.
这位女子的工作已经堆积成堆了。
🔸 accumulation n 积聚 / gather v 积聚 / accumulated value ph 累积结余

137

stack [stæk] n.（整齐的）一堆，一叠

When can you finish the **stack** of documents on the desk?
你什么时候能完成桌子上的那堆档案？

▶ **stacked** a. 妖艳的 / **stack up** 把……堆起 / **stack up to** 加起来共计

---

burnout ['bɜːnaʊt] n. 精疲力竭

The woman suffered from **burnout** after finishing her work.
完成工作以后，这位女子筋疲力尽。

▶ **burn-out** n. 中途退出者，酗酒或吸毒的人

---

code [kəʊd] n. 代码

Sometimes, accounting uses **codes**.
会计工作有时会用到一些代码。

▶ **coder** n. 编码器 / **coded** a. 编成密码的 / **code name** n. 代号 / **code of conduct** n. 行为准则

---

concentrate ['kɒnsntreɪt] v. 专心于……，集中于

The woman is **concentrating** all her attention on her work.
这位女子把她所有的注意力都放在工作上。

▶ **concentration** n. 浓度 / **concentrate on** n. 全神贯注于…… / **focus** v. 聚焦

---

financial year n. 会计年度，财政年度

The woman has had a good performance for the new **financial year**.
这位女子在新会计年度里做出了不错的业绩。

▶ **financial accounting** n. 财务会计 / **pecuniary** a. 金钱的 / **monetary** a. 金融的，财政的

---

ledger ['ledʒə(r)] n. 会计总账

The manager will check the **ledger** today.
经理今天会查会计总账。

▶ **subsidiary ledger** n. 明细分类账 / **book** n. 账册

---

statistic [stə'tɪstɪk] n. 统计数据

You can refer to the **statistics** I provided for you.
你可以参考我给你的统计数据。

▶ **statistical** a. 统计的 / **statistics** n. 统计（资料）

---

troubled ['trʌbld] a. 为难的，忧虑的

Her **troubled** expression shows that she can't accept your decision.
她为难的表情表示她无法接受你的决定。

▶ **troublous** a. 动荡不安的 / **anxious** a. 焦虑的 / **troublemaker** n. 闹事者

听力测验 | Part 1 图片描述题

(A) There is a computer on the desk.
(B) Everyone has a calculator in their hands.
(C) There is a pen in the woman's hand.
(D) The man is wearing a blue tie.

(A) 桌子上有一台电脑。
(B) 每个人手里都有一个计算器。
(C) 女子手里握有一支笔。
(D) 男子系着蓝色的领带。

答案：(C)
从图片可以看出，女子手里有一支笔，男子系着黑白相间的领带，手里有一个计算器，桌子上有很多纸张，但桌子上没有电脑，所以选 (C)。

听力测验 | Part 3 简短对话题

NEW TOEIC

1. What does the customer want to do?
    (A) He wants to make a deposit.
    (B) He wants to open an account.
    (C) He wants to withdraw money.
    (D) He wants to fill a form.

2. What does the customer need to do if he wants to open an account?
    (A) He needs to make an initial deposit.
    (B) He needs to pay a lot of money.
    (C) He needs to have a minimum balance.
    (D) He needs to sign something.

3. What is the customer's final decision?
    (A) He decides to open an account.
    (B) He doesn't want to open an account.
    (C) He decides to think again.
    (D) He decides to open an account next week.

Customer: Hello! I want to open an account. Would you mind telling me your minimum balance requirement?

Accountant: There is no minimum balance requirement, sir. And you can earn interest no matter how much deposit you make.

Customer: Are there any difficulties in opening an account?

Accountant: No, sir. You just fill out a form and make an initial deposit.

Customer: OK, let me have a look. Is my personal information enough? Do I need to pay or sign anything?

Accountant: No. Your personal information is just for identification purposes. There is nothing you need to do except this.

Customer: OK. I'll fill out this form and open an account.

Unit 14 会计 | Accounting

1. 顾客想要做什么？
- (A) 他想存钱。
- (B) 他想开一个账户。
- (C) 他想领钱。
- (D) 他想填写一个表格。

2. 如果顾客想开账户，他需要做什么？
- (A) 他需要进行首次存款。
- (B) 他需要存一大笔钱。
- (C) 他需要确保账户的最少余额。
- (D) 他需要签订一些东西。

3. 顾客的最终决定是什么？
- (A) 他决定开一个账户。
- (B) 他决定不开账户。
- (C) 他决定再考虑。
- (D) 他决定下周再开账户。

顾客：你好！我想开个账户，你能告诉我你们这里的最少余额是多少吗？
行员：先生，我们这里没有最少余额。无论你存多少都可以获得利息。
顾客：开账户麻烦吗？
行员：不麻烦。你只需填一张表格，然后进行第一次存款就可以了。
顾客：好的，让我看一下表格。只要我的个人信息就够了吗？我还需要付钱或者签什么东西吗？
行员：不用，你的个人信息只是用来确认身份的。除了这个，你不用做其他事。
顾客：好的。那我填一下表格，然后开个账户。

解析与答案

答案：1. (B) 2. (A) 3. (A)

1. 根据听力第一句 I want to open an account 可知，顾客是想要开账户，所以答案选 (B)。
2. 根据内容可知，顾客只需要填一个表格，然后进行第一笔存款就可以了，正确答案只有 (A)。
3. 根据最后一句 I'll fill out this form and open an account 可知，顾客决定当下就开账户。

单词 Vocabulary

account [ə'kaʊnt] n 账户，理由 v 解释，认为
minimum ['mɪnɪməm] a 最小的，最少的 n 最小值
balance ['bæləns] n 平衡，余额，剩余部分 v 保持平衡，结算，抵销
deposit [dɪ'pɒzɪt] n 存款，押金 v 存放，沉淀
initial [ɪ'nɪʃl] a 最初的，开始的 n 首字母 v 签姓名的首字母
identification [aɪˌdentɪfɪ'keɪʃn] n 认同，鉴别，身份证明

阅读测验 | Part 7 文章理解题

Betty Austin

Washington Moblle Communication Co., Ltd.

Dear Ms Austin,

I am your customer. Recently, I found something strange and I don't exactly know why. I think I was overcharged by your company. My assistant noticed the last phone bill was well over fifteen thousand minutes. It showed on the bill that I have used twenty thousand minutes last month, but I don't know why I used so much.

Previous monthly bills have never gone over eight thousand minutes. The point is that I rarely have business outside Washington, so I seldom make long-distance calls. I estimate that I used six thousand long-distance minutes at most last month. I can't really understand this situation. There is a rule in our company that I will be paid two hundred dollars by our company, providing that our phone bill is below fifteen thousand minutes per month. But if it is higher than that standard, I will be paid nothing. So, I invite you to review the attached bill from last month and give me an explanation as to why you charged me so much. I want to avoid this kind of problem. I don't want this kind of thing to happen again. You had better solve it as soon as possible, or more and more customers will complain about it and may not use your service any more.

I look forward to your reply!

Regards,

Jackson Smith

Unit 14 会计 | Accounting

1. What does Jackson complain about?

   (A) Phone bill.
   (B) Phone.
   (C) His clients.
   (D) His work.

2. How many long-distance minutes did Jackson use last month according to what he says?

   (A) Four thousand minutes.
   (B) Five thousand minutes.
   (C) Six thousand minutes.
   (D) Seven thousand minutes.

3. What can Jackson get if his phone bill is below fifteen thousand minutes per month?

   (A) One hundred dollars.
   (B) Two hundred dollars.
   (C) Three hundred dollars.
   (D) Four hundred dollars.

4. Where does Betty work according to Jackson?

   (A) In the same company with Jackson.
   (B) In the company of Jackson's client.
   (C) In Washington Mobile Communication Co., Ltd..
   (D) Not mentioned in the text.

5. What does Jackson ask Betty to do?

   (A) To review his phone bill and give him an explanation.
   (B) To return his money.
   (C) To ask her manager to explain the problem.
   (D) To call other customers.

贝蒂·奥斯丁

华盛顿移动通信有限公司

尊敬的奥斯丁女士：

  我是你们的顾客。最近，我发现一些奇怪的事情，却不知道具体原因。我认为你们公司多收取了我的费用。我的助理注意到上一次的电话账单远远超过 15 000 分钟。账单上显示我上个月使用两万分钟，但是我不知道我怎么使用了这么多。

  我之前每月账单从来没有超过 8 000 分钟。重点是我几乎没有华盛顿以外的业务，因此我很少打长途电话。我估计上个月最多用了 6 000 分钟。我实在无法理解这种情况。我们公司有条规定，如果每月账单低于 15 000 分钟，公司会支付我 200 美元。但是如果超过标准，不会支付我一分钱。因此，我请您查看一下我上个月的账单，给我一个解释，你们为什么向我收取那么多费用。我想避免这种问题，不想这类的事情再发生。你们最好尽快解决问题，否则会有越来越多的顾客抱怨，可能再也不会用你们的服务。

  期待你的回复！

  此致

敬礼！

杰克森·史密斯

1. 杰克森抱怨什么？

 (A) 电话账单。

 (B) 电话。

 (C) 他的客户。

 (D) 他的工作。

2. 根据杰克森所说，他上个月的长途电话时长是多少？

 (A) 4 000 分钟。

 (B) 5 000 分钟。

 (C) 6 000 分钟。

 (D) 7 000 分钟。

3. 如果每月账单低于 15 000 分钟，杰克森能得到什么？

 (A) 100 美元。

 (B) 200 美元。

 (C) 300 美元。

 (D) 400 美元。

4. 根据杰克森所说的话可知，贝蒂在哪里工作？
   (A) 与杰克森在同一家公司。
   (B) 杰克森客户的公司。
   (C) 华盛顿移动通信有限公司。
   (D) 文中未提及。

5. 最后，杰克森让贝蒂做什么？
   (A) 回顾他的电话账单，给他一个解释。
   (B) 还他钱。
   (C) 让她的经理来解决问题。
   (D) 给其他顾客打电话。

解析与答案

答案：1. (A) 2. (C) 3. (B) 4. (C) 5. (A)

1. 此题考信息提取能力，可见第一段第三句、第四句 I think I was overcharged by your company. My assistant noticed the last phone bill was well over fifteen thousand minutes，由此可知在抱怨电话账单的收费问题，因此选 (A)。

2. 此题也是信息提取能力，可见第二段第三句 ... I used six thousand long-distance minutes at most last month，答案要选 (C)。

3. 此题考细节，可见第二段第五句 ... I will be paid two hundred dollars by our company, providing that our phone bill is below fifteen thousand minutes per month，因此选 (B)。

4. 此题考逻辑推理能力，杰克森向贝蒂抱怨自己的话费问题，并让他解释他们为什么会出现这种情况，因此贝蒂的公司就是 Washington Mobile Communication Co., Ltd.，所以这一题要选择 (C)。

5. 此题考信息提取能力，可见第二段倒数第四句 So, I invite you to have a review of the attached bill last month and give me an explanation...，因此选 (A)。

单词 Vocabulary

recently ['ri:sntli] ad 最近地，新近
strange [streɪndʒ] a 奇怪的，陌生的，外行的
overcharge [ˌəʊvəˈtʃɑːdʒ] v 索价过高 n 过高的索价
assistant [əˈsɪstənt] n 助理，起辅助作用的事物 a 助理的，辅助的
standard [ˈstændəd] n 标准 a 标准的，合规格的
review [rɪˈvjuː] n 回顾，复习，评论 v 检查，批评，回顾，温习
explanation [ˌeksplə'neɪʃn] n 解释，说明，辩解
avoid [əˈvɔɪd] v 避免，撤销
complain [kəmˈpleɪn] v 抱怨，控诉

Unit 15
仓库 | Warehouse

New TOEIC

Picture 15

情境中可明确指出的单词

1. **cardboard** ['kɑːdbɔːd]
   n 硬纸板 a 硬纸板制的
2. **check** [tʃek] n / v 检查，核对
3. **label** ['leɪbl] n 标签，贴纸，称号
4. **lifter** ['lɪftə] n （英）起重机
5. **stock** [stɒk] n 存货，库存
6. **pallet** ['pælət]
   n （装载、搬运货物用的）货板
7. **tape** [teɪp] n 胶带
8. **warehouse** ['weəhaʊs] n 仓库 v 入仓

情境中可延伸记忆的单词

1. **bustle** ['bʌsl] v 忙碌
2. **clerk** [klɑːk] n 职员
3. **compensation** [ˌkɒmpen'seɪʃn] n 赔偿金
4. **delayed shipment** ph 延迟交货
5. **inspection** [ɪn'spekʃn] n 检查，检验
6. **inventory** ['ɪnvəntri]
   n 存货（清单）v 盘存
7. **packing list** ph 装箱单，送货明细
8. **plaster** ['plɑːstə(r)] v 粘贴

146

Unit 15 仓库 | Warehouse

cardboard ['kɑːdbɔːd] n 硬纸板 a 硬纸板制的
All the goods will be packed in the cardboard boxes.
所有的货物都会装入纸板箱。
- cardboard box n 纸箱

---

check [tʃek] n / v 检查，核对
The warehouse employee is checking the order list.
库管员正在核查订货单。
- checker n 检验员 / check off 在……上加符号表示 / check up n 核对，调查 / hold in check n 抑制

---

label ['leɪbl] n 标签，贴纸，称号
Each box has a white label stuck on it.
每个箱子上都贴有白色的标签。
- labeled a 有标签的 / sticker n（背面有黏胶的）标签 / tag n 标签

---

lifter ['lɪftə] n（英）起重机
He is loading the wagon with a lifter.
他正用起重机给货车装货。
- liftman 升降机操作工 / jack n 起重机 / liftoff 起飞 / forklift n（英）起重机

---

stock [stɒk] n 存货，库存
You know that we have run out of all our stock.
你知道，我们已经没有库存了。
- inventory n 存货清单，存货 / stockholder n 股东 / stock certificate n 股票

---

pallet ['pælət] n（装载、搬运货物用的）栈板
It is more convenient to move the boxes with pallets.
用栈板搬箱子比较方便。
- wooden pallet n 木托盘 / palleted a 印有装订者名字的

---

tape [teɪp] n 胶带
The boxes are sealed with tape.
箱子用胶带封口。
- tape measure n 卷尺 / get sth. taped 彻底了解某事 / red tape n 繁文缛节

---

warehouse ['weəhaʊs] n 仓库 v 入仓
Nobody is allowed to go in the warehouse without permission.
未经允许，任何人不得进入仓库。
- warehousing n 储仓 / storehouse n 仓库 / depository n 储藏所

bustle ['bʌsl] v 忙碌

He is bustling about in the warehouse, so you had better not bother him.
他正在仓库忙碌，因此你最好不要去烦他。
● busy v 使忙于 / busyness n 忙碌 / soothe v 缓和，平静

---

clerk [klɑːk] n 职员

The clerk is going to quit her job because of the poor management of the company.
由于公司管理不善，这位职员将要辞职。
● office worker n 公司职员 / personnel n 员工，人事部门 / clerical n 牧师

---

compensation [ˌkɒmpenˈseɪʃn] n 赔偿金

If they can't deliver on time, they have to pay compensation.
如果他们不能按期交货，就要支付赔偿金。
● compensable a 可补偿的 / reimbursement n 偿还，退款，赔偿 / indemnify v 保障，赔偿

---

delayed shipment ph 延迟交货

The losses incurred from a delayed shipment should be compensated by the manufacturer.
延期交货的损失应该由厂商负责。
● delayed action n 延迟作用，（审管）延期爆炸的

---

inspection [ɪnˈspekʃn] n 检查，检验

The goods must pass a strict inspection.
货物必须经过严格的检查。
● inspectorate n 检查员 / examination n 检查，调查 / scrutiny n 详细的检查

---

inventory ['ɪnvəntri] n 存货（清单）v 盘存

The warehouse keeper does a full and complete inventory of the machines.
仓管员对机器做出一份详尽、完整的清单。
● inventory list n 存货清单 / inventory turnover n 库存周转 / in stock n 有库存的

---

packing list ph 装箱单，送货明细

Before delivery, you must check the packing list.
在递送之前，你必须核查送货明细。
● packing case n 装运货物的箱子 / listed a 列在单子上的

---

plaster ['plɑːstə(r)] v 粘贴

The woman plastered stickers all over the box.
女子把贴纸贴在整个箱子上。
● plaster on n 粘贴 / plasterer n 泥水匠 / stick v 粘贴

听力测验 | Part 1 图片描述题

NEW TOEIC

题目
(A) Everyone is wearing uniforms.
(B) There are two women and two men.
(C) There is nothing on the table.
(D) This warehouse is open.

中译
(A) 所有人都穿着制服。
(B) 图片中有两名女子和两名男子。
(C) 桌子上什么东西都没有。
(D) 这个仓库很空旷。

解析与答案
答案：(B)
从图片可以看出，共有两名女子和两名男子，有两个人穿着工作服，仓库里面堆放了很多东西，桌子上也是，所以选 (B)。

听力测验 | Part 3 简短对话题

1. Why is Bash so happy today?
    (A) Because he will be transferred to the warehouse.
    (B) Because he will be transferred to the Jewelry Department.
    (C) Because he bought a new suit.
    (D) Because he will be promoted.

2. Why will Bash be transferred to the warehouse?
    (A) Because the warehouse needs an assistant.
    (B) Because he asks the manager.
    (C) Because he has some experience.
    (D) There is no mention of it.

3. What's Bash's attitude to this decision?
    (A) He is confused.
    (B) He is satisfied.
    (C) He is indecisive.
    (D) He is unsatisfied.

Manager: Hello, Bash! You are in good mood today.

Bash: Yes. This is my new suit. Do I look good?

Manager: Sure. But now I want to say something to you. Would you like to work in the warehouse some time?

Bash: Sorry. The warehouse? Why?

Manager: We are badly in need of an assistant in the warehouse. So, I hope you can help.

Bash: Why me?

Manager: I think you are the best man. Have you heard that the Jewelry Department will need an assistant manager?

Bash: Yes, but what does that have to do with me?

Manager: If you do well in the warehouse, I'll make sure that you get promoted.

Bash: Well, I don't think I can make a decision now.

♪ 150

Unit 15 仓库 | Warehouse

中译

1. 巴斯为什么今天特别高兴？
   - (A) 因为他今天要调到仓库去了。
   - (B) 因为他要调到珠宝部门了。
   - (C) 因为他买了新的西装。
   - (D) 因为他要升迁了。

2. 巴斯为什么要被调到仓库？
   - (A) 因为仓库需要一名助手。
   - (B) 因为是他要求经理的。
   - (C) 因为他有这方面的经验。
   - (D) 文中没有提到。

3. 巴斯对这个决定的态度是什么样的？
   - (A) 他很困惑。
   - (B) 他很满意。
   - (C) 他很犹豫。
   - (D) 他很不满意。

经理：巴斯，你好！你今天心情很好呀。
巴斯：对啊。这是我新买的西装。好看吗？
经理：的确。但是我现在要跟你说些事情。你是否愿意去仓库工作一段时间？
巴斯：抱歉，你是说仓库吗？为什么？
经理：仓库现在急需一名助手。所以，我希望你可以去帮忙。
巴斯：为什么是我？
经理：我认为你是最佳人选。你听说珠宝部门最近需要一名副经理了吗？
巴斯：我听说了，但是和我有什么关系呢？
经理：如果你的仓库工作做得出色，我保证你会得到升迁。
巴斯：我觉得我需要时间考虑一下。

解析与答案

答案：1. (C) 2. (A) 3. (C)

1. 对话刚开始经理就提到巴斯心情很开心，然后巴斯就说他买了新西装的事，由此可推断他高兴的原因就是买了新西装，所以选 (C)。
2. 根据 We are badly in need of an assistant in the warehouse 可知，巴斯被调到仓库的原因是仓库需要一名助手，所以选 (A)。
3. 由全文可知，巴斯刚得知这个消息的时候很困惑，但根据最后一句 I don't think I can make a decision now 可判断，他在犹豫要不要调到仓库，所以选 (C)。

单词 Vocabulary

mood [muːd] n 情绪，气氛，语气

warehouse ['weəhaus] n 仓库，大商店 v 以他人名义购入（股票），存入仓库

decision [dɪˈsɪʒn] n 决定，决心，法院判决，会议决议

To: Mike Stuart

From: Jeremy King

Dear Mr. Stuart,

I have a question to ask you. Just now, I went to the warehouse. I found that the five pellet machines were still there. I remember that you told me they had been delivered to our client. So, why were they still there? I hope we didn't forget to deliver them to our client, otherwise, our boss will certainly be mad at us. Please explain this to me as soon as possible.

Also, another client called me just now. He wants three crushing machines and three grinding machines. He requires us to deliver them within two days. It is an urgent order. You need to assist our salesman with this.

At this time, I have to remind you of your responsibilities again. I would like to tell you that you, as a warehouse keeper, should know your responsibilities. I hope that you can do this job well. Here are your responsibilities:

First, you must guarantee the supply of machines and you should guarantee your work efficiency. Orders that have been made, must be dealt with as required by our clients. No delay is allowed, otherwise you will be fired.

Second, you should keep a record of all inventory and submit this record by each weekend.

For now, I have nothing further to ask. Please explain the pellet machine matter to me as soon as possible.

I look forward to your reply.

Regards,

Jeremy King

Unit 15 仓库 | Warehouse

1. What is Jeremy's question?

    (A) Why are the five pellet machines still there?

    (B) When will the crushing machines be delivered?

    (C) Where should the pellet machines be delivered to?

    (D) How to deliver the pellet machines?

2. What does Mike do?

    (A) Warehouse keeper.

    (B) Salesman.

    (C) Boss.

    (D) Manager.

3. When does the client request delivery of the crushing machines and grinding machines?

    (A) Today.

    (B) Within two days.

    (C) Within three days.

    (D) Within four days.

4. Which of the following is NOT listed as Mike's responsibilities?

    (A) To guarantee the supply of machines.

    (B) To guarantee work efficiency.

    (C) To monitor the salesmen's work.

    (D) To keep a record of all inventory.

5. When must the record be submitted?

    (A) On Monday.

    (B) On Tuesday.

    (C) On Thursday.

    (D) By the weekend.

收件人：麦克・斯图尔特

寄件者：吉米・金

尊敬的斯图尔特先生：

  我有一个问题要问你。刚才我去了仓库，发现那五台颗粒机还在那里。我记得你告诉过我，已经送给客户了，但是为什么它们还在那里呢？我不希望是我们忘了把它们递送给我们的客户，否则老板肯定会对我们很生气。请尽快向我解释。

  刚才另一位客户打电话给我。他想要三台粉碎机和三台磨粉机。他要求两天之内发送给他。这是份紧急订单，你应该协助我们的业务员处理。

  同时，我想再次提醒你的责任。我想对你说，作为一名仓库管理人员，你应该知道自己的责任。我希望你能将这份工作做好。这是你的责任：

  首先，你必须保证机器的供应；你应该保证你的工作效率。已经下的订单应按照客户的要求处理。不允许拖延，否则你会被开除。

  其次，你应该对所有货物进行记录，每周周末交给我。

  现在，我没有什么要问的了。请尽快向我解释颗粒机的事情。

  期待你的回复。

此致

敬礼！

吉米・金

1. 吉米的问题是什么？
 (A) 为什么那五台颗粒机还在那里？
 (B) 什么时候发送粉碎机？
 (C) 颗粒机应该发送到哪里？
 (D) 如何发送颗粒机？

2. 麦克做什么工作？
 (A) 仓库管理员。
 (B) 销售员。
 (C) 老板。
 (D) 经理。

Unit 15 仓库 | Warehouse

3. 客户要求什么时候发送粉碎机以及磨粉机？
   (A) 今天。
   (B) 两天之内。
   (C) 三天之内。
   (D) 四天之内。

4. 下列哪项没有被罗列为麦克的责任？
   (A) 保证机器的提供。
   (B) 保证工作效率。
   (C) 监督业务员的工作。
   (D) 记录所有货物。

5. 应在什么时候递交记录？
   (A) 周一。
   (B) 周二。
   (C) 周四。
   (D) 截止到周末。

解析与答案

答案：1. (A) 2. (A) 3. (B) 4. (C) 5. (D)

1. 此题可见第一段第五句 So, why were they still there，知道问题在于"为什么颗粒机还在"，因此答案选 (A)。
2. 此题可见第三段第二句 ... you, as a warehouse keeper, should know your responsibilities，得知职位是 warehouse keeper（仓库管理员），因此选 (A)。
3. 从第二段第三句 He requires us to deliver them within two days 可推测出答案，因此选 (B)。
4. 此题可见第三段下面列举的麦克的责任 First, you must guarantee the supply of machines and you should guarantee your work efficiency 以及 Second, you should keep a record of all inventory and submit this record by each weekend，因此选 (C)。
5. 此题可见第三段最后一句 ... submit the record by each weekend，答案要选 (D)。

单词 Vocabulary

deliver [dɪˈlɪvə(r)] v 递送，发送，宣布，解救，实现
mad [mæd] a 发疯的，疯狂的 v 激怒 n 狂怒
another [əˈnʌðə(r)] a 另一个的
urgent [ˈɜːdʒənt] a 紧急的，急迫的
again [əˈɡen] ad 再一次
supply [səˈplaɪ] v 提供，供应，补充 n 供给，供应量，补给品，库存货
allow [əˈlaʊ] v 允许，准许，提供，考虑
pellet [ˈpelɪt] n 颗粒，药丸 v 把……制成药丸
reply [rɪˈplaɪ] n 回复，答复

Unit 16
生产线 | Assembly Line

New TOEIC

Picture 16

情境中可明确指出的单词

1. **apparatus** [ˌæpəˈreɪtəs] n 仪器，装置
2. **assembly line** ph 装配线
3. **conveyor** [kənˈveɪə(r)] n 传送（递）带
4. **factory building** ph 厂房
5. **overall** [ˈəʊvərɔːl] n 工作服
   [ˌəʊvəˈrɔːl] ad 从头到尾
6. **production line** ph 生产线
7. **steel** [stiːl] n 钢铁
8. **trolley** [ˈtrɒli] n 手推车

情境中可延伸记忆的单词

1. **assemble** [əˈsembl] v 组合，配装
2. **automation** [ˌɔːtəˈmeɪʃn] n 自动化
3. **collaboration** [kəˌlæbəˈreɪʃn] n 合作
4. **exhausted** [ɪgˈzɔːstɪd] a 精疲力竭的
5. **mechanization** [ˌmekənaɪˈzeɪʃn] n 机械化
6. **latest** [ˈleɪtɪst] a 最新的
7. **operate** [ˈɒpəreɪt] v 操作
8. **output** [ˈaʊtpʊt] n 产量 v 生产

Unit 16 生产线 | Assembly Line

apparatus [ˌæpəˈreɪtəs] n 仪器，装置
They will deliver the apparatuses which the client ordered this afternoon.
客户订购的仪器，他们将于下午发货。
- apparent a 表面上的 / equipment n 装备

assembly line ph 装配线
We decided to replace the assembly line next month.
我们决定下个月更换生产线。
- assembly hall ph 会馆 / assemble v 集合，装配

conveyor [kənˈveɪə(r)] n 传送（递）带
We are responsible for producing conveyors.
我们负责生产传送带。
- conveyance n 运输 / convey v 运送，搬运 / conveyor belt ph 传送带

factory building ph 厂房
The client will visit our assembly lines in the factory building.
客户将去厂房参观我们的生产线。
- factory site ph 厂房 / factory n 工厂

overall [ˈəʊvərɔːl] n 工作服 a 从头到尾的 [ˌəʊvərˈɔːl] ad 从头到尾
The workers are all wearing blue overalls.
工人们都穿着蓝色的工作服。
- overbearing a 傲慢的 / entire a 全部的 / whole n 全部的

production line ph 生产线
The manager is walking around the production line.
经理正在生产线旁走动。
- productive a 生产的，富有成效的 / productive of ph 产生……的

steel [stiːl] n 钢铁
They are all made of steel.
它们都是钢制的。
- steely a 似钢的 / steelmaker n 钢铁制造商 / steelwork n 钢铁制品，钢铁厂

trolley [ˈtrɒli] n 手推车
He moves the goods with a trolley.
他用手推车移动货物。
- trolley bus ph 无轨电车 / trolley car ph 电车 / trolly n （英）手推车

assemble [əˈsembl] v 组合，配装
The production line is assembled with many parts.
生产线是由许多零件组合而成的。
- assembling n 装配 / assemblage n 装配，装置

automation [ˌɔːtəˈmeɪʃn] n 自动化
Automation reduces the number of the workforce.
自动化减少了工人的数量。
- automatic a 自动机械 / automatize v 使自动化 / robot n 自动控制装备

collaboration [kəˌlæbəˈreɪʃn] n 合作
The collaboration among the workers is integral to the work.
工作离不开工人之间的团结协作。
- collaborative a 合作的 / work together n 合作 / cooperation n 合作，协力

exhausted [ɪɡˈzɔːstɪd] a 筋疲力尽的
After having worked for such a long time, the workers must be exhausted.
工作了那么长时间，工人们一定都筋疲力尽了。
- exhaustive a 详尽的 / tired 疲倦的，厌倦的 / outspent a 筋疲力尽的

mechanization [ˌmekənaɪˈzeɪʃn] n 机械化
The factory raised work efficiency through mechanization.
工厂用机械化来提高生产效率。
- mechanical a 机械的 / mechanize v 使机械化 / mechanist n 机械技师

latest [ˈleɪtɪst] a 最新的
We must introduce the latest equipment to raise work efficiency.
我们必须引进最新设备来提高工作效率。
- latest news 最新消息 / latest fashion n 最新流行

operate [ˈɒpəreɪt] v 操作
The equipment we will purchase must be easy to operate.
我们将要购买的设备必须容易操作。
- operation n 操作 / manipulate v 熟练地操作 / maneuver v 巧妙地操纵

output [ˈaʊtpʊt] n 产量 v 生产
Automation has raised the output.
自动化提高了产量。
- annual output n 年产量 / output quality control n 出货品质管制 / input n 输入

听力测验 | Part 1 图片描述题

题目
(A) The woman is working hard.
(B) The woman is wearing a pair of glasses.
(C) There are many female workers on the assembly line.
(D) There is a hammer in her hand.

中译
(A) 这位女子在努力工作。
(B) 这位女子戴着一副眼镜。
(C) 这条生产线上有很多的女员工。
(D) 这位女子的手里有一把锤子。

解析与答案

答案：(A)
从图片中可以看出，这里只有一位在认真工作的女员工，她的手里握的明显不是锤子，她并没有戴眼镜，所以答案要选 (A)。

听力测验 | Part 4 简短独白题

NEW TOEIC

1. What's the main idea of this passage?
   (A) The declining labor cost of the textile machinery plant.
   (B) The application of automated technology.
   (C) The new guidelines for the packing section.
   (D) The efficiency of staff.

2. When will the textile machinery plant test the mechanical prototype?
   (A) On Friday, November 5th.
   (B) On Friday, November 15th.
   (C) On Thursday, November 5th.
   (D) On Thursday, November 15th.

3. What's the result of applying automated technology?
   (A) The labor costs have dropped.
   (B) The output has been maximized.
   (C) The textile machinery plant is going through a difficult time.
   (D) A and B.

The textile machinery plant will test some mechanical prototypes on Friday, November 5th. This test is for the packaging and labeling assembly line. If it succeeds, these mechanical prototypes will be supplied for practice in some sectors. Then, other sectors will follow. The packing and labeling assembly line will be the first automated production line.

The automated technology is up to standard. The textile machinery plant has gone through a difficult time last year. Profits decreased and returns diminished, so the board of directors decided to streamline the company, including applying automated technology. As a result, the labor costs have dropped and output has been maximized.

Unit 16 生产线 | Assembly Line

中译

1. 这篇文章的主要观点是什么？
   (A) 纺织机械厂的人工成本下降。
   (B) 自动化技术的应用。
   (C) 包装部门的新指导方针。
   (D) 员工的效率。

2. 纺织机械厂什么时候对机械产品进行测试？
   (A) 11 月 5 日，星期五。
   (B) 11 月 15 日，星期五。
   (C) 11 月 5 日，星期四。
   (D) 11 月 15 日，星期四。

3. 应用自动化的结果是什么？
   (A) 人工成本下降。
   (B) 产量达到了最大化。
   (C) 纺织机械厂进入困难时期。
   (D) A 选项和 B 选项。

纺织机械厂将在 11 月 5 日星期五对一些机械产品的标准进行测试。这是为了测试包装和贴标签的生产线。如果成功的话，这些机械产品就会进入一些部门并开始使用，然后，其他的部门也会跟进。包装和贴标签的生产线会是第一个自动化的生产线。

自动化技术合乎标准。纺织机械厂经历了整整一年的困难期。利润下降，收益也减少，因此，董事会决定对公司进行简化，包括应用自动化技术。结果，人工成本下降了，产量也达到了最大化。

解析与答案

答案：1. (B) 2. (A) 3. (D)

1. 这篇听力中提到机械厂经历了一段时间的困难期，但是自动化应用后，达到了很好的效果，所以主要是讲自动化的应用，答案选 (B)。
2. 根据第一句 The textile machinery plant will test some mechanical prototypes on Friday, November 5th 可知，答案选 (A)。
3. 根据最后一句 As a result, labor costs have dropped and output has been maximized 可知，(A) 选项和 (B) 选项都是自动化应用带来的结果，所以选 (D)。

单词 Vocabulary

textile ['tekstaɪl] n 纺织品 a 纺织的
prototype ['prəʊtətaɪp] n 原型，模范，标准
assembly [ə'semblɪ] n 装备，集合，集会，与会者
automated ['ɔːtəʊmeɪtɪd] a 自动化的，机械化的
standard ['stændəd] n 标准，水准，规格 a 优秀的，标准的
diminish [dɪ'mɪnɪʃ] v 减少，变小，削弱……的权势
streamline ['striːmlaɪn] v 使合理化，使简单化，使现代化 n 流线（型）

阅读测验 | Part 7 文章理解题

To: All staff

From: Matthew Perry

Subject: Adjustments and changes

Hello everyonge,

First, we will implement a new system. Workers with good performance will be rewarded with a pay increase and be considered for promotion. If you work hard, you can seize this opportunity easier.

Second, our assembly lines are kind of outdated to some degree, so the board of directors has decided to improve them. Within two weeks, there will be an improvement of the assembly lines. We ask that related departments are prepared.

Third, I want to make it clear that the test team should test the products we produce as well as the assembly lines and submit your ideas about them. All of the problems that workers encounter in the production process should be collected and submitted. Not only the problems, but also your good suggestions can be submitted too. And we also welcome ideas, advice, or suggestions from all of the people in our company, from workers on the assembly lines to the manager, not only the test team. Whoever submits a valuable idea will receive twenty hundred dollars as reward, providing that your idea is put into practice by the company. Try to submit valuable information and we will give you feedback.

So, contact us as soon as possible. We appreciate your participation. If you have any question, feel free to contact us at 666-5656.

Regards,

Matthew Perry

Unit 16 生产线 | Assembly Line

1. What does Matthew Perry announce?
   (A) A job offer.
   (B) His promotion.
   (C) Some adjustments and changes.
   (D) His retirement.

2. What does Matthew Perry say about the assembly lines in the second paragraph?
   (A) There will be an improvement of the assembly lines.
   (B) The assembly lines are the most advanced so far.
   (C) Workers are urged to replace the assembly lines.
   (D) There is no need to replace the assembly lines.

3. What will the test team do according to the third paragraph?
   (A) Test the products and assembly lines.
   (B) Do research on the products.
   (C) Develop new products.
   (D) Replace old assembly lines right now.

4. Who can submit ideas, advice or suggestions according to the e-mail?
   (A) Only the test team.
   (B) Only the workers on the assembly lines.
   (C) Only mangers.
   (D) All the people in the company.

5. Which of the following is NOT right?
   (A) The assembly lines are a little outdated to some degree.
   (B) Whoever submits a valuable idea will receive two hundred dollars as reward.
   (C) They want to improve the assembly lines.
   (D) They can be reached at 666-5656.

收件人：全体员工

寄件者：马修·派瑞

主题：生产线调整

大家好！

　　首先，我们将实行一个新的系统。表现好的工人将会奖励加薪，以及考虑晋升。努力工作者会更容易抓住机会。

　　其次，在一定程度上，我们的生产线有点过时，因此董事会决定予以改善。两周内，将会对生产线进行改善。请相关部门做好一切准备。

　　再次，我想清楚地表明，测试组应该对我们生产的产品以及生产线进行测试，并提交你们的想法。工人们在生产过程中所遇到的所有问题都应该收集并提交。不仅是问题，你们有什么好的建议也可以提出。我们也欢迎公司所有人员的想法、意见或建议，不仅仅是测试组，无论是从生产线工人还是到经理都可以。提出有价值的想法，并被公司采纳者，将会得到 2 000 美元作为奖励。尽量提交一些有价值的信息，我们将会予以回馈。

　　那么，尽快联系我们吧。我们十分感激您的参与。如果您有任何问题，请拨打 666-5656 联系我们。

　　此致

敬礼！

马修·派瑞

1. 马修·派瑞宣布了什么？
   (A) 工作。 (B) 他的晋升。
   (C) 一些调整与变化。 (D) 他的退休。

2. 在第二段中关于生产线，马修·派瑞说了什么？
   (A) 生产线将做改善。 (B) 目前，生产线最为先进。
   (C) 工人们要求更换生产线。 (D) 没有必要更换生产线。

3. 根据第三段，测试组将做什么？
   (A) 测试产品与生产线。 (B) 做产品研究。
   (C) 开发新产品。 (D) 立即替换掉旧生产线。

Unit 16 生产线 | Assembly Line

4. 根据邮件可知，谁可以提交想法、意见或者建议？
   (A) 只有测试组。
   (B) 只有生产线上的工人。
   (C) 只有经理。
   (D) 公司所有人员。

5. 下列说法哪一项不正确？
   (A) 在一定程度上，生产线有点过时。
   (B) 无论谁提出有价值的想法，都会收到 200 美元作为奖励。
   (C) 他们想改善生产线。
   (D) 拨打 666-5656 可以联系他们。

解析与答案

答案：1. (C) 2. (A) 3. (A) 4. (D) 5. (B)

1. 此题的答案在邮件主题 Subject: Adjustments and Changes，所以答案要选 (C)。
2. 此题考信息提取能力，答案可见第二段第二句 ... there will be an improvement of the assembly lines，因此选 (A)。
3. 从第三段第一句 ... the test team should test the products we produce and assembly lines... 可知，答案选 (A)。
4. 此题可见第三段第四句 And we also welcome ideas, advice or suggestions from all of the people...，因此选 (D)。
5. 此题考细节，可见最后三段倒数第四、五句 Whoever submitted a valuable idea will receive twenty hundred dollars as reward, providing that your idea is put into practice by the company...，提出有价值的想法且被接纳的人会收到 2 000 美元的奖励，因此选 (B)。

单词 Vocabulary

adjustment [ə'dʒʌstmənt] n 调整，校正，保险索赔的金额
performance [pə'fɔ:məns] n 表现，成绩，实现
reward [rɪ'wɔ:d] n 奖励，报答 v 报答，报酬，报应
consider [kən'sɪdə(r)] v 考虑，细想，认为
team [ti:m] n 团队 v 合作，组成一队
process ['prəʊses] n 过程，步骤，程序 v 加工，处理
test [test] n 测验，考试 v 试验，检验
valuable ['væljuəbl] a 有价值的，值钱的，贵重的 n 贵重物品
appreciate [ə'pri:ʃieɪt] v 感激，欣赏，体会

Unit 17
工厂 | Factory

New TOEIC

Picture 17

情境中可明确指出的单词

1. **bracket** [ˈbrækɪt]
   n 托架（座） v 给……装托架
2. **boiler suit** ph 连裤工作服
3. **cutter** [ˈkʌtə(r)] n 切割机，裁剪机
4. **drawer** [drɔː(r)] n 抽屉
5. **hammer** [ˈhæmə(r)] n 锤子
6. **latex glove** ph 橡胶手套
7. **stabber** [ˈstæbə] n 锥子
8. **tape measure** ph 卷尺

情境中可延伸记忆的单词

1. **cautious** [ˈkɔːʃəs] a 十分小心的，谨慎的
2. **ensure** [ɪnˈʃʊə(r)] v 确保
3. **improvement** [ɪmˈpruːvmənt] n 改进，改善
4. **iron** [ˈaɪən] n 铁 a 铁的
5. **measure** [ˈmeʒə(r)] v 测量 n 测量器具
6. **segment** [ˈsegmənt] v 切割，切成片
7. **size** [saɪz] n 尺寸，大小
8. **skill** [skɪl] n 专门技能

Unit 17 工厂 | Factory

bracket ['brækɪt] n 托架（座） v 给……装托架
The **bracket** for the cutter is fixed to the table.
切割机的托架固定在桌子上。
● supporting bracket ph 座架 / bracketed a 相等的

---

boiler suit ph 连裤工作服
Both of them are working in **boiler suits**.
他们两个都身穿连裤工作服正在工作。
● boiler n 锅炉 / boiler room ph 锅炉室 / suit oneself 随自己的意愿行事

---

cutter ['kʌtə(r)] n 切割机，裁剪机
A man is cutting marble with a **cutter**.
男子正在用切割机切割大理石。
● hay cutter ph 切草机

---

drawer [drɔː(r)] n 抽屉，支票的开票人
Just put the documents in my **drawer** if I am not there.
如果我不在，档案放到抽屉里就可以了。
● drawee n 受票人 / drawing n 提款 / drawing of lots ph 抽签方式

---

hammer ['hæmə(r)] n 锤子
The man put the **hammers** near the warehouse.
男子将锤子放置在仓库旁边。
● hammerhead n 锤头 / hammer out ph 设计出 / hammer price ph 拍卖成交价

---

latex glove ph 橡胶手套
Each of them is wearing a pair of **latex gloves**.
他们两个都戴着一副橡胶手套。
● latex paint ph 乳胶漆 / glove n 手套 / take off the gloves 强硬起来

---

stabber ['stæbə] n 锥子
I can't work without a **stabber**.
没有锥子，我无法工作。
● stabbing a 刺穿的 / tack n 图钉，大头钉 / nail n 钉子

---

tape measure ph 卷尺
The worker is holding a **tape measure** and standing next to the assembly line.
工人手拿卷尺，站在生产线旁边。
● ruler n 直尺 / measure up ph 符合标准 / scale n 刻度，刻度尺

cautious ['kɔːʃəs] a 十分小心的，谨慎的
The man using the cutter is being cautious.
男子十分小心地使用切割机。
● **cautiousness** n 谨慎 / **careful** a 小心的 / **discreet** a 谨慎的 / **considerate** a 考虑周到的

ensure [ɪnˈʃʊə(r)] v 确保
In order to ensure correctness, the workers should check the measurements carefully.
为确保准确性，工人应该仔细核对测量资料。
● **ensure from** n 保护 / **assure** v 向……保证，确保 / **guarantee** v 保证

improvement [ɪmˈpruːvmənt] n 改进，改善
They need to make improvements in their working conditions.
他们需要改善工作环境。
● **improvable** a 可改良的 / **improver** n 改进者（物）/ **reform** v 革新，改造

iron [ˈaɪən] n 铁 a 铁的
We know that iron needs to be cast in high temperatures.
我们都知道，铸铁需要高温。
● **ironical** a 讽刺的 / **iron out** v 消除 / **ferrous** a 铁的

measure [ˈmeʒə(r)] v 测量 n 测量器具
The man is measuring carefully with a tape measure.
这位男子正在用卷尺仔细地测量。
● **measurement** n 测量 / **measureless** a 无限的 / **measure up** v 符合标准

segment [ˈsegmənt] v 切割，切成片
The cutter can be used to segment metal.
切割机可用来切割金属。
● **segmentation** n 分割 / **segmentalize** v 使分割

size [saɪz] n 尺寸，大小
The man is measuring the size of a part with the tape measure.
这位男子正在用卷尺测量一个零件的尺寸。
● **sizable** a 相当大的 / **size-up** v 估计 / **dimension** n 尺寸，面积

skill [skɪl] n 专门技能
Certain skills are requited to do this job well.
做好这份工作，需要一定的技巧。
● **skillful** a 熟练的 / **skilled** a 熟练的，有技能的 / **ability** n 才能，专门技能

听力测验 | Part 1 图片描述题

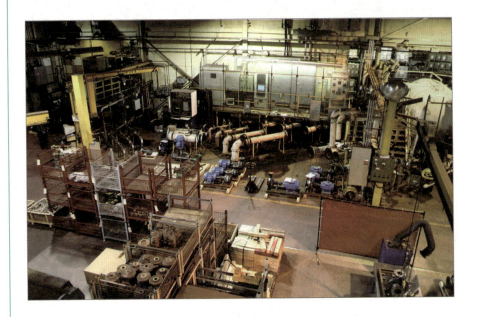

题目
(A) There are many people in the factory.
(B) There are many types of equipment in the factory.
(C) The floor of the factory is dirty.
(D) There are many tables and chairs in the factory.

中译
(A) 工厂里有很多人。
(B) 工厂里有很多不同的设备。
(C) 工厂的地板很脏。
(D) 工厂里有很多桌椅。

解析与答案
答案：(B)
从图片可以看出，工厂里没有人，几乎没有桌椅，但是有很多不同的设备，地面也很干净，所以选 (B)。

听力测验 | Part 4 简短独白题

1. When did the Department of Public Safety suffer a massive fire?
   (A) On Monday.
   (B) On Tuesday.
   (C) On Wednesday.
   (D) On Thursday.

2. Is the Department of Public Safety safe now?
   (A) Yes, it's safe now.
   (B) No, it will be safe after a week.
   (C) No, it will be safe after one month.
   (D) No, it will be safe until the next Monday.

3. What equipment will be compulsive instead of optional for the next month?
   (A) The standard protective eye goggles.
   (B) Full body suits and rubber gloves.
   (C) Extra protective gear.
   (D) Masks.

A section of the Department of Public Safety and its chemical supplies was burned by a massive fire on Monday, but they have announced that it's time to go back to work for all employees, because it's safe now. However, the Environmental Protection Agency reports that there are still some harmful gases in the air. They speculate that it will be one month before all of the harmful gases have dissipated fully. Just in case, the agency suggests that extra protective gears should be used during this period. All employees should be well equipped, including the standard protective eye goggles. Beyond that, when they enter the manufacturing area, they are supposed to put on masks. Lastly, full body suits and rubber gloves will be mandatory for the next month, rather than optional.

Unit 17 工厂 | Factory

1. 公共安全部什么时候发生的火灾？
   (A) 星期一。 (B) 星期二。
   (C) 星期三。 (D) 星期四。

2. 公共安全部现在安全吗？
   (A) 是的，现在安全。 (B) 不，一周之后才安全。
   (C) 不，一个月之后才安全。 (D) 不，下周一才安全。

3. 什么装备下个月会成为强制性用品而不是选择性用品？
   (A) 标准保护眼睛的护目镜。 (B) 全身装备和橡胶手套。
   (C) 额外的护具。 (D) 面罩。

公共安全部的一部分在星期一发生了火灾，其化学物品都被烧毁了，但是他们宣布所有的员工都该回到自己的工作岗位，因为，现在已经安全了。然而，环境保护署报告空气中仍然存在有害气体。他们估计还需一个月才能完全驱散有害气体。为了以防万一，环境保护署建议他们在这段时间要使用额外的护具。所有的员工都应该装备齐全，包括标准的保护眼睛的护目镜。除此之外，当进入生产区域的时候，他们要戴上面罩。最后，全身装备和橡胶手套下个月会成为强制性用具，而不是选择性用具。

答案：1. (A) 2. (C) 3. (B)

1. 根据第一句可知，火灾发生在星期一，所以选 (A)。
2. 公共安全部宣称已经安全了，但是环境保护署的人员说空气中还存在有害气体，一个月之后才会完全消散，所以答案要选 (C)。
3. 根据最后一句 Lastly, full body suits and rubber gloves will be mandatory for the next month, rather than optional 可知答案应选 (B)。

单词 Vocabulary

massive ['mæsɪv] a 大量的，魁梧的，厚重的，大规模的
announce [ə'naʊns] v 宣布，播报，述说
dissipate ['dɪsɪpeɪt] v 驱散，消散，浪费，消失
gear [ɡɪə(r)] n 装置，设备，工具，齿轮 v 搭上齿轮，开动（机器），准备好
goggle ['ɡɒɡl] n 护目镜 v 瞪眼看 a 瞪眼的，睁眼的
mandatory ['mændətəri] a 强制的，托管的，义务的 n 受托者
optional ['ɒpʃənl] a 可选择的，随意的 n 选修科目

阅读测验 | Part 7 文章理解题

With the development of our factory, there is a lack of production space, so we have decided to move our factory to the suburbs to enlarge our facilities to meet the requirements of development. The workshop is too small and not beneficial for large scale production, and the crushing machines we produced were too simple due to outdated production equipment. Our new working site is better for production, as it has larger workshops and is equipped with advanced equipment.

In the meantime, the system has been updated to meet the requirements of production. With the hardware and software improved, there will be a huge increase in productivity, which will bring us greater profits. I think this year we can make a difference.

Our top priority is that we should perfect the new assembly lines. Everyone should hand in the problems you encounter in production as well as suggestions you come up with on how to solve it. Our professionals will do an analysis of existing problems for us as soon as possible. Any good suggestions can be sent to my e-mail by this afternoon. If you have problems, you can consult with our professionals.

Lastly, all of the staff should have a good rest tomorrow and prepare to move to the new working site next week. Thank you!

Unit 17 工厂 | Factory

1. What does this factory produce?
   (A) Cars.
   (B) Crushing machines.
   (C) Computers.
   (D) Phones.

2. Why does the factory need to move to the suburbs?
   (A) Because the suburbs can provide workshops with more space which is beneficial for large scale production.
   (B) Because there is no noise in the suburbs.
   (C) Because the environment in the suburbs is very nice.
   (D) Because the staff urged that it should move there.

3. What does the announcement say about the assembly lines?
   (A) They will make them completely automatic.
   (B) They will stop production for a month.
   (C) There may be a decrease in the production of the new assembly lines.
   (D) Everyone should hand in the problems about the production of the assembly lines.

4. Who will help to solve the problems in production?
   (A) The announcer himself.
   (B) The professionals.
   (C) The manager.
   (D) The president of the factory.

5. When will they move to the suburbs?
   (A) Today.
   (B) Tomorrow.
   (C) Next week.
   (D) Next year.

中译

　　随着我们工厂的发展，我们缺乏发展生产空间，因此我们决定将公司搬到郊区，来扩大我们工厂的规模，满足发展需要。由于工厂狭小，不利于大规模生产，况且生产设备落后，我们过去生产的粉碎机过于简单。然而，我们新的工作地点提供宽阔的生产车间，配有先进装置，有利于生产。

　　同时，为了满足生产要求，系统已经升级。硬件与软件都已经升级，生产上将会有大幅提高，能给我们带来巨额的利润。我认为，今年，我们能有所作为。

　　最重要的是我们应该完善新的生产线。每个人都应该递交你们在生产过程中遇到的问题，你也可以提出解决的办法。任何好的建议都可以发送到我的电子信箱，时间截止到今天下午。如果你有问题，可以咨询我们的专业人员。

　　最后，所有的员工明天都应该好好休息，准备下周搬到新的工作地点。谢谢！

1. 这家工厂生产什么？
   (A) 汽车。
   (B) 粉碎机。
   (C) 电脑。
   (D) 手机。

2. 这家工厂为什么要搬到郊区？
   (A) 因为郊区能够提供空间比较大的工厂，有利于生产。
   (B) 因为郊区没有杂讯。
   (C) 因为郊区环境好。
   (D) 因为员工要求应该搬到那里。

3. 关于生产线的问题，这则公告表达了什么？
   (A) 他们将生产线完全自动化。
   (B) 他们将停止生产一个月。
   (C) 新生产线生产可能会下降。
   (D) 每个人都应该提出在生产线生产的过程中遇到的问题。

4. 谁会帮助解决生产中的问题？
   (A) 公告者自己。
   (B) 专业人员。
   (C) 经理。
   (D) 厂长。

Unit 17 工厂 | Factory

5. 他们何时搬到郊区？
   (A) 今天。
   (B) 明天。
   (C) 下周。
   (D) 下一年。

解析与答案

答案：1. (B) 2. (A) 3. (D) 4. (B) 5. (C)

1. 此题考细节，答案可见第一段第二句 ... and the crushing machines we produced...，因此选 (B)。
2. 此题考推理能力，在第一段讲述迁移的原因，从第一段第一句 With the development of our factory, there is a lack of production space... 可知搬到郊区的原因是缺乏空间，郊区能够提供足够的空间，因此选 (A)。
3. 此题考细节，从第三段第二句 Everyone should hand in the problems you encounter in the production... 可知答案选 (D)。
4. 此题考细节，可见第三段第三句 Our professionals will do analysis of existing problems for us as soon as possible，因此选 (B)。
5. 此题考阅读能力，从最后一段的第一句 ... prepare to move to the new working site next week 可知答案选 (C)。

单词 Vocabulary

factory ['fæktri] n 工厂，制造厂
suburb ['sʌbɜːb] n 郊区，边缘，外围
enlarge [ɪn'lɑːdʒ] v 扩大，放大，详述
scale [skeɪl] n 规模，尺度，天平，鱼鳞 v 把……过程，按比例排列，攀登
outdated [ˌaʊt'deɪtɪd] a 过时的
supply [sə'plaɪ] v 供给，供应 n 补给，补给品，生活用品
meantime ['miːntaɪm] ad 同时
productivity [ˌprɒdʌk'tɪvəti] n 生产力，丰饶
priority [praɪ'ɒrəti] n 优先，优先权，重点
analysis [ə'næləsɪs] n 分析

Unit 18
实验室 | Laboratory

New TOEIC

Picture 18

情境中可明确指出的单词

1. **beaker** ['biːkə(r)] n 烧杯
2. **device** [dɪ'vaɪs] n 仪器，设备
3. **goggle** ['gɒgl] n 护目镜
4. **lab** [læb] n 实验室，研究室
5. **saran wrap** ph 保鲜膜
6. **test tube** ph 试管
7. **tinfoil** ['tɪnfɔɪl] n 锡纸
8. **vessel** ['vesl] n 容器，器皿

情境中可延伸记忆的单词

1. **chemical** ['kemɪkl] n 化学品 a 化学的
2. **experiment** [ɪk'sperɪmənt] n / v 实验
3. **calibration** [ˌkælɪ'breɪʃn] n 刻度
4. **microbe** ['maɪkrəʊb] n 微生物
5. **mingle** ['mɪŋgl] v 使混合
6. **pipette** [pɪ'pet] n 吸量管，滴管
7. **precise** [prɪ'saɪs] a 精确的，清晰的
8. **sample** ['sɑːmpl] n 样本

Unit 18 实验室 | Laboratory

beaker ['biːkə(r)] n 烧杯
Everyone should put everything back, including the beakers.
大家应该将所有东西都放回原位，包括烧杯在内。
- plastic beaker ph 塑胶杯

device [dɪ'vaɪs] n 仪器，设备
We have introduced the latest chemical devices to our laboratory.
我们引进最新的化学设备到实验室。
- medical device ph 医疗设备 / apparatus n 仪器，设备 / equipment n 设备

goggle ['gɒgl] n 护目镜
While doing a chemical experiment, you had better wear a pair of goggles.
做化学实验时，你最好带上护目镜。
- safety goggle ph 安全护目镜 / goggle box ph （英）电视机

lab [læb] n 实验室，研究室
Besides laboratory supplies, we can see only one woman in the lab.
在实验室，除了实验用品，我们只看到一名女子。
- media lab ph 媒体实验室 / laboratory n 实验室

saran wrap ph 保鲜膜
I wonder what the saran wrap is used for.
我想知道保鲜膜是用来做什么的。
- wrap account ph 共管账户 / fresh a 新鲜的

test tube ph 试管
He poured some liquid into the test tubes.
他往试管中倒了一些液体。
- test for ph 测试 / test out ph 充分检验 / testable a 可试验的

tinfoil ['tɪnfɔɪl] n 锡纸
We should seal the beaker with tinfoil after we finish the experiment.
做完实验后，我们应该用锡纸把烧杯封口。
- tin n 锡箔 / foil n 金属薄片

vessel ['vesl] n 容器，器皿
No vessels are allowed to be taken outside the lab.
容器不被允许带出实验室。
- blood vessel ph 血管 / container n 容器，货柜 / receptacle n 容器

chemical [ˈkemɪkl] n 化学品 a 化学的
The **chemicals** in the lab must be carefully stored.
实验室的化学品必须小心存放。
- chemist n 化学家 / chemistry n 化学 / chemical abuse n 吸毒，饮酒成瘾

experiment [ɪkˈsperɪmənt] n / v 实验
The woman is alone doing an **experiment** in the lab.
这名女子独自在实验室做实验。
- test n 实验，试验 / experimental a 实验性的

calibration [ˌkælɪˈbreɪʃn] n 刻度
The **calibration** of the measuring cup must be clear.
量杯上的刻度一定要清晰。
- calibrate v 校准，使……标准化 / calibrated a 标刻度的 / scale n 刻度

microbe [ˈmaɪkrəʊb] n 微生物
The woman can use a microscope to observe the **microbe**.
这位女子可以用显微镜来观察微生物。
- microbiology n 微生物学 / microbiological a 微生物学的 / microbicide n 杀菌剂

mingle [ˈmɪŋgl] v 使混合
First, **mingle** sulfuric acid with sodium hydroxide.
首先，将硫酸与氢氧化钠混合。
- mingling a 混合的 / mingle-mangle n 混合 / mix v 混合 / blend v 混合，混杂

pipette [pɪˈpet] n 吸量管，滴管
The **pipette** is an indispensable piece of equipment in the lab.
吸量管是实验室必不可少的用品。
- pipet n 滴管 v 用滴管移 / pipework n 管道

precise [prɪˈsaɪs] a 精确的，清晰的
The experimental data must be **precise**.
实验资料必须精确。
- precision a 精密的 / exact a 确切的，精确的 / to be precise ad 确切地说

sample [ˈsɑːmpl] n 样本
Every **sample** must be translated in detail.
每一个样本都必须详细标注。
- sampler n 采样器 / sample size n 样品尺寸 / specimen n 样品，样本

听力测验 | Part 1 图片描述题

(A) They are all wearing white uniforms.
(B) Everyone has a sample in their hands.
(C) Everyone has a computer.
(D) They are sedentary at work.

(A) 他们都穿着白色的制服。
(B) 每个人手里都有一个样品。
(C) 每个人都有一台电脑。
(D) 他们都是坐着工作。

答案：(A)
从图片可以看出，共有三个人，一位男子和两位女子，他们都穿着白色的制服，其中一人是坐着的，另外两个人是站着的，桌子上只有一台电脑，他们在观察同一个样品，所以选(A)。

听力测验 | Part 4 简短独白题

NEW TOEIC

1. When will the thing talked about at this week's meeting be sent out?
   (A) Next week.
   (B) This week.
   (C) Next month.
   (D) This month.

2. How long will the meeting last?
   (A) One hour.
   (B) Two hours.
   (C) Three hours.
   (D) Two or three hours.

3. When is the speaker free?
   (A) All morning today.
   (B) Tomorrow.
   (C) All morning today and five hours tomorrow afternoon.
   (D) Today.

I have come up with some suggestions of sources of finance for the new laboratory facilities. Everything we talked about in this week's meeting will be sent out to the selected venture capital firms next month. I'm sure we will get a positive response.

It will be a couple of weeks before the suggestions go out, so if we could sit down and talk it over, I would appreciate it very much. The meeting won't be too long, maybe just a couple of hours. I'm available this morning today and tomorrow afternoon before 5 p.m. So, if it's convenient for you during either of these times, please let me know.

Unit 18 实验室 | Laboratory

1. 他们本周在会议上谈论的事项在什么时候会发送？
   (A) 下周。
   (B) 这周。
   (C) 下个月。
   (D) 这个月。

2. 这次会面将要持续多长时间？
   (A) 一个小时。
   (B) 两个小时。
   (C) 三个小时。
   (D) 两个小时或三个小时。

3. 说话者什么时候有时间？
   (A) 今天整个早上。
   (B) 明天一天。
   (C) 今天整个早上，还有明天下午五点前。
   (D) 今天一天。

我已经提出了一些针对实验室设施的融资建议。我们在这周的会议上讨论的所有事项将会在下个月发送给已选定的风险投资公司。我保证我们会得到肯定的回复。

这个建议发送出去还需要两三周的时间，所以，如果我们可以坐下来谈一谈，我会非常感激。这次的会面时间不会太长，也许只要两三个小时的时间。我今天上午和明天下午五点之前都有空，因此，如果这段时间对你来说方便的话，请告诉我。

答案：1. (C) 2. (D) 3. (C)

1. 从 Everything we talked about in this week's meeting... next month 这句话可知，答案要选 (C)。
2. 独白中提到 a couple of hours，所以两个小时或三个小时都对，答案要选 (D)。
3. 根据 I'm available for this morning today and tomorrow afternoon before 5 p.m. 可知，答案选 (C)。

单词 Vocabulary

finance ['faɪnæns] n 金融，财政，资金援助 v 筹措资金，供资金
venture ['ventʃə(r)] n 冒险，投机活动，企业 v 冒险，以……为赌注
capital ['kæpɪtl] n 资金，首都，大写字母 a 重要的
convenient [kən'viːniənt] a 方便的，实用的

Welcome to our laboratory. To begin with, please allow me to do an introduction. Our laboratory was set up two years ago. We have the latest chemical equipment and professional chemical experts. I believe you will be shocked after you enter. If you want to come to the laboratory, please first get permission. Here are the things you should know:

First, our laboratory is under rigorous control. Whoever wants to enter must show his ID card to the security guard. The guard will scan the bar code on your ID card into the computer system before you enter. In this way, visits can be recorded in case of unexpected matters. Nobody is allowed to enter the laboratory without permission, or his name will be blacklisted. The laboratory is available twenty-four hours a day, so you can come any time.

Second, you should prepare before entering the laboratory. You should know how to do the experiment. You should prepare a notebook to take down experimental data.

Third, you should follow the instructions in the laboratory. Do not touch anything that is not allowed, in case of danger. While doing the experiment, you can't be too careful. You may cause danger if you do things improperly.

Last, you should put everything back after doing the experiment.

If you have any problem, you can contact me at jackgreen@gmail.com.

Unit 18 实验室 | Laboratory

1. What is this announcement about?
   (A) A library.
   (B) A school.
   (C) A laboratory.
   (D) A classroom.

2. How many years ago was the laboratory founded?
   (A) One year.
   (B) Two years.
   (C) Three years.
   (D) Four years.

3. What do we have to show when going to the laboratory?
   (A) Drivers license.
   (B) ID card.
   (C) Notebook.
   (D) Library card.

4. What does the writer advise us to bring according to the third paragraph?
   (A) Money.
   (B) Notebook.
   (C) Chemical apparatus.
   (D) Mobile phone.

5. What does the writer remind us to do after the experiment?
   (A) To put everything back.
   (B) To close the door.
   (C) To close the window.
   (D) To call the chemical experts.

欢迎来到我们的实验室,请允许我做一些介绍。我们的实验室建于两年前。我们有最先进的化学仪器和专业的化学专家。我相信,你进入之后,肯定会震惊。如果你想来实验室,请先获得许可。你应该知道这些事情:

首先,我们的实验室控制十分严格。无论谁想进入实验室,都必须向保安出示身份证。在进入之前,保安会将你身份证上的条码扫描到电脑系统。只有这样,才能记录访问,以防突发事件。未经允许,不可进入,否则会上黑名单。实验室全天二十四小时开放,因此你们随时都可以来。

其次,在进入实验室之前,应该做好准备。你应该知道如何做实验。你最好准备一台笔记本电脑,记录下实验信息。

再次,你们应该遵循实验室指示。不允许碰的东西不能碰,以防危险。做实验时,再小心都不为过。如果操作不当,可能会引起危险。

最后,做完实验后,我们应该将所有东西归回原位。

如果你有任何问题,可以用电子信箱 jackgreen@gmail.com 联系我。

1. 这则公告是关于什么的?
   (A) 图书馆。
   (B) 学校。
   (C) 实验室。
   (D) 教室。

2. 实验室建立多少年?
   (A) 一年。
   (B) 二年。
   (C) 三年。
   (D) 四年。

3. 去实验室,我们必须出示什么?
   (A) 驾驶证。
   (B) 身份证。
   (C) 笔记本电脑。
   (D) 借阅证。

Unit 18 实验室 | Laboratory

4. 第三段中作者建议我们带什么？
   (A) 钱。
   (B) 笔记本电脑。
   (C) 化学仪器。
   (D) 手机。

5. 实验后，作者提醒我们做什么？
   (A) 将所有东西归回原位。
   (B) 关门。
   (C) 关窗。
   (D) 打电话给化学专家。

解析与答案

答案：1. (C) 2. (B) 3. (B) 4. (B) 5. (A)

1. 由第一段第一句 Welcome to our laboratory 可知此题答案应选 (C)。
2. 可见第一段第三句 Our laboratory was set up two years ago，因此选 (B)。
3. 可见第二段第二句 Whoever wants to enter must show his ID card to the security guard，由此可知进入实验室要出示身份证，因此答案选 (B)。
4. 可见第三段最后一句 You had better prepare a notebook...，因此选 (B)。
5. 这类问题的信息会出现在文章的后半部分，答案可见倒数第二段 Last, you should put everything back after doing the experiment，因此选 (A)。

单词 Vocabulary

set [set] v 设立，放置，开始
chemical ['kemɪkl] a 化学的 n 化学制品
apparatus [ˌæpə'reɪtəs] n 仪器，设备，机关
admission [əd'mɪʃn] n 进入许可，门票，承认，录用
rigorous ['rɪgərəs] a 严格的，严厉的，精确的
security [sɪ'kjʊərəti] n 安全（感），防备，保证
permission [pə'mɪʃn] n 允许，许可，同意
improperly [ɪm'prɒpəli] ad 不正确地

学习重点

- 页数
- 笔记内容

NEW TOEIC

Chapter 4

房地产、交通

Real Estate and Traffic

Unit 19
建筑 | Building

New TOEIC

Picture 19

情境中可明确指出的单词

1. **brick** [brɪk] n 砖块
2. **building site** ph 建筑工地
3. **construction** [kənˈstrʌkʃn] n 建筑物
4. **drawing** [ˈdrɔːɪŋ] n 制图
5. **helmet** [ˈhelmɪt] n 安全帽
6. **material** [məˈtɪəriəl] n 材料，原料
7. **motion** [ˈməʊʃn] n 手势，动作
8. **scaffold** [ˈskæfəʊld] n 鹰架，支架

情境中可延伸记忆的单词

1. **architecture** [ˈɑːkɪtektʃə(r)] n 建筑学
2. **beam** [biːm] n 梁 v 以梁支撑
3. **building laws** ph 建筑法规
4. **engineer** [ˌendʒɪˈnɪə(r)] n 工程师，技师
5. **expertise** [ˌekspɜːˈtiːz] n 专门知识，专门技术
6. **illustrate** [ˈɪləstreɪt] v（用图实测等）说明
7. **inspect** [ɪnˈspekt] v 视察
8. **intend** [ɪnˈtend] v 想要，打算

Unit 19 建筑 | Building

brick [brɪk] n 砖块
The boss asked us to move the pile of bricks to the construction site.
老板要求，那堆砖块应该挪到建筑工地去。
- brick wall ph 砖墙 / brick red 红棕色

building site ph 建筑工地
The woman and man are working at the building site.
这位女子和这位男子正在建筑工地工作。
- building contractor ph 建筑承包商 / build v 建筑（过去式与过去分词为 built）

construction [kənˈstrʌkʃn] n 建筑物
There is a great increase in the salaries of the construction industry this year.
今年，建筑行业工资大幅提升。
- constructive a 建设性的 / construction in progress 未完工程 / structure n 建筑物

drawing [ˈdrɔːɪŋ] n 制图
They are examining the drawing of the building.
他们正在探讨建筑物的制图。
- drawn a 拔出的 / sketch n 草图 / drafting n 制图

helmet [ˈhelmɪt] n 安全帽
Nobody is allowed to enter the construction site without wearing a helmet.
不戴安全帽，任何人都不允许进入工地。
- steel helmet ph 钢盔 / helmeted a 佩戴头盔的 / safety belt ph 安全带

material [məˈtɪəriəl] n 材料，原料
The construction site is full of building materials.
施工场地堆满了工业原料。
- materialist n 唯物主义者 / material girl ph 拜金女 / ingredient n （烹饪）原料

motion [ˈməʊʃn] n 手势，动作
To express himself better, the man made hand motions.
为了更好地表达自己，这位男子做了手势。
- motivation n 动机 / motivate v 给……动机 / motion picture ph 电影

scaffold [ˈskæfəʊld] n 鹰架，支架
Standing on the scaffold scared me to death.
站在支架上，我害怕得要命。
- falsework n 鹰架，临时搭的架子

architecture [ˈɑːkɪtektʃə(r)] n 建筑学
She told me that architecture is the man's line of work.
她告诉我说，建筑是这位男子的本行。
🔄 architect n 建筑师 / architectural a 有关建筑的

---

beam [biːm] n 梁 v 以梁支撑
We usually use concrete beams to replace wooden ones.
我们通常用水泥梁柱取代木制的梁柱。
🔄 beam bridge n 梁桥 / beamy a 光亮的 / beaming a 发光的

---

building laws n 建筑法规
Builders have to abide by building laws.
建筑商得遵守建筑法规。
🔄 buildup n 把空地盖满房子 / building coverage ratio n 建蔽率

---

engineer [ˌendʒɪˈnɪə(r)] n 工程师，技师
Both of them, I imagine, are engineers.
我想他们两个都是工程师。
🔄 engineering n 工程 / engine n 发动机 / technician n 技术人员

---

expertise [ˌekspɜːˈtiːz] n 专门知识，专门技术
This will take the abundant expertise, patience, and circumspection of an engineer.
这需要工程师有丰富的专业知识、耐心和细心。
🔄 expert n 专家 / expertness n 专门性 / knowledge n 学识，学问

---

illustrate [ˈɪləstreɪt] v （用图实测等）说明
The woman pointing at the drawing is illustrating her opinion.
女子指着图纸，正在表明自己的观点。
🔄 illustration n 说明 / illustrative a 说明的 / picture v 描绘 / portray v 画，描绘

---

inspect [ɪnˈspekt] v 视察
They should inspect the building site at regular intervals.
他们应该每隔一段时间就来视察工地。
🔄 inspection n 视察 / inspector n 检查员 / observe v 观测，观察

---

intend [ɪnˈtend] v 想要，打算
They intended to improve the designs.
他们打算改进设计。
🔄 intend to n 想要做 / intend for n 本意是 / propose v 提议，建议

听力测验 | Part 1 图片描述题

题目
(A) It's going to rain.
(B) There is a fence around the construction site.
(C) The building has been built.
(D) There are many workers at the construction site.

中译
(A) 快要下雨了。
(B) 施工场地外有一个围栏。
(C) 这栋建筑物已经建好了。
(D) 建筑场地上有很多工人。

解析与答案
答案：(B)
从图片中可以看出来，天气非常好，一座大楼正在修建中，建筑场地外面有一个红色的围栏，从图片中看不到有施工人员，所以选 (B)。

NEW TOEIC

听力测验 | Part 4 简短独白题

1. Which of the following features is not mentioned about the department?
   (A) It's situated in a fine location.
   (B) It's still in good condition.
   (C) It has a spiral staircase.
   (D) It has a balcony offering sweeping views.

2. Which year was the apartment constructed?
   (A) The apartment was constructed in 1950.
   (B) The apartment was constructed in 1915.
   (C) The apartment was constructed in 1919.
   (D) The apartment was constructed in 1918.

3. What's special about every room?
   (A) Original.
   (B) Capacious.
   (C) Narrow.
   (D) Elegant and classic.

Even the most judgmatic buyer could hardly find such a good opportunity as to buy this large Art Deco style apartment. This apartment with its original decorative features was constructed in 1915. It is situated in a good location and it's still in perfect condition. There are five bedrooms, a separate dining room and a large living room. In addition, there is a balcony with a nice view. Every room is exquisite and classic. What's more, the apartment is located in a place with convenient transportation. So, if you are thinking of buying, please call Blair at 816-3717.

Unit 19 建筑 | Building

1. 下列公寓的特点中没有被提到的是哪一个？
(A) 房子坐落在黄金地段。
(B) 房子状况良好。
(C) 房子里有旋转楼梯。
(D) 房子带有视野良好的阳台。

2. 这所公寓什么时候建成的？
(A) 1950 年。
(B) 1915 年。
(C) 1919 年。
(D) 1918 年。

3. 每个房间都有什么特色？
(A) 独特的。
(B) 宽敞的。
(C) 狭窄的。
(D) 高雅而且古典的。

即使是眼光独到的买家也很难有这么好的机会来购买这种极具艺术风格的公寓。这座有独特装饰风格的公寓建立于 1915 年，坐落在黄金地段，而且至今各种设备依然完好无损。公寓里面有五个卧室、一个独立的餐厅，还有一个很大的客厅。除此之外，还有一个视野极好的阳台。每个房间都是既高雅又古典。更重要的是，这个公寓处在交通便利的地段。所以，如果你有购买的意愿，请拨打布雷尔的电话：816-3717。

答案：1. (C) 2. (B) 3. (D)
1. 根据听力内容可知，(A)、(B)、(D) 选项都有提到，所以选 (C)。
2. 根据 This apartment with its original decorative features was constructed in 1915 可知公寓是 1915 年建成的，所以答案选 (B)。
3. 根据 Every room is exquisite and classic 可知，答案选 (D)，elegant 和 exquisite 都可以表示"高雅的"。

单词 Vocabulary

judgmatic [dʒʌdʒ'mætɪk] ⓐ 明智的，眼光敏锐的，考虑周到的
original [ə'rɪdʒənl] ⓐ 原始的，独特的，新颖的 ⓝ 原型，原件
decorative ['dekərətɪv] ⓐ 装饰性的
separate ['seprət] ⓐ 单独的，个别的，不同的 ['spreɪt] ⓥ 分开，分离，区分
balcony ['bælkəni] ⓝ 阳台，包厢
exquisite [ɪk'skwɪzɪt] ⓐ 精致的，高雅的，剧烈的

阅读测验 | Part 7 文章理解题

Awarded Architecture Company of This year

It is being reported that German Architecture Co., Ltd. has been selected as the leading company in the architecture industry this year. That is to say, it has become the top architecture company out of all of the architecture companies in Europe this year.

Bill Clinton, the president of German Public Works, and Jason Green, the head of German Regional Development, awarded a certificate of commendation to Andrew Queen, the chairman of German Architecture Co., Ltd. This ten-year-old company has finished a few construction projects in the past few years and won a bid to construct a huge bridge in Germany. German Architecture Co., Ltd. is known for its ability to accomplish an administrative building in a very short term and on a limited budget.

However, I know this is just its latest success. Last May, German Architecture Co., Ltd. and some artists worked out a plan together to replace a park with a museum in Lyon. Their efforts made a great contribution to tourism in Lyon. There has been an increasing number of tourists there. Due to its good quality and high efficiency, German Architecture Co., Ltd. has gained the honor as the best company in the architecture industry.

At the award ceremony, Mr. Queen accepted the award on behalf of all his staff. He said at the ceremony that, "It is our people who make our company so successful. We can't ignore their contribution to our company and to our country."

Unit 19 建筑 | Building

1. What does the awarded company do?
   (A) Tourism.
   (B) Machinery.
   (C) Software.
   (D) Architecture.

2. Who is the chairman of German Architecture Co., Ltd.?
   (A) Bill Clinton.
   (B) Jason Green.
   (C) David Bright.
   (D) Andrew Queen.

3. How many years ago was German Architecture Co., Ltd. founded?
   (A) Five years.
   (B) Ten years.
   (C) Fifteen years.
   (D) Twenty years.

4. What plan did the company work out with artists?
   (A) To construct a park.
   (B) To construct a bridge.
   (C) To construct a museum.
   (D) To construct a administrative building.

5. Who makes the company so successful according to Mr. Queen?
   (A) Himself.
   (B) Mr. Green.
   (C) Mr. Clinton.
   (D) All of his staff.

今年获奖的建筑公司

据报道,德国建筑有限公司当选今天建筑行业中的领先者。也就是说它是今年欧洲建筑公司中的第一名。

比尔·克林顿,德国公共工厂主席,杰森·格林,德国地区发展首席,颁发给安德鲁·奎恩——德国建筑有限公司的主席一份荣誉证书。这家十岁的公司在过去的几年中,完成了几项建筑工程,并且中标建设德国一座巨桥。德国建筑有限公司在短期内以有限预算完成一座行政大楼,它因这种能力而著名。

然而,我知道这只是它最近的成功。去年五月,德国建筑有限公司和一些艺术家一起制订出一项计划,就是将里昂的一家公园改建为一个博物馆。他们的努力将对里昂的旅游业做出巨大贡献。那里的游客数量会明显上升。由于高质高效,德国建筑有限公司获得建筑业中最佳公司的荣誉。

在颁奖仪式上,奎恩先生代表全体员工接受奖项。他在仪式上说道:"我们的员工让我们公司如此成功。我们不能忽略他们对我们公司以及对我们国家的贡献。"

1. 获奖公司是关于什么的?
    (A) 旅游。
    (B) 机器。
    (C) 软件。
    (D) 建筑。

2. 德国建筑有限公司的主席是谁?
    (A) 比尔·克林顿。
    (B) 杰森·格林。
    (C) 大卫·布莱特。
    (D) 安德鲁·奎恩。

3. 德国建筑公司成立多少年?
    (A) 五年。
    (B) 十年。
    (C) 十五年。
    (D) 二十年。

Unit 19 建筑 | Building

4. 这家公司与艺术家制订出什么计划？
   (A) 建造公园。
   (B) 建造桥梁。
   (C) 建造博物馆。
   (D) 建造行政大楼。

5. 根据奎恩先生的讲话，是谁使得公司如此成功？
   (A) 他自己。
   (B) 格林先生。
   (C) 克林顿先生。
   (D) 他的全体员工。

解析与答案

答案：1. (D) 2. (D) 3. (B) 4. (C) 5. (D)

1. 这一题从文章的标题 "Awarded Architecture Company of This year" 就可以得出答案，选 (D)。
2. 此题考判断能力，可见第二段第一句 ... the chairman of German Architecture Co., Ltd.，因此选 (D)。
3. 此题考思维转换能力，从第二段第一句 This ten-year-old company... 可知公司十岁了，因此选 (B)。
4. 此题考信息提取能力，可见第三段第二句 ... German Architecture Co., Ltd. and some artists worked out a plan together to replace a park with a museum in Lyon，因此选 (C)。
5. 此题考信息提取能力，可见最后一段第二句 He said at the ceremony that "It is our people who make our company so successful..."，因此选 (D)。

单词 Vocabulary

report [rɪˈpɔːt] v 报道，报告，告发 n 报告书，报道，风评
architecture [ˈɑːkɪtektʃə(r)] n 建筑，建筑物，结构
Europe [ˈjʊərəp] n 欧洲
president [ˈprezɪdənt] n 主席，会长，董事长，总统
chairman [ˈtʃeəmən] n 主席
accomplish [əˈkʌmplɪʃ] v 完成，实现，达到
bid [bɪd] n 招标，命令，邀请
ability [əˈbɪləti] n 能力，才能，专门技能
artist [ˈɑːtɪst] n 艺术家，某行业的大师，艺人
behalf [bɪˈhɑːf] n 代表，利益

Unit 20
购买和租赁 | Purchase and Rent

New TOEIC

Picture 20

情境中可明确指出的单词

1. **glass door** [ph] 玻璃门
2. **house** [haʊs] [n] 房子，住宅
3. **lawn** [lɔːn] [n] 草皮，草坪
4. **move** [muːv] [n] / [v] 搬迁，移居
5. **porter** ['pɔːtə(r)] [n] 搬运工人
6. **plush toy** [ph] 毛绒玩具
7. **potted plant** [ph] 盆栽
8. **van** [væn] [n] 有厢小货车，厢型车

情境中可延伸记忆的单词

1. **denote** [dɪ'nəʊt] [v] 标志，指示
2. **deliver** [dɪ'lɪvə(r)] [v] 运送
3. **deliveryman** [dɪ'lɪvərimen] [n] 送货员
4. **recline** [rɪ'klaɪn] [v] 斜倚，向后仰
5. **satisfying** ['sætɪsfaɪɪŋ] [a] 满意的
6. **take** [teɪk] [v] 拿取
7. **thrilled** [θrɪld] [a] 激动的，兴奋的
8. **unload** [ˌʌn'ləʊd] [v] 卸货

Unit 20 购买和租赁 | Purchase and Rent

glass door ph 玻璃门
The building is supposed to install glass doors.
这座建筑应安装玻璃门。
- door n 门口 / next door to ph 与……相邻 / out of doors ph 露天

house [haʊs] n 房子，住宅
We can deliver these goods to your house.
我们可以将这些货物送到你家。
- dwelling house ph 住宅 / on the house ph 免费 / house arrest ph 软禁 / house guest ph 暂住的客人

lawn [lɔːn] n 草皮，草坪
I want to buy a house with a lawn.
我想买有草坪的房子。
- lawn mower ph 割草机 / meadow n 草地 / grassland n 草原

move [muːv] n/v 搬迁，移居
If you don't pay the rent on time, you will be asked to move out.
如果你不按时交付房租的话，将会让你搬出去。
- movement n 活动 / move about ph 四处走动 / move in ph 搬进新家

porter ['pɔːtə(r)] n 搬运工人
The porters are moving the goods to the warehouse.
搬运工人正在往仓库搬运货物。
- portal n 大门 / portable a 便于携带的 / baggageman n 行李员

plush toy ph 毛绒玩具
The little girl is taking the plush toy out of the box.
这个小女孩正将毛绒玩具从箱子里拿出来。
- plush a 长绒毛制的

potted plant ph 盆栽
We decide to buy some potted plants to decorate our office.
我们决定买些盆栽来装扮我们的办公室。
- potted a 盆栽的 / plant n 植物 / plant oneself ph 站立不动

van [væn] n 有盖小货车，厢型车
He is driving a van downtown.
他驾驶货车驶往商业区。
- vanity n 虚荣 / wagon n 运货马车 / truck n 卡车

denote [dɪˈnəʊt] v 标志，指示
The sign in front of the house denotes that it is a shop.
房子前面的指示牌标志着这座房子是一家商店。
- denotation n 符号 / indicate v 指示，指出 / signify v 表明，示意

deliver [dɪˈlɪvə(r)] v 运送
Many shops deliver free of charge.
很多商店都免费送货。
- deliverer n 拯救者 / transfer v 转移 / hand over 交出

deliveryman [dɪˈlɪvərɪmen] n 送货员
The deliveryman called me so he could deliver goods.
送货员打电话给我，让他能递送货品。
- delivery n 投递 / delivery room 收发室

recline [rɪˈklaɪn] v 斜倚，向后仰
The woman is reclining against the van and staring at the shop.
那位女子正斜靠在货车上，盯着商店看。
- reclining n 倾斜

satisfying [ˈsætɪsfaɪɪŋ] a 满意的
It was a satisfying experience to purchase this dress.
买这件连衣裙真是一次满意的体验。
- satisfy v 满意，满足 / satisfaction n 满意 / pleasant a 令人愉快的

take [teɪk] v 拿取
The little girl is taking the toy out of the box.
小女孩正在从箱子里取出玩具。
- take part n 参与 / take... in account 考虑到…… / take a seat n 坐下

thrilled [θrɪld] a 激动的，兴奋的
The little girl must be very thrilled to see so many toys.
小女孩看到如此多的玩具时，一定十分兴奋。
- thrill v 兴奋，激动 / thriller 惊险小说 / thrill through 穿过

unload [ˌʌnˈləʊd] v 卸货
The porter is unloading the van.
这位搬运工正在从货车上卸货。
- load v 装货 / unloading 抛售股票

听力测验 | Part 1 图片描述题

题目
(A) The real estate agent is a man.
(B) There is an elderly couple viewing the house.
(C) The house is a mess.
(D) The lights in the room are dim.

中译
(A) 房地产代理商是一位男子。
(B) 来看房的是一对老夫妻。
(C) 房间很凌乱。
(D) 房间的灯光很暗。

解析与答案

答案：(A)

从图片可以看出，房产代理商是一位男子，来看房的是一对年轻夫妇，房间非常整洁，灯光也很明亮，所以答案选 (A)。

听力测验 | Part 4 简短独白题

NEW TOEIC

1. Why does Tyco Electrical Appliance Supplies want to offer an apology?
   (A) Because the customer didn't receive the purchase in time.
   (B) Because the customer didn't receive a gift token.
   (C) Because Tyco didn't leave the hot-line.
   (D) There is no mention of it.

2. What measure has Tyco Electrical Appliance Supplies taken to express its regret?
   (A) They decided to give a discount.
   (B) They don't charge anything for service.
   (C) They send the customer a gift voucher.
   (D) They decided to leave the hot-line.

3. Which number should be called if customers have any problems?
   (A) 806-0317.
   (B) 186 0317.
   (C) 806-0371.
   (D) 186-0371.

I would like to express my apologies on behalf of Tyco Electrical Appliance Supplies. Inappropriate handling has contributed to a delay in your order. You must be yearning to get your electric space heater that you bought a few days ago, as winter is coming. But we have worked out the problem. You can expect to have your order by tomorrow afternoon or the following day. In an effort to show good faith, we are sending you a gift token, which you can use at any Tyco Electrical Appliance Supplies store. You can call me at 806-0317, if you have any problem.

Unit 20 购买和租赁 | Purchase and Rent

中译

1. 泰科电器用品为什么想要表示歉意？
   (A) 因为顾客没有按时收到购买品。
   (B) 因为顾客没有收到礼品兑换券。
   (C) 因为泰科电器用品没有留热线电话。
   (D) 文中没有提到。

2. 泰科电器用品用什么方式来表示歉意？
   (A) 打折。
   (B) 不收取任何的服务费用。
   (C) 送给顾客礼品兑换券。
   (D) 留下热线电话。

3. 如果顾客有问题，他们应该拨打哪个电话？
   (A) 806-0371。
   (B) 186-0317。
   (C) 806-0317。
   (D) 186-0371。

我想代表泰科电器用品表示我们的歉意。我们对您的订单所出现的状况感到抱歉。您的订单发货延误是由于我们处理不当造成的。由于冬天马上就要到了，您肯定急切想收到购买的物品：电器供暖装置。现在问题已经解决了，您可以期待明天下午或后天收到您订购的物品。为了表示我们的诚意，我们送给您一张礼品兑换券，您可以在泰科电器用品的任何一个商店消费使用。最后，如果您有任何问题，您可以拨打我们的热线 806-0371。

解析与答案

答案：1. (A) 2. (C) 3. (A)

1. 听力一开始就提到由于处理不当，顾客的订单发货时间延误了，也就是说顾客没有按时收到购买物品，所以选 (A)。
2. 根据 In an effort to show good faith, we are sending you a gift token, ... 可知，泰科电器用品为了表示歉意决定送给顾客礼品兑换券，所以选 (C)。
3. 根据最后一句可知正确答案是 (A)。

单词 Vocabulary

contribute [kən'trɪbjuːt] v 贡献，捐献，投稿
inappropriate [ˌɪnə'prəʊprɪət] a 不适当的
yearn [jɜːn] v 渴望，怜悯，思念
effort ['efət] n 成就，努力，努力的成果
token ['təʊkən] n 代表，记号 v 象征，表示 a 象征的，作为标记的
consume [kən'sjuːm] v 吃掉，挥霍，耗尽（生命）

203

Jason Auto Rental
Headquarters
345 Franklin Street
Seattle, Washington

Customer Name: Peter Green
Pick-up time: 2 pm, Nov. 18th
Drop-off time: 3 pm, Nov. 18th
Charges: $280

Terms and Conditions:

The total expenses shall consist of the vehicle rental fees but not include additional expenses such as the cost of other equipment, fuel, insurance and so on. Please note this clearly. The renter shall pay a ten percent tax on the total due amount. In the case that you want to cancel the reservation, you shall do it within three days before picking up and will be liable for a fifty dollar cancellation fee. If the car is picked up late, a thirty percent charge will be due. Our autos, as our advertisement says, are available any time of the day or year. Customers are allowed to return the vehicles within sixty minutes. In the case of a late return, customers need to pay extra expenses to the total expenses.

Drivers must have valid driver's licenses and be over eighteen years old. Jason Auto Rental will not be responsible for any liability if you fail to meet the demands of the terms and conditions. All customers shall read this announcement carefully before making a reservation. If you are interested, contact us at 777-3535.

Unit 20 购买和租赁 | Purchase and Rent

1. What does this company do?
   (A) Bike rental.
   (B) Auto rental.
   (C) Issue of loan.
   (D) International trade.

2. Where is Jason Auto Rental from?
   (A) England.
   (B) America.
   (C) Japan.
   (D) Canada.

3. How much tax shall the renter pay?
   (A) Ten percentage of the total expenses.
   (B) Fifteen percentage of the total expenses.
   (C) Twenty percentage of the total expenses.
   (D) Twenty-five percentage of the total expenses.

4. Who is the business of Jason Auto Rental available to?
   (A) Anybody, regardless of age.
   (B) Children who are under eighteen.
   (C) Only men.
   (D) People who have driver's licenses and are above eighteen.

5. How can customers contact Jason Auto Rental according to the announcement?
   (A) Search for their contact information on the Internet.
   (B) Call them at 777-3535.
   (C) Write to them.
   (D) Send them e-mails.

杰森汽车租赁公司

总部

华盛顿，西雅图

富兰克林街，345 号

客户名称：皮特·格林

提取时间：11 月 18 日，下午两点

结束时间：11 月 18 日，下午三点

费用：280 美元

条款和条件：

  全部费用包含汽车租用费，不包含其他额外费用，例如其他设备的费用、燃油费、保险费等。请将它们标注清楚。同时，租用者应付全部费用的 10% 作为税金。如果你想取消预订，你应该提前 3 天之内取消，并且你仍然应该支付 50 美元。如果逾期提车，你应该支付全部费用的 30%。正如广告商所说，我们的汽车全年全天任何时候都开放使用。客户被允许在 60 分钟之内归还汽车。如果逾时归还，那么除收取全部费用外，客户需要额外支付费用。

  需要声明的是，汽车驾驶者应当持有驾驶证，并且年满 18 岁。如果你不符合条款和条件，杰森汽车租赁公司不承担任何责任。客户在预订之前，都应当仔细阅读这份声明。如果你感兴趣，就打电话 777-3535 联系我们。

1. 这家公司是做什么的？
    - (A) 自行车租赁。
    - (B) 汽车租赁。
    - (C) 发放贷款。
    - (D) 国际贸易。

2. 杰森汽车租赁公司来自哪里？
    - (A) 英国。
    - (B) 美国。
    - (C) 日本。
    - (D) 加拿大。

3. 租用者应缴多少税费？
    - (A) 全部费用的 10%。
    - (B) 全部费用的 15%。
    - (C) 全部费用的 20%。
    - (D) 全部费用的 25%。

Unit 20 购买和租赁 | Purchase and Rent

4. 杰森汽车租赁公司对谁开放？
   (A) 任何人，无论年龄。
   (B) 18 岁以下的孩子。
   (C) 只有男子。
   (D) 18 岁以上，持有驾照者。

5. 根据声明，客户如何联系杰森汽车租赁公司？
   (A) 在网上搜索他们的联系方式。
   (B) 拨打 777-3535。
   (C) 给他们写信。
   (D) 给他们发邮件。

解析与答案

答案：1. (B) 2. (B) 3. (A) 4. (D) 5. (B)

1. 此题十分简单，可见开头的标题，因此选 (B)。
2. 此题考常识，文中第三行与第四行便点出公司位址，华盛顿州，根据常识可知，华盛顿位于美国，因此选 (B)。
3. 此题考阅读能力，可见正文的第一段第三句 The renter shall pay a ten percent tax on the total due amount，因此选 (A)。
4. 此题考阅读能力，在正文的第二段第一句便点明公司业务的开放对象 automobilists must have driver's licenses and be over eighteen years old，因此选 (D)。
5. 此题考细节，答案在最后一段的最后一句 If you are interested, just contact us at 777-3535，因此此题选 (B)。

单词 Vocabulary

headquarters [ˌhedˈkwɔːtəz] n 总部
term [tɜːm] n 条款，期限，学期，关系
vehicle [ˈviːəkl] n 车辆，工具，手段
rental [ˈrentl] n 租赁，租金，出租 a 租赁的
percentage [pəˈsentɪdʒ] n 百分比，比例，利润
cancel [ˈkænsl] v 取消，删去，废止，销账
overdue [ˌəʊvəˈdjuː] a 过期的
announce [əˈnaʊns] v 宣布，播报
driver [ˈdraɪvə(r)] n 汽车驾驶者，司机，电脑驱动程序
demand [dɪˈmɑːnd] n 要求，请求 v 要求，请求，盘问

Unit 21
机场 | Airport

Picture 21

情境中可明确指出的单词

1. **ceiling** ['si:lɪŋ] n. 天花板
2. **hall** [hɔ:l] n. 大厅
3. **luggage** ['lʌgɪdʒ] n.（英）行李
4. **passenger** ['pæsɪndʒə(r)] n. 乘客
5. **ticket agent** ph. 票务人员
6. **waiting line** ph. 等候线
7. **warning sign** ph. 警告标志
8. **look** [lʊk] v. 看

情境中可延伸记忆的单词

1. **barrier** ['bæriə(r)] n. 检票处，路障
2. **carry-on** ['kæri ɒn] a. 可随身携带的
3. **check** [tʃek] v. 检查，核对
4. **contraband** ['kɒntrəbænd] n. 违禁品，走私品
5. **flight** [flaɪt] n.（飞机的）班次，航程
6. **query** ['kwɪəri] v. 询问
7. **round-trip ticket** ph. 来回票
8. **timetable** ['taɪmteɪbl] n. 时间表

Unit 21 机场 | Airport

ceiling ['siːlɪŋ] n 天花板
The loudspeaker is installed in the ceiling of the waiting room.
扩音器安装在等候室的天花板上。
● hit the ceiling ph 勃然大怒 / floor n 地板

hall [hɔːl] n 大厅
Passengers can not enter the hall without showing an ID card.
不出示身份证的旅客，不能进入大厅。
● city hall ph 市政厅 / hall of fame ph 名人堂 / lobby n 大厅，门廊 / foyer n 旅馆门厅

luggage ['lʌɡɪdʒ] n （英）行李
Passengers put their luggage at their feet.
乘客把他们的行李放在脚边。
● luggage rack ph 行李架 / luggage compartment ph 行李置物架 / baggage n （美）行李

passenger ['pæsɪndʒə(r)] n 乘客
Passengers are supposed to arrive half an hour early.
乘客们应该提前半个小时到。
● passer n 过路人 / passerby n 行人 / commuter n 通勤者

ticket agent ph 票务人员
Some ticket agents are dimly visible behind the glass.
一些票务人员在玻璃后面隐约可见。
● ticket n 车票，票券 / ticket window ph 售票窗口

waiting line ph 等候线
Please stand in line beyond the waiting line.
请在等候线外排队。
● rank v 排队 / waiting n 等候 / waiter n 服务生

warning sign ph 警告标志
Warning signs are used to remind us of dangers.
警告标志用于提醒我们有危险。
● warning n 警告 a 警告的 / alarm n 警报 v 向……报警 / caution n 警告

look [luk] v 看
The man gave me a strange look.
男子用奇怪的目光看着我。
● looker n 检察员 / look about 环顾 / look after 照顾，目送

barrier ['bæriə(r)] n 检票处，路障
Passengers should show their tickets at the barrier.
乘客应该在检票处出示票券。
- trade barrier n 贸易壁垒 / barring prep 除……以外 / obstruction n 阻碍，障碍

---

carry-on ['kærɪ ɒn] a 可随身携带的
Passengers can take carry-on luggage on the plane.
乘客可以把随身携带的东西带上飞机。
- carry-on bag n 手提行李 / carryout n 外卖的 n 外卖的餐点

---

check [tʃek] v 检查，核对
Passengers need to check their luggage in advance.
乘客需要提前检查行李。
- checker n 检验员 / check point n 检查点 / checkage n 核对，经核对过的项目

---

contraband ['kɒntrəbænd] n 违禁品，走私品
Customs will check the passenger's luggage for contraband.
海关会搜查乘客的行李，看他们是否带有违禁品。
- contrabandist n 走私者 / smuggle v 走私 / smuggler n 走私者，走私船

---

flight [flaɪt] n （飞机的）班次，航程
Passengers can also check flight information on the Internet.
乘客也可以在网上查询航班。
- direct flight n 直航 / flight attendant n 空中服务人员

---

query ['kwɪəri] v 询问
Some passengers are querying the ticket agent.
一些乘客正在询问票务人员。
- inquire v 询问，查问 / question v 询问 / answer v 回答

---

round-trip ticket n 来回票
Buying round-trip tickets may save passengers money.
购买来回票，旅客可以节省钱财。
- one-way ticket 单程票

---

timetable ['taɪmteɪbl] n 时间表
The timetable for flights will be displayed on the screen in the hall.
航班的时间表会在大厅的屏幕上显示。
- timeline n 时间轴 / time-tested a 受过时间考验的 / schedule n 时间表，计划表

听力测验 | Part 1 图片描述题

NEW TOEIC

题目
(A) The plane is full of people.
(B) There are many female passengers in this plane.
(C) The men in this plane are dressed in suits.
(D) There are several airline stewardesses.

中译
(A) 飞机上坐满了人。
(B) 飞机上有很多女乘客。
(C) 这架飞机里的男子穿着西装。
(D) 飞机上有好几名空姐。

解析与答案

答案：(C)
从图片可以看出，飞机上共有两名穿着西装的男乘客和一名空姐，因此 (A)、(B)、(D) 都可以排除，看到男子都穿着西装，所以答案要选 (C)。

♪ 211

听力测验 | Part 4 简短独白题

NEW TOEIC

1. What's the main idea of this passage?
   (A) The airport provides a safe route for passengers.
   (B) The airport announces it will be closing down.
   (C) The airport announces all passengers can enjoy the service of all the shops.
   (D) The airport announces all flights will be delayed for four hours.

2. What will happen to some flights during this time?
   (A) They will depart on schedule.
   (B) They will arrive on schedule.
   (C) They will land at the nearest airport.
   (D) They will offer special discounts for passengers.

3. What does the speaker suggest?
   (A) The weather report will be heard in four hours.
   (B) All shops and restaurants will be open during the delay.
   (C) All flights are going to depart.
   (D) Not all passengers will be on board today.

Ladies and gentlemen, attention please. The airport will be closing down because of the bad weather. All flights will be delayed and all passengers here should wait with patience. The airport should be back to normal operation in four hours. During this time, all flights scheduled to arrive will be delayed, or will land at the nearest airport, which is 300 kilometers away from here. You can get further information about rescheduling from ticket counters. We are sorry for any inconvenience this may cause to you. During this time, you will receive wholehearted service from all shops and restaurants in the airport concourse.

Unit 21 机场 | Airport

1. 这段话的主要观点是什么？
(A) 机场为乘客们提供了一条更加安全的路线。
(B) 机场宣布停业。
(C) 机场宣布乘客们可以享受所有商店的服务。
(D) 机场宣布飞机将会延迟四个小时。

2. 这段时间，飞机会出现哪种情况？
(A) 飞机会按时起飞。
(B) 飞机会按时到达。
(C) 飞机会降落到附近最近的机场。
(D) 飞机会为乘客提供特殊的折扣。

3. 说话者建议了什么？
(A) 四个小时后会再次听到天气预报。
(B) 在飞机延迟期间，所有的商店和餐厅都会正常营业。
(C) 所有的飞机都准备起飞。
(D) 不是所有的乘客今天都可以登机。

各位先生、女士请注意，由于恶劣的天气，机场将会关闭。也就是说所有的飞机都要延后，请乘客们耐心等待。机场于 4 个小时后恢复正常运营。在这期间，所有预计到达的飞机也会延迟，或者降落到离这里 300 千米的最近的机场。另外，你可以从售票处获知更多关于重新指定时间表的信息。对此给你造成的不便表示歉意。在此期间，你会得到机场内所有商店和餐厅的贴心服务。

答案：1. (D) 2. (C) 3. (B)

1. 这段话主要是讲飞机因天气原因不得不延迟起飞和到达的时间，所以选 (D)。
2. 根据 ..., or will land at the nearest airport 可知，(C) 选项是会发生的事情，文中说所有飞机的起飞和到达时间都会延迟，所以 (A)、(B) 选项错误，(D) 选项没有提到，因此选 (C)。
3. 根据最后一句 During this time, you will receive the wholehearted service... 可知，在飞机延迟期间，所有的商店和餐厅都正常营业，所以选 (B)。

单词 Vocabulary

patience ['peɪʃns] n 耐心，忍耐，毅力
normal ['nɔːml] a 标准的，正常的 n 标准，常态
counter ['kaʊntə(r)] n 柜台，计数器 a 相反的 v 反驳，反向移动
inconvenience [ˌɪnkən'viːniəns] n 不便，麻烦 v 打扰
wholehearted [ˌhəʊl'hɑːtɪd] a 一心一意的，全神贯注的
concourse ['kɒŋkɔːs] n 广场，机场或车站的大厅，群众，集合

听力测验 | Part 4 简短独白题

1. Where can the announcement be heard?
   (A) At the airport.
   (B) At the train station.
   (C) At school.
   (D) In a restaurant.

2. How early should the passengers arrive at the airport before their flight departure?
   (A) Half an hour early.
   (B) One hour early.
   (C) Two hours early.
   (D) Half day early.

3. What are the passengers not allowed to take on the plane?
   (A) Food.
   (B) Drinks.
   (C) Drugs.
   (D) Books.

4. How will the passenger be dealt with if taking flammable and explosive goods?
   (A) They will be allowed to board a plane.
   (B) They will be executed by shooting immediately.
   (C) They will be sent to the police.
   (D) They will be held in the airport for three days.

5. Which of the following is true according to the announcement?
   (A) Passengers can go to the registration desk if they have questions.
   (B) Passengers can call 777-3838 if they have questions.
   (C) While boarding, young passengers should pick the priority seats.
   (D) No pregnant women are allowed to board the plane.

Ladies and Gentlemen, may I have your attention, please? We are Atlantic Airlines. We have something important to inform you of. VIP passengers are welcome to have a rest in the VIP rooms of Europe Atlantic Airlines and other passengers may relax in the regular rooms. Take care not to lose your luggage. Please keep children and the elderly in your sight.

We want to remind you that all passengers should arrive two hours before your flight is scheduled to take off. We are sorry that our service is a little slow today due to an unexpected situation, so please arrive early for the security check. You had better be here two hours ahead of time rather than take the risk of missing your flight. You are not allowed to take flammable and explosive goods, daggers, drugs and so on, and if you are found to have the things mentioned above, you will be sent to the police.

While boarding, you can get into the plane and pick your seat. We should emphasize that the priority seats should be left to the elderly, the disabled, pregnant women and children.

If you have any question, please come to the registration desk or call 777-3535, we will help you solve it as soon as possible. We hope you have an enjoyable trip!

Thank you for listening!

1. 在哪里能听到这则公告？
   (A) 机场。
   (B) 火车站。
   (C) 学校。
   (D) 餐厅。

2. 在航班起飞之前，乘客应什么时候到达机场？
   (A) 早到半小时。
   (B) 早到一个小时。
   (C) 早到两个小时。
   (D) 早到半天。

3. 乘客不允许将什么带上飞机？
   (A) 食物。
   (B) 饮料。
   (C) 毒品。
   (D) 书籍。

4. 如果乘客携带易燃、易爆物品，将会怎么处理？
   (A) 允许登机。
   (B) 立即执行死刑。
   (C) 送到警察局。
   (D) 在机场扣留三天。

5. 根据这则公告，下列哪一项是正确的？
   (A) 乘客如果有问题，可以去登记台。
   (B) 乘客如果有问题，可以拨打 777-3838。
   (C) 登记时，年轻乘客应选择优先座位。
   (D) 孕妇不允许登机。

　　女士们、先生们，请注意！我们是大西洋航空公司，有重要的事情通知您。欢迎贵宾人员到贵宾休息室休息，其他乘客到普通室休息。您应该管理好自己的物品，以防丢失。如果您带有儿童或老人，请保证他们在您的视线范围内。

　　我们想提醒您的是所有乘客应在航班起飞前两个小时到达。由于突发原因，今天服务稍慢，我们感到十分抱歉，因此请您提前到达进行安检。您最好提前两个小时到达，否则可能赶不上航班。您不允许携带易燃易爆物品、匕首、毒品等；一旦查获您带有上述物品，将会把您送到警察局。

Unit 21 机场 | Airport

登机时，您可以进行登机选座。需要强调的是优先座位应当留给老人、残疾人、孕妇以及儿童。

如果您有任何问题，请到登记台或拨打 777-3535，我们将尽快帮您解决问题。我们希望您有一个愉快的旅程！

解析与答案

答案：1. (A) 2. (C) 3. (A) 4. (C) 5. (A)

1. 从最前面的 We are Atlantic Airlines 可知发布公告者是航空公司，会听到航空公司公告的地点是机场，因此答案选 (A)。
2. 此题可见第二段第一句 ... all the passengers should arrive two hours before your flight is scheduled to take off，因此选 (C)。
3. 此题可见第二段的倒数第一句 You are not allowed to take inflammable and explosive goods, daggers, drugs and so on，因此选 (A)。
4. 从第二段的倒数第一句 ..., and if you found to have the things mentioned above, you will be sent to the police 可知此题答案要选 (C)。
5. 此题可见第四段第一句 If you have any question, please come to the registration desk...，因此答案选 (A)。

单词 Vocabulary

gentlemen ['dʒentlmən] n. 绅士，先生
Atlantic [ət'læntɪk] n. 大西洋 a. 大西洋的
airline ['eəlaɪn] n. 航线，航空公司
inform [ɪn'fɔːm] v. 通知，告知，告发
passenger ['pæsɪndʒə(r)] n. 乘客
elderly ['eldəli] a. 较老的，年长的，上了年纪的，过时的
unexpected [ˌʌnɪk'spektɪd] a. 未预料到的，意外的
flammable ['flæməbl] a. 易燃的，可燃的 n. 易燃物，可燃物
explosive [ɪk'spləʊsɪv] a. 爆炸性的，暴躁的 n. 爆炸物，炸药
dagger ['dæɡə(r)] n. 敌意，短剑 v. 用短剑刺
emphasize ['emfəsaɪz] v. 强调，着重，加强语气
pregnant ['preɡnənt] a. 怀孕的，意味深长的，富有的
solve [sɒlv] v. 解决，解释，解答（数学题）
enjoyable [ɪn'dʒɔɪəbl] a. 享受的，快乐的

Unit 22
火车 | Train

New TOEIC

Picture 22

情境中可明确指出的单词

1. **drink** [drɪŋk] n 饮料
2. **handbag** ['hændbæɡ] n（女用）手提包
3. **guardrail** ['ɡɑːdreɪl] n 栏杆
4. **muffler** ['mʌflə(r)] n 围巾
5. **stand** [stænd] v 站立
6. **track** [træk] n 铁轨
7. **train** [treɪn] n 火车 v 训练
8. **platform** ['plætfɔːm] n 月台

情境中可延伸记忆的单词

1. **berth** [bɜːθ] n 卧铺
2. **carriage** ['kærɪdʒ] n（火车）客车厢
3. **conductor** [kən'dʌktə(r)] n 列车长
4. **embrace** [ɪm'breɪs] n / v 拥抱
5. **express** [ɪk'spres] n 快车
6. **pick up** ph 接（某）人
7. **traveler** ['trævələ(r)] n 旅客
8. **trot** [trɒt] n / v 小跑，急行

Unit 22 火车 | Train

drink [drɪŋk] n. 饮料
The waiter brought me a bottle of soft drink.
服务生给我拿来一杯软饮料。
● drinker n. 酒徒 / drink down 一口气喝完 / drink driving 酒后驾车

handbag ['hændbæg] n. （女用）手提包
The guard was checking my handbag at that time.
那时，保安正在检查我的手提包。
● leather handbag n. 皮手袋 / pocketbook n. （无背带）女用手提包 / bag n. 提袋，手提包

guardrail ['gɑ:dreɪl] n. 栏杆
Two women in black are leaning against the guardrail.
穿黑衣服的两名女子倚在栏杆上。
● railing n. 栏杆，扶手 / handrail n. 栏杆，扶手

muffler ['mʌflə(r)] n. （英）围巾
It was so hot on the train that she took off her muffler.
火车上太热了，她摘掉了围巾。
● muffle v. 蒙住 / scarf n. 围巾，披肩 / neckpiece n. 装饰的围巾

stand [stænd] v. 站立
The woman is standing at the gate with a cup of tea in one hand and a hamburger in the other.
女子站在门口，一手端着茶杯，一手拿着汉堡。
● stand against n. 反对，对抗 / stand back 退后，不参与 / stand for 代表，象征，支持

track [træk] n. 铁轨
The track disappeared into the distance.
铁轨消失在远方。
● trackless a. 无路的 / keep track of n. 记录 / rail n. 铁轨，铁路

train [treɪn] n. 火车 v. 训练
We can make it to the train station by five o'clock.
五点之前，我们能赶到火车站。
● trainer n. 助理教练 / trainee n. 实习生 / derail v. 出轨

platform ['plætfɔ:m] n. 月台
We are waiting for the train on the platform.
我们正在月台上等待火车。
● service platform 工作台 / platform shoe n. 厚底鞋 / stage n. 舞台

berth [bɜːθ] n. 卧铺
Berths are more comfortable than soft seats.
卧铺比软座舒服得多。
- hard berth 硬卧 / to give a wide berth 远离 / berthage 泊位

carriage [ˈkærɪdʒ] n. （火车）客车厢
During rush hour, the **carriage** will be very crowded.
在高峰期，车厢内会很挤。
- carriageable 马车可通行的，可携带的 / carry on 继续

conductor [kənˈdʌktə(r)] n. 列车长
The **conductor** will remind travelers of the arrival of the train over the intercom.
列车长会通过广播提醒旅客到站。
- conduct v. 引导，带领 / conduction 传导 / conductress n. 女车长

embrace [ɪmˈbreɪs] n. / v. 拥抱
He **embraced** his family and friends before the departure of the train.
火车开动前，他与家人、朋友拥抱。
- embracement n. 拥抱 / hug 拥抱，怀抱 / cuddle 抚爱地拥抱

express [ɪkˈspres] n. 快车
It will save you a lot of time to take an **express** train.
坐快车能大大节省时间。
- expressionism 表现主义 / express oneself 表达自己的想法 / express mail 快件

pick up ph. 接（某）人
My sister asked me to **pick** her **up** at the train station.
我妹妹让我在火车站接她。
- pick on 指责，挑选 / pick out 挑选 / pick over 检查挑选

traveler [ˈtrævələ(r)] n. 旅客
The **travelers** are waiting for their train at the station.
旅客在车站等车。
- travel v. 旅行 / traveler's check 旅行支票 / traveling salesman 旅行推销员

trot [trɒt] n. / v. 小跑，急行
Some passengers **trotted** to the train.
一些游客小跑着上火车。
- trotter n. 快步走的人，猪脚 / sprint 冲刺 / 全速疾跑 / run v. 奔跑，逃跑

听力测验 | Part 1 图片描述题

题目
(A) There is only one man at the train station.
(B) The man is wearing a black hat.
(C) The man is carrying a backpack.
(D) The man is waiting for the train.

中译
(A) 火车站只有一位男子。
(B) 这位男子戴着黑色的帽子。
(C) 这位男子背着一个背包。
(D) 这位男子在等火车。

解析与答案
答案：(C)
从图片的背景可以看出，火车站有很多人，我们可以看清楚的是一位在看公布栏信息的男子，他背着背包，没有戴帽子，所以选 (C)。

听力测验 | Part 3 简短对话题 NEW TOEIC

1. Where does the man want to leave for?
   (A) Vancouver.　　　　　　　(B) Ottawa.
   (C) Washington.　　　　　　 (D) New York.

2. Which train would require the man to make a transfer?
   (A) The train to Vancouver.　　(B) The train to Ottawa.
   (C) The train to Washington.　 (D) The train to New York.

3. How many hours does it take to get to Vancouver?
   (A) About five hours.　　　　 (B) About one hour.
   (C) About two hours.　　　　 (D) There is no mention of it.

Passenger: Is there a train going to Vancouver around three tomorrow afternoon?
Conductor: Yes, we have an express at three-fifty and a local train at four.
Passenger: How many hours does it take to get to Ottawa by express?
Conductor: About five hours.
Passenger: When is the next express to Ottawa?
Conductor: In one hour.
Passenger: Do I have to transfer?
Conductor: No, you don't have to.
Passenger: What time does the train for Washington leave?
Conductor: It will leave in ten minutes.
Passenger: What about the train to New York?
Conductor: You can take the train in two hours and you have to transfer.
Passenger: Where do I wait for the express to Vancouver?
Conductor: You can wait at track No. 5.
Passenger: OK. Thank you.
Conductor: My pleasure.

♪ 222

Unit 22 火车 | Train

中译

1. 男子想去哪里？
   (A) 温哥华。
   (B) 渥太华。
   (C) 华盛顿。
   (D) 纽约。

2. 男子坐哪一辆车需要转车？
   (A) 开往温哥华的列车。
   (B) 开往渥太华的列车。
   (C) 开往华盛顿的列车。
   (D) 开往纽约的列车。

3. 去温哥华需要多长时间？
   (A) 大约五个小时。
   (B) 大约一个小时。
   (C) 大约两个小时。
   (D) 文中没有提到。

乘　客：你们这里有明天下午三点左右开往温哥华的火车吗？
售票员：有。明天下午三点五十分有一趟快车，四点整有一趟普通车。
乘　客：坐快车去渥太华需要多长时间？
售票员：大约五个小时。
乘　客：下一趟开往渥太华的快车是什么时候？
售票员：一个小时之后。
乘　客：我需要转车吗？
售票员：不需要。
乘　客：开往华盛顿的列车什么时候离开？
售票员：十分钟之后。
乘　客：开往纽约的列车呢？
售票员：你需要在两个小时之后才能坐车，而且需要转车。
乘　客：我需要在哪里等开往温哥华的列车？
售票员：你可以在第五车道等候。
乘　客：好的。谢谢！
售票员：不客气！

解析与答案

答案：1. (A)　2. (D)　3. (D)

1. 听力中男子（乘客）提到了多个地点，但是他问的最后一个问题是他要在哪里等候开往温哥华的列车，由此可判断他是想去温哥华，所以选 (A)。
2. 只有问到开往纽约的列车时，才提到需要转车，可推论其他列车不需要转车，所以选 (D)。
3. 只提到开往温哥华的发车时间以及候车地点，没有提到总路程需要多长时间，所以选 (D)。

单词 Vocabulary

express [ɪk'spres] n 快车，快递 v 表达，快递 a 明确的，专门的
pleasure ['pleʒə(r)] n 快乐，希望 v 高兴，满意

阅读测验 | Part 7 文章理解题

Nowadays, the system of selling real-name train tickets has been put into practice by all of the railway stations and related authorized agencies all over the country. We can't purchase train tickets without an ID card. This system of selling real-name train tickets, I think, aims to make purchasing tickets more fair. It also protects passenger safety and stops some people from buying bulk tickets to resell at a higher price.

The introduction of a real-name system does bring us some benefits, but it also has hidden problems. First, the system may leak our personal information, such as our names, ID numbers, addresses and so on, that lawless people may use to make counterfeit certificates or for other illegal purposes. Second, the complex system brings more trouble to the railway staff. The railway staff have to spend more time to deal with the complex system. That is still OK with young staff, but it is a little more difficult for older staff. Third, if we forget to bring our ID cards with us, we can't purchase train tickets.

In my point of view, the system of selling real-name tickets has been practiced all over the country for years. It is an effective measure to fight against scalping. What I want to emphasize is that we should protect our information from being used for illegal purposes, so we had better not throw our used train tickets away.

In general, I think it is of great benefit and convenience to us.

1. What does the text mainly talk about?
   (A) The decoration of the train station.
   (B) Moving the train station.
   (C) The system of selling real-name train tickets.
   (D) Rebuilding of the train station.

2. What is the aim of a system of selling real-name train tickets?
   (A) To make purchasing tickets more fair.
   (B) To make purchasing tickets quicker.
   (C) To make purchasing tickets slower.
   (D) To make purchasing tickets inconvenient.

3. Which of the following is NOT a hidden problem of the system?
   (A) We can't purchase train tickets without ID cards.
   (B) We can purchase train tickets online.
   (C) It brings more trouble to the railway staff.
   (D) It may leak our personal information.

4. What does the announcer emphasize according to the third paragraph?
   (A) To always bring your ID cards with you.
   (B) To protect our information from being used for illegal purposes.
   (C) To throw used train tickets away.
   (D) To make others buy tickets for you.

5. What does the announcer think of the system in general?
   (A) Inconvenient.
   (B) Beneficial and convenient.
   (C) Bad.
   (D) Just so so.

现在,火车票实名制售票系统已经在全国的火车站以及相关权威部门实行了。没有身份证,不能购票。我认为,火车票实名制售票系统旨在使购票更加公平,也保护了旅客的安全,并且防止了一些人多购票,以高价售出。

实名制系统的引进确实给我们带来了一些好处,但是也有潜在的问题。首先,它可能会泄露我们的个人信息,比如名字、身份证号码、地址等,不法分子可能会因非法意图用它们做假证。其次,复杂的系统给火车站工作人员也带来了更多的麻烦。火车站工作人员不得不花费更多的时间处理复杂的系统。对于年轻员工还可以,但是对于年长员工有点困难。再者,如果忘记带身份证,我们不能购买车票。

在我看来,实名制售票系统已经在全国实行了几年。这是一项阻止囤票的有效方法。我想强调的是我们应该保护我们的个人信息不被非法意图利用,因此我们最好不要扔掉我们用过的火车票。

总而言之,我认为它对我们十分有好处并且便利。

1. 这篇文章主要讨论什么?
    (A) 火车站的装修。
    (B) 火车站的搬迁。
    (C) 实名制售票系统。
    (D) 火车站的重建。

2. 实名制售票系统的目的是什么?
    (A) 使购票更公平。
    (B) 使购票更快速。
    (C) 使购票更慢速。
    (D) 使购票更不便。

3. 下列哪项不是系统的隐藏问题?
    (A) 没有身份证不能购票。
    (B) 我们可以线上购票。
    (C) 它给火车站工作人员带来更多麻烦。
    (D) 可能会泄露我们的个人信息。

4. 根据第三段,宣称者强调什么?
    (A) 一直将身份证带在身上。
    (B) 保护你的个人信息不被非法利用。
    (C) 将用过的火车票扔掉。
    (D) 让别人给你买票。

5. 总体上来说，宣称者认为系统怎么样？
   (A) 不方便。
   (B) 有好处并且便利。
   (C) 糟糕。
   (D) 一般般。

> 答案：1. (C) 2. (A) 3. (B) 4. (B) 5. (B)
>
> 1. 考主旨的题目，答案通常在第一段，可见第一段第一句 ... the system of selling real-name train tickets has been put into practice...，由此可知此文在讨论实名制售票系统，因此选 (C)。
>
> 2. 从第一段第三句 The system of selling real-name train tickets, I think, aims to make purchasing tickets more fair 可知答案是 (A)。
>
> 3. 文章中并未提及线上购票事宜，因此选 (B)。
>
> 4. 此题可见第三段第三句 What I want to emphasize is that we should protect our information from being used for illegal purposes...，宣称者强调要保护个人信息不被非法利用，因此选 (B)。
>
> 5. 从最后一段 In general, I think it is of great benefit and convenience to us 可知作者认为这个系统有好处且便利，答案选 (B)。

单词 Vocabulary

system ['sɪstəm] n 系统，体制
ticket ['tɪkɪt] n 票券，证明书
practice ['præktɪs] v 实行，实践，练习 n 实施，习惯
railway ['reɪlweɪ] n 铁路
authorize ['ɔːθəraɪz] v 授权给，委托，批准
purchase ['pɜːtʃəs] v 购买，赢得 n 购买，所购之物
benefit ['benɪfɪt] n 利益，好处，优势 v 对……有益
complex ['kɒmpleks] a 复杂的，合成的 n 复合物，集团
effective [ɪ'fektɪv] a 有效的，给人印象深刻的
emphasize ['emfəsaɪz] v 强调，着重
illegal [ɪ'liːgl] a 非法的，不合法的 n 非法移民
purpose ['pɜːpəs] n 目的，意图，用途，意志，议题 v 意图，打算

Unit 23
出租车 | Taxi

Picture 23

情境中可明确指出的单词

1. **edifice** ['edɪfɪs] n 大厦
2. **handle** ['hændl] n 把手
3. **girdle** ['gɜːdl] n 腰带
4. **overhead light** ph 顶灯
5. **necklace** ['nekləs] n 项链
6. **shopping bag** ph 购物袋
7. **sunflower** ['sʌnflaʊə(r)] n 向日葵
8. **vehicle** ['viːəkl] n 车辆，运载工具

情境中可延伸记忆的单词

1. **arrive** [əˈraɪv] v 到达
2. **carriage way** ph 马路，行车道
3. **fare** [feə(r)] n 车费
4. **open** [ˈəʊpən] v 打开
5. **park** [pɑːk] v 停车
6. **shopping** [ˈʃɒpɪŋ] n 购物
7. **seat belt** ph 安全带
8. **refuel** [ˌriːˈfjuːəl] v 为……补给燃料

edifice ['edɪfɪs] n 大厦

I want to take a taxi to the edifice.
我想乘出租车去那栋大厦。

edification n 启迪 / mansion n 大厦，大楼 / construction n 建筑物

handle ['hændl] n 把手

We can clearly see the door handles of the car.
我们可以清晰地看见车门的把手。

handling a 操作的 / handleable a 可操作的

girdle ['gɜːdl] n 腰带

A brown girdle is worn on the woman's waist.
这位女子的腰上束着一条棕色的腰带。

girth n 周长 / belt n 皮带 / waistband n 腰带

overhead light ph 顶灯

The overhead light doesn't work, you should have it repaired.
顶灯坏了，你应该找人修一下。

overhead projector n 高架投影机 / overhead a 在头顶上的

necklace ['nekləs] n 项链

I lost my necklace on the way home this evening.
在今晚回家的路上，我把项链弄丢了。

pearl necklace ph 珍珠项链 / neck n 颈部，脖子，衣领

shopping bag ph 购物袋

You need to pay extra money for the shopping bag.
你需要另外付钱买购物袋。

shopping n 买东西，购物 / shopping center n 购物中心 / shopping list n 购物清单

sunflower ['sʌnflaʊə(r)] n 向日葵

One of the shopping bags contains several sunflowers.
其中的一个购物袋里装着几朵向日葵。

sunflower seed n 香瓜子 / Sunflower State n 美国堪萨斯州的别名

vehicle ['viːəkl] n 车辆，运载工具

Through the vehicle's window, we can vaguely see the driver.
通过车窗，我们隐约可以看见司机。

conveyance n 运输工具，交通工具 / transportation n 运输工具，交通车辆

arrive [əˈraɪv] v 到达
The client told me that he would arrive at our office before ten o'clock.
客户对我说，他十点之前到我们办公室。
- arrival n 到达 / arrive in 到达 / arrive at 到达，达成

carriage way ph 马路，行车道
The taxi stopped at the side of the carriage way.
这辆出租车停在马路旁边。
- road 马路 / street 街道 / lane 巷弄，车道 / avenue 大街，大道

fare [feə(r)] n 车费
He was overcharged for the fare this morning.
今天上午，他被索要了高价车费。
- reasonable fare 合理的车费 / fare forth 动身 / farer 旅行者

open [ˈəʊpən] v 打开
When opening the car door, passengers need to be careful with the traffic.
开车门的时候，乘客要小心来往的车辆。
- openness n 公开 / open with 以……开始 / open circuit 断路

park [pɑːk] v 停车
The driver parked the car on the roadside.
司机把车停在路边。
- parking n 停车 / parking lot 停车场 / parking ticket 违规停车罚单

shopping [ˈʃɒpɪŋ] n 购物
I want you to go shopping with me this weekend.
这周末，我想要你和我去购物。
- go shopping 去购物

seat belt ph 安全带
The pilot and the co-pilot should fasten their seat belts.
驾驶员和副驾驶员应该系好安全带。
- airbag n 安全气囊

refuel [ˌriːˈfjuːəl] v 为……补给燃料
The driver drives his car to refuel in a gas station.
司机开车到加油站加油。
- refueling stop 补给站 / fuel 燃料，加燃料 / fuel up 加油

听力测验 | Part 1 图片描述题

题目
(A) There are just a few cars on the road.
(B) A woman is waiting for a taxi.
(C) A man is waiting for a taxi.
(D) The woman has long, straight hair.

中译
(A) 路上的车很少。
(B) 一位女子在等出租车。
(C) 一位男子在等出租车。
(D) 这位女子留着长直发。

解析与答案
答案：(B)
从图片中可以看出，一位留着短卷发的女子在路边等出租车，而且路上有很多车，所以选 (B)。

听力测验 | Part 3 简短对话题

1. What happened to Jane?
   (A) She doesn't know the license plate number of the taxi.
   (B) She left the speech in a taxi.
   (C) She doesn't recall the content of the speech.
   (D) She has to put off the presentation.

2. Why does Blair want to make a phone call?
   (A) He wants to know the exact time of the presentation.
   (B) He wants to find his speech.
   (C) He wants to express his regret for being late for the presentation.
   (D) He wants to know the taxi driver's name.

3. What will Blair do next?
   (A) He will call the conference center.
   (B) He will try to recall the content of the speech.
   (C) He will wait for the taxi driver in the underground parking garage.
   (D) He will find the taxi driver by taxi.

Blair: Jane, the presentation is going to start. I want to brush up on the speech. Please give me the blue document folder.

Jane: Where did you put it?

Blair: I asked you to bring it with me this morning, have you forgotten it?

Jane: Oh, no! I left it in the taxi this morning. What should we do?

Blair: Time is running out. I'll call the taxi company right now, and ask him to come back. You come to the underground parking garage as soon as possible. You should stay there and wait for the taxi driver.

Jane: Sorry, Blair. I will wait for the taxi driver. Meanwhile, in case the driver doesn't arrive in time, I hope you can be relaxed and try to remember as much as you can.

Blair: OK. I will.

Unit 23 出租车 | Taxi

中译

1. 珍发生了什么事情？
   (A) 她不知道出租车的车牌号码。
   (B) 她将演讲稿留在出租车上了。
   (C) 她忘记了演讲的内容。
   (D) 她不得不延后演讲。

2. 布雷尔为什么要打电话？
   (A) 他想知道演讲的确切时间。
   (B) 他想找到他的演讲稿。
   (C) 他想对演讲迟到表示歉意。
   (D) 他想知道出租车司机的名字。

3. 布雷尔接下来会做什么？
   (A) 他会打电话给会议中心。
   (B) 他会尽可能回想起演讲的内容。
   (C) 他会去地下停车场等候出租车司机。
   (D) 他会坐出租车去找出租车司机。

布雷尔：珍，演讲马上就要开始了，我想再复习一下演讲稿，你把那个蓝色的资料夹给我。
珍：你放在哪里了？
布雷尔：我让你今天早上带来给我的，你忘记了吗？
珍：天啊，不。我今天早上来的时候把它掉在出租车里了。现在该怎么办？
布雷尔：没多少时间了。我现在马上打电话给出租车公司，让那个司机到这里来。你现在尽快赶到地下停车场，然后，在那里等出租车司机。
珍：抱歉，布雷尔。我现在马上就去等出租车司机。在这期间，万一他不能及时赶到，我希望你不要那么紧张，试着尽可能回忆起演讲的内容。
布雷尔：好的，我会的。

解析与答案

答案：1. (B) 2. (B) 3. (B)

1. 根据 I left it in the taxi this morning 可知，珍将演讲稿忘在出租车上了，所以选 (B)。
2. 听力中提到布雷尔要打电话给出租车公司是因为他的演讲稿忘在出租车上了，而他想再复习一下他的演讲稿，也就是说他想找到他的演讲稿，所以选 (B)。
3. 根据听力内容可知，布雷尔要打电话给出租车公司，而不是会议中心，所以 (A) 选项错误，去地下停车场等出租车司机的是珍而不是布雷尔，所以 (C) 选项错误，(D) 选项文中没有提到，所以选 (B)。

单词 Vocabulary

presentation [ˌprezn'teɪʃn] n 陈述，展示，介绍，赠送
brush [brʌʃ] n 刷子，争吵，矮树丛 v 刷，擦过
folder ['fəʊldə(r)] n 资料夹，文件夹
garage ['gærɑːʒ] n 车库，汽车修理厂 v 把……送入车库

阅读测验 | Part 7 文章理解题

A taxi, also called a cab, is a kind of public transport vehicle for a single passenger or several passengers. The ride is non-shared. What is different from a bus, is that a passenger does not have to go along with a certain route and can go to the destination directly.

A taxi is used for delivering passengers to their destination. However, in other means of public transport, such as buses, trains, planes, etc., the places of departure and destination are decided by service providers rather than passengers.

But there are many problems about taking taxis in our city now, among which some are getting more and more serious. First, there are a few dishonest taxi drivers cheating passengers from other places. These taxi drivers charge unnecessary mileage to make more money or charge passengers at a very high price, which makes passengers very angry. I hope the government can take effective measures to stop this from happening. We are ashamed of this.

Second, it has been difficult to take a taxi for the last two years, especially in bad weather. Many passengers complain about it, but no improvement has been made. It is urgent that we get this problem solved.

Third, to earn more money, some taxi drivers drive very fast. It is dangerous to drive at a high speed in city areas, not only for pedestrians, but also for taxi drivers themselves. So, there should be some measures taken by government on speeding.

In general, the taxi industry should be paid more attention to. These are my points of view on taxis.

1. What is the text about?
   (A) Taxis.
   (B) Buses.
   (C) Trains.
   (D) Planes.

2. Who decides the places of departure and destinations for taxis?
   (A) Taxi drivers.
   (B) Passengers.
   (C) Government.
   (D) Officers.

3. How many problems does the writer list in the text?
   (A) One.
   (B) Two.
   (C) Three.
   (D) Four.

4. What is the writer ashamed of?
   (A) Dishonesty of taxi drivers.
   (B) Honesty of taxi drivers.
   (C) Loyalty of taxi drivers.
   (D) Modesty of taxi drivers.

5. What does the writer appeal to the government to do?
   (A) To take effective measures for the taxi industry.
   (B) To decrease the number of taxis.
   (C) To have more taxes on taxis.
   (D) To arrest taxi drivers.

出租车也叫的士，是一种交通工具，可供单个乘客或几个乘客使用。行程不能分摊。与公交车不同的是乘客不必按照某种特定路线行走，可以直接奔赴目的地。

出租车是用于载运乘客去目的地的。然而，对于其他形式的交通，比如公交车、火车、飞机等，起点与终点都是由服务提供者决定，而非乘客。

但是现在，我们在城市中乘出租车方面有很多问题，其中一些问题变得越来越严重。

第一，有一些不诚实的出租车司机欺骗外地乘客。那些出租车司机为了多赚钱，走不必要的路程，或者向乘客索要高价，这让乘客十分恼怒。我希望政府可以采取有效措施来阻止这种情况发生。我们以此为耻。

第二，这两年想要乘坐出租车是一件很困难的事，尤其在天气不好的时候。很多乘客抱怨，但是没有任何改善。这个问题急需解决。

第三，为了多赚钱，一些出租车司机开车很快。在城市区域高速行驶，这不论对行人来说，还是对出租车司机自己来说，都十分危险。因此，政府在超速方面应当采取一些措施。

总之，应当多关注出租车行业。这就是我在出租车方面的看法。

1. 这篇文章是关于什么的？
   (A) 出租车。
   (B) 公交车。
   (C) 火车。
   (D) 飞机。

2. 对于出租车来说，起点与终点是由谁决定的？
   (A) 出租车司机。
   (B) 乘客。
   (C) 政府。
   (D) 官员。

3. 文中，作者列举了几个问题？
   (A) 一个。
   (B) 两个。
   (C) 三个。
   (D) 四个。

4. 作者以什么为耻？
   (A) 出租车司机的不诚实。
   (B) 出租车司机的诚实。
   (C) 出租车司机的忠诚。
   (D) 出租车司机的谦逊。

5. 作者呼吁政府做什么？
   (A) 对出租车行业采取有效措施。
   (B) 减少出租车数量。
   (C) 对出租车加税。
   (D) 拘留出租车司机。

解析与答案

答案：1. (A) 2. (B) 3. (C) 4. (A) 5. (A)

1. 此题可见第一段第一句 A taxi, also called a cab, is a kind of public transport vehicle...，因此选 (A)。
2. 此题考推断能力，从第二段 A taxi is used for delivering passengers to their destination 可知出租车载乘客去目的地，之后又提到 However, in other means of public transport... the places of departure and destination are decided by service providers rather than passengers，指出出租车和其他交通工具不同，不是由服务提供者而是由乘客决定起点与目的地，所以选 (B)。
3. 从文章中的 Frist... Second... Third... 可知作者提了三个要点，因此答案选 (C)。
4. 从第三段的第二句与第五句 First, there are a few dishonest taxi drivers cheating passengers from other places... We are ashamed of this 可推断此题选 (A)。
5. 此题可见第三段第四句 I hope the government can take effective measures to stop this from happening 与第五段最后一句 So, there should be some measures taken by government on speeding，因此选 (A)。

单词 Vocabulary

taxi ['tæksi] n 出租车 v 搭出租车，飞机滑行
cab [kæb] n 出租车 v 搭出租车
vehicle ['vi:əkl] n 交通工具，传播媒介，工具
passenger ['pæsɪndʒə(r)] n 乘客
route [ru:t] n 路线，途径
destination [ˌdestɪ'neɪʃn] n 目的地，目标
cheat [tʃi:t] v 欺骗，诈取，作弊 n 骗子，欺骗，作弊
especially [ɪ'speʃəli] ad 尤其，特别
improvement [ɪm'pru:vmənt] n 改善，改进（处），改善的事物
speeding ['spi:dɪŋ] n 超速 a 高速行驶的

Unit 24
汽车 | Car

New TOEIC

Picture 24

情境中可明确指出的单词

1. **boot** [buːt] n 靴子
2. **car** [kɑː(r)] n 汽车
3. **engine** ['endʒɪn] n 发动机
4. **engineer** [,endʒɪ'nɪə(r)] n 机械工，技师
5. **headlight** ['hedlaɪt] n 汽车的前灯
6. **overall** ['əʊvərɔːl] n 工作服
7. **rear-view mirror** ph 后视镜
8. **tire** ['taɪə(r)] n 轮胎

情境中可延伸记忆的单词

1. **carburetor** [,kɑːbə'retə(r)] n 汽化器
2. **garage** ['gærɑːʒ] n 车库，汽修厂
3. **install** [ɪn'stɔːl] v 安装，装上
4. **jack** [dʒæk] n 千斤顶
5. **maintain** [meɪn'teɪn] v 维修，保养
6. **remove** [rɪ'muːv] v 移除 n 移动
7. **spanner** ['spænə(r)] n 扳手
8. **squat** [skwɒt] v 蹲（下） a 蹲着的

Unit 24 汽车 | Car

boot [buːt] n. 靴子
She left her newly-bought clothes and boots in the taxi.
她把新买的衣服和靴子忘在出租车上了。
- boot up ph. 启动 / boot out ph. 驱逐，开除 / bootable a. 可开机的

---

car [kɑː(r)] n. 汽车
I couldn't afford a car until last year.
直到去年，我才买得起车。
- by car 乘汽车 / automobile n.（美）汽车 / machine n. 汽车

---

engine ['endʒɪn] n. 发动机
The engine always makes a lot of noise, so I want to have it repaired.
这部发动机总是产生很多噪声，因此我想找人修一下。
- engineer n. 工程师 / engine displacement ph. 发动机排气量

---

engineer [ˌendʒɪ'nɪə(r)] n. 机械工，技师
The engineer can certainly help you with it.
机械工一定可以帮你解决的。
- engineering n. 工程

---

headlight ['hedlaɪt] n. 汽车的前灯
I can't figure out why the headlights don't work.
我不知道为什么前车灯坏了。
- taillight n. 车辆的尾灯 / turn signal ph. 方向灯 / brake light ph. 刹车灯

---

overall ['əʊvərɔːl] n. 工作服
The engineer is wearing blue overalls.
这位工程师穿着一件蓝色的工作服。
- overbearing a. 傲慢的

---

rear-view mirror ph. 后视镜
Before changing lanes, you must look in the rear-view mirror to see if there are vehicles behind you.
在变换车道之前，我们应该看后视镜，看后面是否有车辆。
- mirror n. 镜子 / traffic jam ph. 塞车 / traffic light ph. 交通信号灯

---

tire ['taɪə(r)] n. 轮胎
The engineer is pointing at the tire and talking with the woman.
工程师正指着轮胎和这名女子讨论。
- flat tyre ph. 瘪胎 / flat tire ph. 爆胎

carburetor [ˌkɑːbəˈreɪtə(r)] n 汽化器

The **carburetor** in a vehicle mixes air with fuel properly so the engine can run smoothly.
汽车的汽化器恰当地混合空气和燃料，使发动机能顺畅运转。
🔄 **carburet** n 碳化物

---

garage [ˈgærɑːʒ] n 车库，汽修厂

I have sent my car to a **garage**.
我已经将我的汽车送去汽修厂。
🔄 **parking garage** n 停车场 / **garage sale** n 在家里的车库拍卖物品 / **garageman** n 汽车修理工人

---

install [ɪnˈstɔːl] v 安装，装上

The worker will **install** a new tire on the car.
这位工人会给汽车安装一个新轮胎。
🔄 **installation** n 安装 / **establish** v 设立，安置 / **set up** v 建立

---

jack [dʒæk] n 千斤顶

The car mechanic will use a **jack** when he replaces the tire.
当要换轮胎的时候，汽车维修工会使用千斤顶。
🔄 **jack up** n 顶起 / **Jack and Jill** n 男男女女 / **lifter** n 起重机

---

maintain [meɪnˈteɪn] v 维持，保养

The woman **maintains** her car well, it runs just like new.
这位女子的汽车保养得很好，跑起来像新车一样。
🔄 **maintenance** n 维护 / **sustain** v 维持 / **preserve** v 维持 / **upkeep** n （房屋或设备的）保养

---

remove [rɪˈmuːv] v 移除 n 移动

What the engineer decides to do next is to **remove** the old tire.
工程师接下来要做的是拆掉旧轮胎。
🔄 **removal** n 免职 / **removed** a 分离的 / **shift** v 转移

---

spanner [ˈspænə(r)] n 扳手

During maintenance, the engineer uses a **spanner**.
在维修的过程中，维修工会用到扳手。
🔄 **span** n 跨度 / **wrench** n 扳手

---

squat [skwɒt] v 蹲（下） a 蹲着的

The woman and the engineer **squatted** down and examined the car.
女子和工程师蹲下来仔细检查汽车。
🔄 **squatty** a 矮胖的 / **crouch** v 蹲伏

听力测验 | Part 1 图片描述题

题目

(A) The man is checking the car.
(B) This is a white car.
(C) There are many scrapped cars.
(D) There are many maintenance crews.

中译

(A) 这位男子正在检修汽车。
(B) 这是一辆白色的汽车。
(C) 这里有很多报废的车辆。
(D) 这里有很多的维修人员。

解析与答案

答案：(A)

从图片中我们可以看出，有一位男维修人员正在检修一辆黑色的汽车，(B) 和 (D) 都可以排除，而选项 (C) 描述的场景在图片中没有看到，因此此题选择 (A)。

听力测验 | Part 3 简短对话题

1. Where does this conversation take place?
    (A) At a garage.
    (B) At a factory.
    (C) At an office.
    (D) In a grocery store.

2. Why does the man want to apologize?
    (A) Because he didn't repair the car well.
    (B) Because it took a long time to repair the car.
    (C) Because the price of the automobile maintenance is high.
    (D) Because he didn't replace the tires for woman.

3. What does the man suggest?
    (A) He suggests that the woman should buy a new car.
    (B) He suggests that the woman should pay more.
    (C) He suggests that the woman should have the car's tires replaced.
    (D) He suggests that the woman shouldn't drive the car anymore.

Woman: Hello, sir. Have you repaired my car yet?

Man: Yes, it's done. The power steering fluid was the most serious problem, but we have changed it. We are shorthanded recently. So we want to apologize for making you wait for such a long time.

Woman: It doesn't matter. It's not urgent.

Man: OK. But there is one other thing I want to tell you. The tires are looking a bit worn. So, I suggest that you should replace them as soon as possible.

Woman: OK. Thank you.

Unit 24 汽车 | Car

中译

1. 这段对话发生在什么地方？
   (A) 汽车修理厂。
   (B) 工厂。
   (C) 办公室。
   (D) 杂货店。

2. 男子为什么要道歉？
   (A) 因为他没有把车修好。
   (B) 因为他修车花了很长时间。
   (C) 因为修理费用很高。
   (D) 因为他没有替女子换新轮胎。

3. 男子提出了什么建议？
   (A) 他建议女子买一辆新车。
   (B) 他建议女子付更多的维修费。
   (C) 他建议女子更换新的轮胎。
   (D) 他建议女子不要再开这辆车了。

女子：您好，先生！我的车修好了吗？
男子：已经修好了。动力机油是最主要的问题，但是我们已经换过了。由于最近人手不够，所以很抱歉让您等这么长时间。
女子：没关系。我也不急着用车。
男子：嗯。还有一件事我想告诉您。您的车轮胎已经有点磨损了，所以我建议您尽快换新的轮胎。
女子：好的，谢谢！

解析与答案

答案：1. (A) 2. (B) 3. (C)

1. 根据听力内容可知，对话是和修车有关的，所以是在汽车修理厂，答案选 (A)。
2. 根据 So we want to apologize for making you wait for such a long time 可知，答案选 (B)。
3. 根据男子说的最后一句 I suggest that you should replace them as soon as possible 可知，他建议女子更换新的轮胎，所以选 (C)。

单词 Vocabulary

repair [rɪ'peə(r)] v 修理，补救 n 修理，修补
fluid ['fluːɪd] n 液体，流质 a 液体的，流动的，不固定的
shorthanded [ˌʃɔːtˈhændɪd] a 人手不够的
urgent ['ɜːdʒənt] a 紧急的，急迫的
worn [wɔːn] a 用旧的，疲倦的，憔悴的

To: Adam Bright

From: Matt LeBlanc

Subject: Test of car GPS

Dear Mr. Bright,

I'd like to thank you for your speech at the meeting yesterday. The documents you distributed were very easy to understand and rich with information. But there is one thing I am worried about, and that is the function of GPS units in mountains. You know, no test has been done in mountains, and this is something to worry about. Our routes cover everywhere, so we must make sure the GPS units can work properly everywhere and in all conditions. We must test them in all conditions before installing them in our SUVs.

To ensure that our GPS units can work in mountains, I invite you to work out a test plan for mountains. In the meantime, the GPS units should function with agreements with all of the European countries, such as England, France, Germany, Spain, and so on, because of our planned routes. In the case that the units don't work properly in some European countries, we will not use them anymore.

I advise you to work with Jack on this, because he has a lot of experience with this. Jack can certainly help you a lot. I think you two will finish it in a short time. Last, you should first work out the test plan and submit it to me by this weekend. If you have any question, just send me an e-mail.

I look forward to your reply!

Regards,

Matt LeBlanc

1. What is this e-mail about?
    (A) Clients.
    (B) Foreigners.
    (C) Testing of car GPS units.
    (D) Manufacturers.

2. Where will they have a car GPS test?
    (A) In the city.
    (B) In mountains.
    (C) In the office.
    (D) In the countryside.

3. Who does Matt appoint to assist Adam?
    (A) Mike.
    (B) Jack.
    (C) Jason.
    (D) Jeremy.

4. How many times have they done such a test in the mountains?
    (A) Once.
    (B) Twice.
    (C) Three times.
    (D) Never.

5. Which of the following is false?
    (A) Jack will work with Adam together on the car GPS test.
    (B) They may finish the test in a short time.
    (C) Matt gave a speech at the meeting yesterday.
    (D) Their routes cover all of Europe.

收件人：亚当·布莱特

寄件者：马特·勒布朗

主题：汽车定位测试

尊敬的布莱特先生：

　　我想感谢你昨天在会议上的发言。你分发的文件很容易理解，并且信息丰富。但是，有件事情我很担心，就是设备在山区的定位功能。你知道还未在山区做过测试，我们对此十分担心。我们的路径都会覆盖到每一个角落，因此我们必须保证定位装置在每种地方以及任何条件下都能正常运转。在安装到运动型多用途汽车上之前，我们必须在所有的条件下对其进行测试。

　　为了保证定位装置能在山区正常运转，我邀请你制订山区测试计划。同时，我们的定位装置应符合所有欧洲国家的协议，例如英国、法国、德国、西班牙等。在欧洲国家，如果装置不能正常运转，我们将不会再使用。

　　在这件事情上，我建议你与杰克一起工作，因为在这方面，他有许多经验。杰克一定会帮助你很多。我认为你们两个在短时间内就能将之完成。最后，你应该先做出测试计划，这周末前交给我。如果你有任何问题，发邮件给我。

　　期待你的回复！

此致

敬礼！

马特·勒布朗

1. 这封邮件是关于什么的？
   - (A) 客户。
   - (B) 外国人。
   - (C) 汽车定位测试。
   - (D) 厂商。

2. 他们将在哪里进行汽车定位测试？
   - (A) 城市。
   - (B) 山区。
   - (C) 办公室。
   - (D) 乡村。

3. 马特指派谁去协助亚当？
   - (A) 麦克。
   - (B) 杰克。
   - (C) 杰森。
   - (D) 杰若米。

4. 他们在山区做过多少次此类测试？
   (A) 一次。
   (B) 两次。
   (C) 三次。
   (D) 从来没有。

5. 下列哪项说法错误？
   (A) 杰克将和亚当一起工作，完成汽车定位测试。
   (B) 他们可能会在短时间内完成测试。
   (C) 马特昨天在会议上做演讲。
   (D) 他们的路径覆盖整个欧洲。

答案：1. (C) 2. (B) 3. (B) 4. (D) 5. (C)

1. 此题的阅读材料为邮件，关于询问主旨的问题可见邮件标题 Title: Test of Car GPS，因此选 (C)。
2. 此题考信息提取能力，可见第二段第一句 ... I invite you to work out a test plan for mountains，由此得知要在山区做测试，所以选 (B)。
3. 此题考细节，可见第三段第一句 I advise you to work with Jack on this, ...，因此选 (B)。
4. 此题考信息提取能力，从第一段第四句 You know, no test has been done in mountains... 可知，此题答案应选 (D)。
5. 此题考查信息分辨能力，可见第一段第一句 I'd like to thank you for your speech at the meeting yesterday，由此可知进行演讲的是亚当，此文并没有提及马特是否演讲，因此选 (C)。

单词 Vocabulary

speech [spiːtʃ] n 演讲，说话能力，演说
document [ˈdɒkjumənt] n 文件，证件
distribute [dɪˈstrɪbjuːt] v 分发，分配，散布
worry [ˈwʌri] v 担心，忧虑
everywhere [ˈevriweə(r)] ad 到处，完完全全 n 每个地方
properly [ˈprɒpəli] ad 正确地，恰当地，严格地
unit [ˈjuːnɪt] n 装置，单元，组
meantime [ˈmiːntaɪm] ad 同时，期间
Spanish [ˈspænɪʃ] n 西班牙语 a 西班牙的
certainly [ˈsɜːtnli] ad 确实地，必然地，当然

学习重点

页 数	笔记内容

NEW TOEIC

餐厅
Restaurant

Chapter 5

Unit 25
订位 | Reservation

New TOEIC

Picture 25

情境中可明确指出的单词

1. **alcohol** ['ælkəhɔl] n 酒精，酒
2. **arm** [ɑːm] n 手臂 v 挽着
3. **bar** [bɑː(r)] n 吧台，酒吧
4. **collate** [kə'leɪt] v 核对，对照
5. **container** [kən'teɪnə(r)] n 货柜，容器
6. **flaxen** ['flæksn] a 亚麻色的
7. **registration record** ph 登记记录
8. **ballpoint pen** ph 圆珠笔

情境中可延伸记忆的单词

1. **commend** [kə'mend] v 推荐，称赞
2. **telephone** ['telɪfəʊn] n 电话 v 打电话
3. **face-to-face** [feɪs tə 'feɪs] a 面对面的
4. **reception** [rɪ'sepʃn] n 接待，接待处
5. **reservation** [ˌrezə'veɪʃn] n 订位，保留
6. **curly** ['kɜːli] a 弯曲的
7. **time** [taɪm] n 时间，次数
8. **wait** [weɪt] v 等待

Unit 25 订位 | Reservation

alcohol [ˈælkəhɔl] n 酒精，酒
Get a bottle of alcohol off of the shelf for me.
从架子上拿瓶酒给我。
▶ alcoholism n 酗酒 / alcoholic a 酒精的 n 嗜酒者 / ethanol n 乙醇

---

arm [ɑːm] n 手臂 v 挽着
He went into the restaurant with a book under his arm.
他手臂下夹着一本书，走进餐厅。
▶ armored a 装甲的 / arm in arm ph 手挽手

---

bar [bɑː(r)] n 吧台，酒吧
They are celebrating the New Year in a bar now.
现在，他们正在一家酒吧庆祝新年。
▶ barrable a 可以拦阻的 / bar chart ph 长条图 / bar code ph 条码 / behind bars ph 坐牢

---

collate [kəˈleɪt] v 核对，对照
The waitress is collating the booking information.
这位女服务生正在核对订位信息。
▶ collation n 校对 / verify v 核实，证明 / contrast v 对照，对比

---

container [kənˈteɪnə(r)] n 货柜，容器
The shipping container is full of wines and drinks.
货柜里摆满了酒和饮料。
▶ containment n 包含 / container ship ph 货柜船 / containerize v 将货物装入货柜

---

flaxen [ˈflæksn] a 亚麻色的
The lady has short flaxen hair.
这位女子留有一头亚麻色的短发。
▶ flax n 亚麻 / flaxseed n 亚麻子

---

registration record ph 登记记录
The waitress is consulting the registration records.
女服务生正在查阅登记记录。
▶ registration n 登记，记录 / register v 登记，注册 / registration number ph 汽车牌照号码

---

ballpoint pen ph 圆珠笔
The waitress is thumbing through the notebook with a ballpoint pen in her hand.
女服务生手里拿着笔在翻笔记本。
▶ ballpoint n 笔尖 / fountain pen ph 钢笔

commend [kəˈmend] v 推荐，称赞
I will go to the restaurant commended by my friends.
我将去我朋友推荐的那家餐厅。
- commendation n 推荐 / praise v 赞美，表扬 / commend itself to sb. 给某人好印象

telephone [ˈtelɪfəʊn] n 电话 v 打电话
The guests can book seats by making a telephone call to the restaurant.
客人可以通过拨打餐厅的电话来订座。
- telephonist n 话务员 / telephone booth n 电话亭 / telephone number n 电话号码 / telephone receiver n 听筒

face-to-face [ˌfeɪstəˈfeɪs] a 面对面的
I prefer discussing problems face-to-face, rather than over the phone.
我倾向于当面讨论问题，而不是用电话。
- personally ad 当面，亲自 / in person 亲自

reception [rɪˈsepʃn] n 接待，接待处
You can go to the reception desk if you have any questions.
如果你有任何问题，你都可以去接待处。
- receptionist n 接待员 / receptible a 能接受的 / reception room n 接待室，会客室

reservation [ˌrezəˈveɪʃn] n 订位，保留
They must have made a reservation ahead of time.
他们一定是提前订位了。
- without reservation 无保留地 / reserve 保留，预订

curly [ˈkɜːli] a 弯曲的
The waitress has curly black hair.
女服务生有一头黑色的卷发。
- curler n 卷发的人 / curl n 卷发 v 使卷曲 / wavy a 波浪的 / crooked a 弯曲的

time [taɪm] n 时间，次数
They have been to this restaurant many times.
他们已经来过这家餐厅好多次了。
- in time 及时 / on time 准时 / time after time 多次 / time off 请假，休假

wait [weɪt] v 等待
You have to wait another ten minutes here.
你得在这里再等十分钟。
- waiter n 服务生 / wait and see 观望

听力测验 | Part 1 图片描述题

题目
(A) There are many chairs in this room.
(B) There are many tables in this room.
(C) The woman is on the phone, taking notes.
(D) There is a pink wall.

中译
(A) 这个房间里有很多椅子。
(B) 这个房间里有很多桌子。
(C) 这位女子在打电话并做笔记。
(D) 这个房间有一面粉红色的墙。

解析与答案

答案：(C)
从图片可以看出，这个房间有一面绿色的墙，只有一张桌子，椅子也很少，有一位女子在打电话，还在记笔记，所以选 (C)。

听力测验 | Part 3 简短对话题

NEW TOEIC

1. Why will Frank be late for the reservation?
   (A) Because he doesn't know the way to the restaurant.
   (B) Because he has another reservation at that time.
   (C) Because he will be at a meeting at that time.
   (D) Because he remembers the wrong time.

2. When will Frank probably arrive?
   (A) At 5:30.
   (B) At 3:00.
   (C) At 6:00.
   (D) At around 7:00.

3. What will they and the others probably discuss at dinner?
   (A) The delicious food.
   (B) The cost-cutting measures.
   (C) The opening of a new account.
   (D) The way to measure profits.

Alisa: Hello, Frank. We are going to have dinner with the department heads tonight. I have made reservations for 5:30. Can you make it?

Frank: Sorry, I'm afraid I can't. I will attend a meeting this afternoon at 3:00, and it will last for three hours or more. So the soonest I could make it is 6:30 or around 7:00.

Alisa: Oh, I'm sorry to hear that. I will change the reservations for another time, but I need to inform the others first.

Frank: You don't need to reschedule the time for me. You can arrive first. I will get there as soon as possible. Then we can have a drink and discuss the cost-cutting measures together.

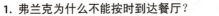

Unit 25 订位 | Reservation

中译

1. 弗兰克为什么不能按时到达餐厅？
   (A) 因为他不知道该怎么去餐厅。
   (B) 因为他那个时候还有其他的预约。
   (C) 因为他那个时候还在开会。
   (D) 因为他记错了时间。

2. 弗兰克可能几点到？
   (A) 五点半。
   (B) 三点。
   (C) 六点。
   (D) 七点左右。

3. 他们和其他人在晚餐期间要商讨什么事情？
   (A) 美味的食物。
   (B) 削减成本的措施。
   (C) 开立新的账户。
   (D) 评估利润的方法。

艾丽莎：你好，弗兰克！我们今天晚上要和系主任一起吃晚饭，我预订了下午五点半的座位，你能按时过来吗？

弗兰克：抱歉，我可能赶不过去了。我今天下午三点要出席一个会议，会议大概要三个小时或者更久。所以，我最快能六点半或七点左右赶到。

艾丽莎：太糟糕了。那我不得不修改预订时间了，但是我要先通知其他人。

弗兰克：你没有必要为我更改时间。你们先去，我尽可能快地赶到那里，然后我们一起讨论削减成本的措施。

解析与答案

答案：1. (C)　2. (D)　3. (B)

1. 听力中弗兰克说他下午三点开始开会，会议会延续三个小时或更久，那个时候已经过了他们预约的晚餐时间，所以他迟到的原因是他那时还在开会，答案选 (C)。

2. 根据 So the soonest I could make it is 6:30 or around 7:00 可知，答案选 (D)。

3. 根据最后一句 Then we can have a drink and discuss the cost-cutting measures together 可知，他们要讨论的是削减成本的措施，所以选 (B)。

单词 Vocabulary

department [dɪˈpɑːtmənt] n 部门，科，局
reservation [ˌrezəˈveɪʃn] n 预约，保留，预订
cost-cutting [kɒst ˈkʌtɪŋ] n 削减成本
measure [ˈmeʒə(r)] n 措施，尺寸，度量单位 v 估量，测量

听力测验 | Part 4 简短独白

1. What is this message about?
   (A) A cancellation.
   (B) A reservation.
   (C) An order.
   (D) A payment.

2. Where does Mary work?
   (A) In a school.
   (B) In a bank.
   (C) In a restaurant.
   (D) In a shop.

3. What does Mary want to check?
   (A) To check if Tom still wants the reservation.
   (B) To check if Tom has paid for his breakfast.
   (C) To check if Tom wants drinks.
   (D) To check if Tom wants to dine in the restaurant tomorrow.

4. When is breakfast served?
   (A) From six o'clock to ten o'clock in the morning.
   (B) From six o'clock to nine o'clock in the morning.
   (C) From five o'clock to ten o'clock in the morning.
   (D) From six o'clock to seven o'clock in the morning.

5. Which of the following is false?
   (A) Business lunch starts from eleven o'clock in the morning and goes to two o'clock in the afternoon.
   (B) The chef of the restaurant is good at making delicious dinners.
   (C) The restaurant provides poor service.
   (D) The restaurant can be reached at 222-3636.

Unit 25 订位 | Reservation

Hello! Is this Tom Green? This is Mary from Family Restaurant. I'm calling to confirm your reservation. You have reserved a table for two for this evening. But you have asked that the table be next to a window. I'm very sorry to tell you that all the tables next to a window have been reserved. I would like to check if you still want to keep the reservation or if you want to cancel it. I think you should keep it, because tables that are not next to window, will be provided with free drinks. This is good news, right?

I would also like to tell you more about our restaurant.

a. Our traditional breakfast is served from six o'clock to ten o'clock in the morning. Some food is served the whole day. Hamburgers and eggs sell best.

b. Business lunch starts from eleven o'clock in the morning and goes to two o'clock in the afternoon. There are many kinds of food to be selected.

c. Family dinners or party dinners are from six o'clock to ten o'clock in the evening. The food is served by our chef; he is good at making a delicious dinner.

d. We welcome you to our restaurant to enjoy the food and service. We provide professional cooks, a graceful atmosphere and good service.

If you have any question, please feel free to contact us at 222-3636. We will help you to solve any problem as soon as possible. Have a nice day!

1. 这条消息是关于什么的？

   (A) 取消。
   (B) 预订。
   (C) 订购。
   (D) 付款。

2. 玛丽在哪里工作？

   (A) 学校。
   (B) 银行。
   (C) 餐厅。
   (D) 商店。

3. 玛丽想确认什么？

   (A) 确认汤姆是否保留预约。
   (B) 确认汤姆是否已经付过早餐。
   (C) 确认汤姆是否想要饮料。
   (D) 确认明天汤姆是否想在这家餐厅用餐。

4. 早餐什么时候供应？

   (A) 早上六点钟到十点钟。
   (B) 早上六点钟到九点钟。
   (C) 早上五点钟到十点钟。
   (D) 早上六点钟到七点钟。

5. 下列哪项叙述错误？

   (A) 上班族午餐从上午十一点开始，到下午两点。
   (B) 餐厅主厨擅长做美味晚餐。
   (C) 餐厅提供的服务差劲。
   (D) 可拨打 222-3636 联系餐厅。

　　您好！是汤姆·格林吗？我是家庭餐厅的玛丽。现在我打电话给您是要确认您的预订。您预订了今晚的两人桌。但是您要求靠近窗户的桌子。很抱歉告诉您所有靠窗的两人桌已经预订完了。我想确认一下您是仍然保留预订还是取消。我认为您应该保留，因为不靠窗的桌子，会提供免费饮料。这是好消息，不是吗？

Unit 25 订位 | Reservation

下面，我向您介绍一下我们的餐厅。

一、早上六点到十点提供传统早餐。一些食物会全天提供。汉堡和鸡蛋卖得最好。

二、上班族午餐从上午十一点开始，到下午两点结束。有很多种食物可供选择。

三、家庭晚餐或聚会晚餐是晚上六点到十点提供。食物由我们主厨提供；他十分擅长做美味晚餐。

四、欢迎到我们餐厅来享受食物与服务。我们提供专业厨师、优雅环境以及良好服务。

如果您有任何问题，请拨打 222-3636 联系我们。我们将尽快帮您解决问题。祝您全天愉快！

解析与答案

答案：1. (B)　2. (C)　3. (A)　4. (A)　5. (C)

1. 从最前面的 I'm calling to confirm your reservation 可知，电话是来确认预订的，因此答案选 (B)。
2. 从自我介绍的部分 This is Mary from Family Restaurant 可得知玛丽在餐厅工作，因此选 (C)。
3. 答案在 I would like to check if you still want to keep the reservation 这句话，因此选 (A)。
4. 在介绍餐厅的时候，玛丽说 our traditional breakfast is served from six o'clock to ten o'clock in the morning，由此得知早餐时间是六点到十点，答案选 (A)。
5. 此题可见倒数第二段第二句 We provide professional cooks, a graceful atmosphere and good service，因此选 (C)。

单词 Vocabulary

confirm [kənˈfɜːm] v 确认，证实，批准
window [ˈwɪndəʊ] n 窗户 v 为……开窗
cancel [ˈkænsl] v 取消，删除，抵销，销账
remain [rɪˈmeɪn] v 保留，剩下，属于
traditional [trəˈdɪʃənl] a 传统的，惯例的
select [sɪˈlekt] v 选择，挑选 a 挑选出来的，精选的
chef [ʃef] n 厨师长，主厨
cook [kʊk] n 厨师 v 烹饪，做菜
solve [sɒlv] v 解决，解释，解答

Unit 26
正式午餐 | Formal Lunch

New TOEIC

Picture 26

情境中可明确指出的单词

1. **waiter** ['weɪtə(r)] n 服务员，服务生
2. **tray** [treɪ] n 托盘
3. **cloth napkin** ph 布餐巾
4. **curtain** ['kɜːtn] n 窗帘
5. **dining table** ph 餐桌
6. **plate** [pleɪt] n 盘子
7. **pinstriped** ['pɪnstraɪpt] a 细条纹的
8. **waistcoat** ['weɪskəʊt] n 背心

情境中可延伸记忆的单词

1. **backpack** ['bækpæk] n 双肩包 v 把……放入背包
2. **busy** ['bɪzi] a 忙碌的 v 使忙于
3. **dessert** [dɪ'zɜːt] n 甜点
4. **invite** [ɪn'vaɪt] v 邀请
5. **lunch break** ph 午休
6. **serve** [sɜːv] v 服务
7. **takeout** ['teɪkaʊt] n 外卖
8. **tip** [tɪp] n 小费，尖端

Unit 26 正式午餐 | Formal Lunch

waiter ['weɪtə(r)] n 服务员，服务生
The **waiter** is putting a cup of red wine on the table.
服务生正在放一杯红酒到桌上。
- waitress n 女服务生 / steward n 管家 / servant n 仆人

tray [treɪ] n 托盘
The waiter is holding a **tray** in his right hand.
服务生的右手端着一个托盘。
- baking tray pn 烤盘 / salver n 盘子，托盘 / trayful n 一盘

cloth napkin pn 布餐巾
Could you please bring me a **cloth napkin**?
请帮我拿一条布餐巾好吗？
- napkin n 餐巾 / serviette n （英）餐巾 / hand towel pn 手巾

curtain ['kɜːtn] n 窗帘
Could you please draw the **curtain** for me?
请帮我拉上窗帘，好吗？
- curtain wall pn 幕墙 / curtained a 装有窗帘的 / shutter n 百叶窗

dining table pn 餐桌
In our house, we always eat at the **dining table**.
在我们家，我们总是在餐桌上吃饭。
- dining n 进餐 / dine v 用餐 / dining room pn 餐厅 / dining car pn 餐车

plate [pleɪt] n 盘子
They put their tableware down on the **plates**.
他们把自己的餐具放在盘子上。
- platy a 板状的 / platter n 大浅盘 / saucer n 浅盘

pinstriped ['pɪnstraɪpt] a 细条纹的
The balding man is wearing a **pinstriped** tie around his neck.
那位秃头的男子脖子上戴着一条细条纹的领带。
- pinstripe n 细条纹 / stripe n 条纹

waistcoat ['weɪskəʊt] n 背心
The waiter is wearing a black **waistcoat** over a white shirt.
服务生在白色衬衫外面套了一件黑色背心。
- strait waistcoat pn 紧身衣 / waisted a 有腰身的 / vest n 背心，马甲

backpack ['bækpæk] n 双肩包 v 把……放入背包

The lady hung her backpack on the back of the chair.
这位女子把她的双肩包挂在椅背上。
▶ backpacker n 背包客 / backpacking n 背背包做徒步旅行

---

busy ['bɪzi] a 忙碌的 v 使忙于

The waiter is busy serving customers in the restaurant.
服务生正在餐厅忙于服务顾客。
▶ bustle v 使忙碌，催促 / busy as a bee ph 忙个不停

---

dessert [dɪ'zɜːt] n 甜点

The lady would like some dessert after dinner.
晚餐过后，这位女子可能会吃一些甜点。
▶ dessertspoon n 甜点匙 / hors d'oeuvre n （法）开胃小菜

---

invite [ɪn'vaɪt] v 邀请

They usually invite one or two colleagues to lunch.
他们通常会邀请一两个同事共进午餐。
▶ invitation n 邀请 / invitee n 被邀者 / call on ph 号召，请

---

lunch break ph 午休

You should have a good rest during your lunch break.
在午休时，你应该好好休息。
▶ take a break ph 休息

---

serve [sɜːv] v 服务

The waiter is serving two glasses of red wine.
服务生正在上两杯红酒。
▶ service n 服务，招待 / serviceable a 有用的 / server n 侍者，餐具

---

takeout ['teɪkaʊt] n 外卖

The restaurant provides takeout service.
餐厅提供外卖服务。
▶ takeaway n 外卖食品 / take-over n 接管，接任 / eat in ph 在家吃饭

---

tip [tɪp] n 小费，尖端

The guests will give the waiter a tip.
客人会给服务生小费。
▶ tippy a 不安定的 / tip of the iceberg ph 冰山一角 / gratuity n 小费

听力测验 | Part 1 图片描述题

 题目
(A) There are many tables and chairs.
(B) There are many dishes on the table.
(C) There are many service staff members.
(D) There are many customers.

中译
(A) 这里有很多的桌椅。
(B) 桌子上有很多菜肴。
(C) 这里有很多的服务人员。
(D) 这里有很多顾客。

 解析与答案
答案：(A)
从图片中可以看出，这里有很多的桌椅，桌子上摆有很多餐具，但是没有菜肴，也没有服务人员和顾客，所以答案选 (A)。

听力测验 | Part 3 简短对话题

NEW TOEIC

1. What are the speakers discussing?
   (A) They are discussing korean food.
   (B) They are discussing a plan for dinner.
   (C) They are discussing a plan for purchasing some groceries.
   (D) They are discussing the coupons.

2. What does the man want to do?
   (A) He wants to pay for the dinner.
   (B) He wants to send Dora some coupons.
   (C) He wants to invite Alice at another time.
   (D) He wants to buy some groceries himself.

3. What can we infer from this conversation?
   (A) They will have dinner together.
   (B) They will have dinner at a korean restaurant at another time.
   (C) Alice doesn't want to have dinner with Jack.
   (D) They will have a free meal with Mary's coupons.

Jack: Alice, are you willing to have dinner with me? I heard there is a new korean restaurant. I want to have a try. It's my treat today.

Alice: I really want to join you for dinner, but I have arranged to meet up with Dora. We will have a free meal with her coupons. Would you like to join us?

Jack: Of course. That sounds nice. I can try the korean food at another time. I also need to buy some groceries.

Alice: Good, we can go together. There is a supermarket near the place we are going to have our meal.

Jack: Fantastic!

Unit 26 正式午餐 | Formal Lunch

1. 说话者在谈论什么？
   (A) 他们在谈论韩国食物。　　　　　　(B) 他们谈论晚餐计划。
   (C) 他们在谈论购买日常用品的计划。　(D) 他们在谈论优惠券。

2. 男子想要做什么？
   (A) 他想要请客。　　　　　　　　　　(B) 他送给朵拉一些优惠券。
   (C) 他想下次再邀请爱丽丝。　　　　　(D) 他想自己去买一些日常用品。

3. 从这段对话我们可以推论出什么？
   (A) 他们会一起去吃晚餐。　　　　　　(B) 他们会下次一起去韩国餐厅吃晚餐。
   (C) 爱丽丝不想和杰克一起吃晚餐。　　(D) 他们用玛丽的优惠券去吃免费的晚餐。

杰　　克：爱丽丝，你愿意今天和我一起吃晚餐吗？我听说新开了一家韩国餐厅，我想去尝一尝。今天我请客。
爱丽丝：我非常愿意和你一起吃饭，但是我今天晚上和朵拉约好了。我们要用她的优惠券去吃免费的晚餐，你愿不愿意和我们一起？
杰　　克：好呀，听起来不错。我可以下次再去吃韩国食物。另外，我还想买一些日常用品。
爱丽丝：好的，我们可以一起去。我们吃饭的地方旁边有一个超市。
杰　　克：太棒了！

答案：1. (B)　2. (A)　3. (A)

1. 根据听力内容可知，他们的谈话和晚餐有关，所以选 (B)。
2. 根据 It's my treat today 可知，男子今天想要请客吃饭，所以选 (A)。
3. 男子（杰克）虽然说会下次再去吃韩国食物，但并没有说是和爱丽丝一起，所以 (B) 选项不对，从 I really want to join you for dinner 可知爱丽丝十分乐意和杰克一起吃晚餐，所以 (C) 选项不对，他们吃饭用的优惠券是朵拉的，所以 (D) 选项不对，答案只能选 (A)。

单词 Vocabulary

treat [tri:t] n 请客 v 探讨，对待，处理，请客
arrange [əˈreɪndʒ] v 安排，整理，排列，改编
coupon [ˈku:pɒn] n 优惠券，配给券
grocery [ˈgrəʊsəri] n 生活用品，杂货，食品杂货店
fantastic [fænˈtæstɪk] a 极好的，空想的，不切实际的

阅读测验 | Part 7 文章理解题

NEW TOEIC

Taste of the Specialties: Country-style Cooking

By Jason Merlyn

There is a restaurant with delicious food that I want to recommend to everyone! Don't be disappointed by the name. What the restaurant offers is Spanish and German dishes; meals are cooked with fresh ingredients and a fancy imagination. A formal lunch at the restaurant is really worth the trip. It only takes thirty minutes from the town center. It is along a river in a village in the countryside.

Since yesterday was a nice day, we went to the restaurant and enjoyed lunch on the boat. We ordered tomato slices, smoked meats, salad and some other dishes. With the pleasant decorations on the boat, we had a great time there.

We believed in the chef's culinary skills and ordered a thirty dollar set menu, which included drinks. My friend ordered a fish as main course. There was all kinds of seafood, lobsters, crab, and more.

I ordered some chicken as main course. I thought it was perfect with the added ham in it. My friend ordered beef. The drinks were an excellent accompaniment to the dishes.

We have never had such delicious food. Even now, I still want to eat their food. My friend and I decided to go there again this weekend. If anyone wants to enjoy a delicious meal, I recommend this restaurant.

Unit 26 正式午餐 | Formal Lunch

1. What does this article mainly talk about?
   (A) A restaurant.
   (B) A hotel.
   (C) A café.
   (D) A club.

2. What does Jason think of the restaurant?
   (A) Bad.
   (B) Just so so.
   (C) Perfect.
   (D) Not mentioned in the article.

3. When did Jason go to the restaurant?
   (A) The day before yesterday.
   (B) Yesterday.
   (C) This morning.
   (D) This afternoon.

4. What does Jason's friend order as a main course?
   (A) Fish.
   (B) Chicken.
   (C) Beef.
   (D) Turkey.

5. When will Jason go to the restaurant again?
   (A) Tomorrow.
   (B) The day after tomorrow.
   (C) This weekend.
   (D) Next weekend.

品尝特色菜：乡村式烹饪

杰森·梅林

　　有家餐厅我要向大家推荐，那里的食物十分美味。但是不要对它的名字感到失望。餐厅提供西班牙菜与德国菜；菜肴是用新鲜材料做的，想象力很丰富，很值得来吃一顿正式午餐。它坐落于乡下一个沿河村庄。从镇中心来这里，只需三十分钟。

　　昨天天气不错，我们去了这家餐厅，在船上享用午餐。我们点了番茄切片、烟熏肉、沙拉以及其他菜肴。船上的装饰很漂亮，我们在那里玩得很开心。

　　我们相信厨师的厨艺，用三十美元点了一份固定菜单，里面包含饮料。我的朋友点了一条鱼作为主菜。那里有各种海鲜，例如龙虾、蟹等。

　　我点了一些鸡肉作为主菜。我认为，里面加火腿十分完美。我的朋友点了牛排。这些菜配饮料，十分不错。我们从未吃过如此美味的食物。

　　就是现在，我还想吃这样的菜。我和我的朋友决定这周末再去那里。如果谁想吃美味佳肴，我推荐这家餐厅。

1. 这篇文章主要在谈论什么？
    (A) 一家餐厅。
    (B) 一家旅馆。
    (C) 一家咖啡厅。
    (D) 一家俱乐部。

2. 杰森觉得这家餐厅如何？
    (A) 不好。
    (B) 还好。
    (C) 完美。
    (D) 在文章中没有评论。

3. 杰森什么时候去餐厅的？
    (A) 前天。
    (B) 昨天。
    (C) 今天早上。
    (D) 今天下午。

Unit 26 正式午餐 | Formal Lunch

4. 杰森的朋友点什么当作主餐？

(A) 鱼肉。

(B) 鸡肉。

(C) 牛肉。

(D) 火鸡。

5. 杰森什么时候会再去这家餐厅？

(A) 明天。

(B) 后天。

(C) 这个周末。

(D) 下个周末。

解析与答案

答案：1.(A) 2.(C) 3.(B) 4.(A) 5.(C)

1. 文章的第一句就说 There is a restaurant with delicious food thatI want to recommend to everyone...，由此可知是要推荐餐厅给大家，因此选 (A)。

2. 在第一段第四句 A formal lunch at the restaurant is really worth the trip 便可以找到杰森对餐厅的评价，因此选 (C)。

3. 第二段第一句 Since yesterday was a nice day, we went to the restaurant... 提到杰森去此餐厅的时间，因此答案选 (B)。

4. 在介绍餐厅时，杰森说明了点餐的内容。由第三段第二句 My friend ordered a fish as main course 可知朋友点鱼肉当主餐，因此选 (A)。

5. 此题可见最后一段第二句 My friend and I decide to go there again this weekend，因此选 (C)。

单词 Vocabulary

recommend [ˌrekəˈmend] v 推荐，介绍，建议

delicious [dɪˈlɪʃəs] a 美味的

style [staɪl] n 风格，作风，流行款式 v 设计，称呼

ingredient [ɪnˈɡriːdiənt] n 材料

formal [ˈfɔːml] a 正式的，表面的，整齐的

enjoy [ɪnˈdʒɔɪ] v 享受，欣赏

order [ˈɔːdə(r)] v 订购，指挥，整理 n 顺序，订购，汇票，命令

lobster [ˈlɒbstə(r)] n 龙虾

beef [biːf] n 牛肉 v 抱怨

accompaniment [əˈkʌmpənɪmənt] n 伴随物，附加物，伴奏

Unit 27
派对 | Party

New TOEIC

Picture 27

情境中可明确指出的单词

1. **beverage** ['bevərɪdʒ] n 饮料
2. **clink** [klɪŋk] v 发出叮当声
3. **informal dress** ph 便服
4. **flower** ['flaʊə(r)] n 花
5. **refectory table** ph （英）长餐桌
6. **salad** ['sæləd] n 沙拉
7. **table cloth** ph 桌巾
8. **tidily** ['taɪdɪli] ad 整齐地

情境中可延伸记忆的单词

1. **bender** ['bendə(r)] n 饮酒作乐
2. **celebrate** ['selɪbreɪt] v 庆祝
3. **clutter** ['klʌtə(r)] v 使凌乱
4. **drinking** ['drɪŋkɪŋ] n 饮酒
5. **party** ['pɑːti] n 派对
6. **polite** [pə'laɪt] a 有礼貌的
7. **relaxed** [rɪ'lækst] a 放松的
8. **atmosphere** ['ætməsfɪə(r)] n 气氛

Unit 27 派对 | Party

beverage ['bevərɪdʒ] n 饮料
They held up their **beverage**.
他们举起自己的饮料。
- beverage bottle ph 饮料瓶 / drink n 饮料

clink [klɪŋk] v 发出叮当声
They **clinked** their glasses together and emptied them in one gulp.
他们碰杯并一口气把它们喝完。
- clinker n 赝品 / clang v 发铿锵声 / jangle v（铃）发出刺耳声

informal dress ph 便服
They were all wearing **informal dress**.
他们都穿着便服。
- formal dress ph 礼服 / informal a 非正式的，不拘礼节的 / attire n 服装

flower ['flaʊə(r)] n 花
The room is decorated with ribbons, **flowers**, and more.
这间房间用缎带、花朵等装饰。
- flowerless a 无花的 / flowerage n（总称）花类 / in flower ph 盛开，在开花 / flower bed 花圃

refectory table ph （英）长餐桌
The picture showed them sitting at a **refectory table**.
这张照片显示他们坐在长餐桌旁边。
- refectory n 食堂，餐厅 / dinner table ph 餐桌 / turntable n 餐桌转盘

salad ['sæləd] n 沙拉
Today, all of the customers will be served **salads** for free.
今天为所有客户提供免费沙拉。
- salad oil ph 沙拉油 / salad bowl ph 沙拉碗 / dressing n 酱汁

table cloth ph 桌巾
The table is covered with a red **table cloth**.
桌子上铺着红色的桌巾。
- tablecloth n 桌布 / table linen ph 餐桌用布

tidily ['taɪdɪli] ad 整齐地
The plates were stacked **tidily** on the table.
盘子整齐地摆放在桌子上。
- tidiness n 整齐 / tidy a 整齐的 / tidy away ph 收拾

bender ['bendə(r)] n 饮酒作乐
I went on a bender last night at the party and drank way too much!
我昨晚去派对饮酒作乐，喝得大醉！
▶ bend v 弯曲 / drink v 饮酒

---

celebrate ['selɪbreɪt] v 庆祝
They held a party to celebrate her birthday.
他们举办聚会庆祝她的生日。
▶ celebration n 庆典 / celebrator n 庆祝者 / congratulate v 祝贺 / celebrity n 名人

---

clutter ['klʌtə(r)] v 使凌乱
After the party, the table became cluttered.
聚会结束后，桌子变得凌乱。
▶ clutter up phr 使杂乱 / in a clutter phr 乱七八糟 / messy a 混乱的

---

drinking ['drɪŋkɪŋ] n 饮酒
Occasionally drinking with some friends is a good way to relax.
偶尔和一些朋友一起喝酒是个很好的放松方式。
▶ drinkable a 可饮用的

---

party ['pɑːti] n 派对
It is just a meeting among friends rather than a formal party.
这只是朋友间的一个聚会，并非正式派对。
▶ third party n 第三方 / party pooper phr 派对上扫大家兴的人

---

polite [pə'laɪt] a 有礼貌的
It is polite to take the host a small present at a party.
派对上，给主人带一份小礼物是有礼貌的。
▶ politeness n 礼貌 / rude a 无礼的 / impolite a 无礼的

---

relaxed [rɪ'lækst] a 放松的
The smile on their faces proves that they are relaxed.
他们脸上的笑容证明他们很放松。
▶ relax v 放松，缓和 / relaxation n 放松 / relaxant n 缓和剂

---

atmosphere ['ætməsfɪə(r)] n 气氛
The atmosphere at this party is joyful.
这次聚会的气氛很好。
▶ atmospherical a 大气的 / atmospheric pressure n 大气压力

听力测验 | Part 1 图片描述题

题目

(A) All of the people here are drinking champagne.
(B) All of them are very excited.
(C) There are just several people.
(D) They are wearing different colored hats.

中译

(A) 这里的所有人都在喝香槟。
(B) 所有人都非常兴奋。
(C) 这里只有几个人。
(D) 他们都戴着不同颜色的帽子。

解析与答案

答案：(B)
从图片中可以看出，派对上有很多人，每个人的脸上都露出微笑，他们都穿着一样的服装、戴着一样的帽子，但不是都在喝香槟，所以答案选 (B)。

听力测验 | Part 3 简短对话题

NEW TOEIC

1. Will the man come to the party?
   (A) Yes, he will be punctual.
   (B) Yes, but he will be late.
   (C) No, he won't, because there is something else he needs to do.
   (D) No, because he didn't prepare for the party.

2. When will the party probably end?
   (A) At 8:00.
   (B) At 9:00.
   (C) At 10:00.
   (D) At 9:30.

3. Will the man stay here until the party is over?
   (A) Yes, he will.
   (B) No, because he has something else to do.
   (C) No, because he will be tired.
   (D) There is no mention of it.

Kelly: Jeffrey, do you have any plans on Friday night?

Jeffrey: Not yet. Why?

Kelly: There is a party at my house on Friday night, so I want to invite you to come. Can you make it?

Jeffrey: Yes, of course. I'm happy to be invited. I will be punctual. When will the party start? Is there anything I should prepare?

Kelly: No, everything is taken care of. You can come at 8:00.

Jeffrey: OK. I will go there after I finish work. But I can't stay more than two hours because I have other things to do.

Kelly: That's all right. The party will last about an hour and a half, so it will end before 10:00. So you can enjoy yourself at the party.

Jeffrey: Great!

Unit 27 派对 | Party

中译

1. 男子会去派对吗？
   - (A) 会，他将准时出现在派对现场。
   - (B) 会，但是他会迟到。
   - (C) 不会，因为他还有别的事情要做。
   - (D) 不会，因为他没有做好准备。

2. 派对可能几点结束？
   - (A) 八点。
   - (B) 九点。
   - (C) 十点。
   - (D) 九点半。

3. 男子会待到派对结束再走吗？
   - (A) 他会等到派对结束再走。
   - (B) 不会，因为他还有其他事情要做。
   - (C) 不会，因为他会感到疲劳。
   - (D) 文中没有提到。

凯　莉：杰弗里，你周五晚上有什么安排吗？
杰弗里：暂时没有。怎么了？
凯　莉：周五晚上我要在家办一个派对，想邀请你参加。你到时可以过来吗？
杰弗里：当然，我非常开心能收到你的邀请。我会准时去的。派对几点开始？我需要准备什么东西吗？
凯　莉：不用，所有东西都会准备好的。你只要晚上八点过来就可以了。
杰弗里：好的。我完成工作就赶过去，但是我待的时间不能超过两个小时，因为我还有其他事情要做。
凯　莉：没关系的。我们的派对会大概持续一个半小时，所以十点之前就会结束。你只需好好享受在派对上的时间就行了。
杰弗里：太好了！

解析与答案

答案：1. (A)　2. (D)　3. (A)

1. 根据男生说 I will be punctual 可知，男子（杰弗里）会准时参加派对，所以选 (A)。
2. 听力中凯莉说派对八点开始，再根据"The party will last about an hour and a half"可知，派对可能九点半的时候结束，所以选 (D)。
3. 听力中杰弗里开始说他不会在派对上待太久，因为他十点的时候还有其他事情，但是凯莉说派对会在十点前结束，让他好好享受派对时光，他非常开心，由此可知他会待到派对结束，所以选 (A)。

单词 Vocabulary

invite [ɪn'vaɪt] n 邀请　v 邀请，招待
punctual ['pʌŋktʃuəl] a 准时的，精确的，正确的
prepare [prɪ'peə(r)] v 准备，筹备，制作，起草
enjoy [ɪn'dʒɔɪ] v 享受，欣赏，使过得快活

阅读测验 | Part 7 文章理解题

To: All Employees

From: Jack Wood, Manager of Administrative Department

Subject: Christmas party

Hello everyone,

Our department has been informed that we will plan the Christmas party this year. Every year, we hold a party to celebrate Christmas and spend the holiday together with all of the employees and their families. All our employees have contributed a lot to our company. We should give them a celebration on this special day.

We are going to hold the Christmas Party at London Mike Restaurant rather than at our company this year. There will be new items added to the the party and I think all of us will be satisfied with it. Our administrative department expects your participation along with that of your family at the celebration.

In addition, we want to invite all employees to contribute suggestions and ideas for the food, drinks, music, dancing, etc. So, tell us what you want the party to be and how the party should be held. We welcome all of your ideas. You can send them to me by e-mail this afternoon.

You are asked to make sure to have your name and the number of people in family on the list at the reception desk by this afternoon. We will inform all the employees about the Christmas Party and all related matters by e-mail this afternoon.

We are looking forward to your ideas and hope you can join us.

Regards,

Jack Wood

Friday, Dec. 14th

Unit 27 派对 | Party

1. What holiday will they celebrate?
   (A) Halloween.
   (B) Valentine's Day.
   (C) Christmas.
   (D) Easter.

2. Which department will plan the Christmas party this year?
   (A) Marketing Department.
   (B) Technology Department.
   (C) Sales Department.
   (D) Administrative Department.

3. Where will the Christmas party be held this year?
   (A) At the company.
   (B) In a restaurant.
   (C) In a club.
   (D) In a hotel.

4. What are the employees asked to do according to the fourth paragraph?
   (A) To give suggestions and ideas.
   (B) To bring their family to the party.
   (C) To get dressed in costume.
   (D) To bring their own bottles.

5. When will the Administrative Department inform the employees about the party?
   (A) Right now.
   (B) This morning.
   (C) This afternoon.
   (D) This evening.

收件人：所有雇员

寄件者：杰克·伍德，行政部门经理

主题：圣诞晚会

大家好！

今年由我们部门筹划圣诞节派对。我们每年都举行派对庆祝圣诞节，与所有员工以及他们的家人度过这个节日。所有员工都对我们的公司做出了极大贡献，我们应该在那个特别的日子里给他们庆祝。

今年，我们准备在伦敦麦克餐厅举行圣诞派对，而不是在我们公司举行。派对中将会添加新项目；我认为我们所有人都会很满意。我们的行政部门期待你和你的家人来参与庆祝。

另外，我们想邀请所有员工对食物、饮料、音乐、舞蹈等提出建议或者意见。告诉我们你期待什么样的派对以及怎样进行。我们欢迎你们所有人提出想法，你们可以将想法发到我的电子信箱，到今天下午截止。

今天下午之前要确保你的名字和你的家庭人数写在前台的名单上。今天下午，我们将以电子邮件的方式通知所有员工有关圣诞派对以及其他相关事项。

我们期待收到你的建议，希望你能加入。

此致

敬礼！

杰克·伍德

12 月 14 日，星期五

1. 他们将要庆祝什么节日？
   (A) 万圣节。　　　　　　　　(B) 情人节。
   (C) 圣诞节。　　　　　　　　(D) 复活节。

2. 今年由哪个部门举行圣诞节派对？
   (A) 营销部门。　　　　　　　(B) 科技部门。
   (C) 销售部门。　　　　　　　(D) 行政部门。

3. 今年在哪里举行圣诞节派对？
   (A) 公司。　　　　　　　　　(B) 餐厅。
   (C) 俱乐部。　　　　　　　　(D) 酒店。

Unit 27 派对 | Party

4. 第四段要求员工做什么？
    (A) 提出建议或意见。
    (B) 将他们的家人带到派对上来。
    (C) 穿戏装。
    (D) 带酒。

5. 行政部门什么时候通知雇员有关派对的情况？
    (A) 立即。
    (B) 今天上午。
    (C) 今天下午。
    (D) 今天晚上。

解析与答案

答案：1. (C) 2. (D) 3. (B) 4. (A) 5. (C)

1. 此题可从主题 Subject: Christmas Party 找到答案，选 (C)。

2. 从寄件者 From: Jack Wood, Manager of Administrative Department 以及第一段第一句 Our department has been informed that we will plan the Christmas party this year 可知今年是行政部门举办，因此选 (D)。

3. 第二段第一句 We are going to hold the Christmas Party at London Mike Restaurant... 指出，想要在餐厅举办派对，因此选 (B)。

4. 此题可见第三段第一句 ... we want to invite all employees to contribute suggestions and ideas...，因此选 (A)。

5. 在倒数第二段第二句 We will inform all employees about the Christmas Party and all related matters by e-mail this afternoon 可知今天下午会以电子邮件方式通知大家有关派对的事宜，所以答案选 (C)。

单词 Vocabulary

Christmas ['krɪsməs] n 圣诞节
party ['pɑːti] n 派对，聚会
family ['fæməli] n 家人，家庭，家族
celebration [ˌselɪ'breɪʃn] n 庆祝
participation [pɑːˌtɪsɪ'peɪʃn] n 参与，参加
raise [reɪz] v 提出，举起，增加，引起
welcome ['welkəm] v 欢迎 a 受欢迎的
idea [aɪ'dɪə] n 想法，主意，意见，了解，概念
reception [rɪ'sepʃn] n 接待，招待会，接受

Unit 28

餐厅点餐 | Ordering

New TOEIC

Picture 28

情境中可明确指出的单词

1. **bow tie** ph 蝶形领结
2. **chandelier** [ˌʃændəˈlɪə(r)] n 吊灯
3. **menu** [ˈmenjuː] n 菜单
4. **knife** [naɪf] n 刀
5. **painting** [ˈpeɪntɪŋ] n 画，油画，水彩画
6. **place mat** ph 餐具垫
7. **order** [ˈɔːdə(r)] v 点餐
8. **tableware** [ˈteɪblweə(r)] n （总称）餐具

情境中可延伸记忆的单词

1. **appetizer** [ˈæpɪtaɪzə(r)] n 开胃菜
2. **family** [ˈfæməli] n 家人，家庭
3. **frequenter** [frɪˈkwentə] n （英）常客
4. **senior** [ˈsiːniə(r)] n 年长者
5. **specialty** [ˈspeʃəlti] n 招牌菜，专长 a 特色的
6. **serving** [ˈsɜːvɪŋ] n 一份食物，上菜
7. **taste** [teɪst] v 品尝
8. **wagon** [ˈwæɡən] n （美）送食品或饮料的推车

Unit 28 餐厅点餐 | Ordering

bow tie [ph] 蝶形领结
The waiter is wearing a white shirt with a bow tie.
服务生穿着白衬衫，打着蝶形领结。
● tie 领带 / necktie 领带

chandelier [ˌʃændəˈlɪə(r)] [n] 吊灯
I think chandeliers are really luxurious.
我认为吊灯真的很奢侈。
● crystal chandelier 水晶吊灯 / chandelier earring 吊灯式耳环

menu [ˈmenjuː] [n] 菜单
The elderly man is holding a menu in his hand.
那位年长的男子手里拿着菜单。
● main menu 主选单 / list 表单

knife [naɪf] [n] 刀
The cook put two table knives on the table.
厨师往桌子上放了两把餐刀。
● fruit knife 水果刀 / knife-edge 刀刃 / blade 刀片 / fork 叉子

painting [ˈpeɪntɪŋ] [n] 画，油画，水彩画
The painting is hanging on the wall between the two windows.
窗户之间的墙上挂着一幅油画。
● wall painting 壁画 / paint 绘画 / painter 画家，油漆工 / paint-in 画图示威

place mat [ph] 餐具垫
The cloth napkins are put on the place mats.
餐具垫上放着餐巾布。
● mat 垫子 / utensil 用具

order [ˈɔːdə(r)] [v] 点餐
The waiter is ordering dishes for the guests.
服务生正在为客人们点餐。
● orderliness 整洁 / ordered 有条理的 / in order to 为了 / in order 按顺序

tableware [ˈteɪblweə(r)] [n] （总称）餐具
How many sets of tableware do you need?
你们需要多少套餐具？
● cutlery 餐具 / pantry 餐具室 / sideboard 餐具柜

appetizer ['æpɪtaɪzə(r)] n 开胃菜
They will order an appetizer before the main course.
在吃主菜之前，他们会先点一道开胃菜。
🔄 starter n 开胃菜 / appetiser n 开胃食品 / appetizing a 开胃的 / aperitif n（法）开胃酒

family ['fæməli] n 家人，家庭
It is just a meal among family members.
这是家人之间的用餐。
🔄 familial a 家族的 / family doctor n 家庭医生 / family name n 姓 / relative n 亲戚

frequenter [frɪ'kwentə] n （英）常客
They are frequenters at this restaurant.
他们是这家餐厅的常客。
🔄 frequent a 频繁的 / frequently ad 频繁地 / regular n 老顾客

senior ['siːniə(r)] n 年长者
I would say that this senior is the two ladies' father.
我敢说这位年长者是两位女子的父亲。
🔄 seniority n 长辈 / senior citizen n 老年人 / junior n 晚辈

specialty ['speʃəlti] n 招牌菜，特长 a 特色的
The waiter doesn't need to introduce the specialty to the frequenters.
服务生不需要向常客介绍招牌菜。
🔄 specific a 特殊的 / specialized a 专门的

serving ['sɜːvɪŋ] n 一份食物，上菜
I can infer that they will order four servings from the four sets of tableware on the table.
从桌上的四套餐具我可以推测出他们会点四份餐。
🔄 service n 服务 / servitor n 仆人 / servile a 奴隶的，屈从的

taste [teɪst] v 品尝
After the meal, the ladies will taste the restaurant's ice cream.
餐后，女士们会品尝店里的冰激凌。
🔄 tasteful a 雅致的 / in taste 得体的 / taste of n 有……味

wagon ['wægən] n （美）送食品或饮料的推车
The waiter will wheel in the serving wagon to begin serving.
服务生将会推着推车上菜。
🔄 wagoner n 车夫 / put the cart before the horse n 本末倒置

听力测验 | Part 1 图片描述题

题目
(A) All the women here are on the phone.
(B) One man is dressed in a short-sleeved shirt.
(C) The table is filled with bread.
(D) A woman is ordering.

中译
(A) 所有的女子都在打电话。
(B) 有一位男子穿着短袖衬衫。
(C) 桌子上堆满了面包。
(D) 有一位女子在点餐。

解析与答案

答案：(B)
从图片中可以看出，有三位女子，其中有一位在打电话；有两位男子，一位穿着短袖，另一位穿着西装的男子在点餐，桌子上有面包，但是并没有堆满，所以选 (B)。

听力测验 | Part 3 简短对话题

1. What did the man order?
   (A) A chicken burger, a cheeseburger and a medium coke.
   (B) A chicken burger, a cheeseburger, a cup of coffee and a small coke.
   (C) Two cheeseburgers, a cup of coffee and a small coke.
   (D) A cheeseburger and a cup of coffee.

2. How many cups of coffee have the man ordered?
   (A) Only one.
   (B) Two.
   (C) Three.
   (D) Four.

3. How much did he pay?
   (A) He paid $15.68.
   (B) He paid $50.68.
   (C) He paid $50.86.
   (D) He paid $15.86.

Waitress: Hello, what would you like to order?

Eason: Please give me a chicken burger and a small coke please. And a cheeseburger and a milkshake.

Waitress: Sorry, our milkshakes are sold out.

Eason: Then please give me a cup of coffee.

Waitress: Is there anything else that you might want?

Eason: No, thanks. How much is it all together?

Waitress: That will be $15.68.

Unit 28 餐厅点餐 | Ordering

1. 男子点了什么？
(A) 他点了一个鸡肉汉堡、一个芝士汉堡和一中杯可乐。
(B) 他点了一个鸡肉汉堡、一个芝士汉堡、一杯咖啡和一小杯可乐。
(C) 他点了两个芝士汉堡、一杯咖啡和一小杯可乐。
(D) 他点了一个芝士汉堡和一杯咖啡。

2. 男子点了几杯咖啡？
(A) 只有一杯。
(B) 两杯。
(C) 三杯。
(D) 四杯。

3. 他一共付了多少钱？
(A) 他一共付了 15.68 美元。
(B) 他一共付了 50.68 美元。
(C) 他一共付了 50.86 美元。
(D) 他一共付了 15.86 美元。

服务生：你好！请问需要点什么？
伊　森：请给我一个鸡肉汉堡和一杯可乐，一个芝士汉堡和一杯奶昔。
服务生：抱歉，奶昔已经卖完了。
伊　森：那么，请给我一杯咖啡。
服务生：还需要点些别的东西吗？
伊　森：不用了，谢谢。一共多少钱？
服务生：一共15.68美元。

答案：1. (B) 2. (A) 3. (A)

1. 伊森一开始说 Please give me a chicken burger and a small coke please. And a cheeseburger and a milkshake，但店员后来回复说奶昔没有了，所以伊森换点咖啡，因此答案要选 (B)。
2. 伊森点了两杯饮料，但因为奶昔没了，所以换成咖啡，因此推论得知只点了一杯咖啡，答案选 (A)。
3. 根据 That will be $15.68 可知，答案选 (A)。

单词 Vocabulary

burger ['bɜːgə(r)] n 汉堡
order ['ɔːdə(r)] n 命令，订单，顺序 v 命令，订购
milkshake ['mɪlkʃeɪk] n 奶昔

阅读测验 | Part 7 文章理解题

When it comes to fast food restaurants, we can't ignore McDonalds. We know that McDonalds is the largest chain of fast food restaurants in the world. In the beginning, McDonalds offered hamburgers, chicken, fried chips, salads, desserts, drinks and so on. However, now it has started to serve fruit, milkshakes, and more. It has introduced many kinds of food and drinks which cater to the taste of customers, especially children. Even more, some McDonalds restaurants have begun to provide playgrounds for children. McDonalds is really popular with customers.

The reasons why McDonalds is so popular are as follows:

First, as a chain of fast food restaurants, it serves plenty of fast food, like hamburgers, chicken, fried chips, and more. There is a wide choice of food, so many people like it.

Second, their service is very fast. After ordering food, you can usually get your food within ten minutes or twenty minutes at most. Since we are living in a fast-paced era and do not have much time to waste in a restaurant, this is another important reason.

Last, it contributes to their good food, clean and comfortable environment and good service. While choosing a restaurant, we tend to choose those that serve good food, have a good environment and service.

In general, McDonalds has a lot of food choices, so it is a good choice to go there.

Unit 28 餐厅点餐 | Ordering

1. What is this article about?
   (A) A chain of fast food restaurants.
   (B) A chain of hotels.
   (C) A clothes shop.
   (D) A fruit shop.

2. Which of the following foods are not served in McDonalds?
   (A) Hamburgers.
   (B) Italian food.
   (C) Chicken.
   (D) Salads.

3. How many reasons for why McDonalds is popular does the writer list?
   (A) One.
   (B) Two.
   (C) Three.
   (D) Four.

4. Which reason of the following does not contribute to the popularity of McDonalds?
   (A) Good food.
   (B) Politeness of waiters.
   (C) Clean and comfortable environment.
   (D) Good service.

5. Which of the following is NOT true?
   (A) McDonalds serves desserts.
   (B) McDonalds is the largest chain of fast food restaurants in the world.
   (C) McDonalds has introduced food recently.
   (D) McDonalds makes customers wait for a long time while dining.

当谈到快餐店时,我们忽略不了麦当劳。我们都知道,麦当劳是世界上最大的连锁快餐店。起初,麦当劳供应汉堡、鸡肉、炸薯条、沙拉、甜点、饮料等。然而,这些日子以来它开始供应水果、奶昔等,还引进了很多种食物以及饮料,以迎合顾客的口味,尤其是儿童。更其者,一些麦当劳餐厅开始为儿童提供游乐场。麦当劳真的十分受顾客欢迎。

麦当劳受欢迎的原因如下:

首先,作为快餐连锁店,它的快餐种类十分丰富,比如汉堡、鸡肉、炸薯条等。可供人们选择的食物比较多,因此人们喜欢它。

其次,上餐快。点过食物之后,通常十分钟以内就可以上餐,最多二十分钟。我们生活在一个快节奏的时代,没有太多时间浪费在餐厅,因此这是另一个重要原因。

最后,这归功于他们的优质食物、干净舒适的环境以及良好的服务。选择餐厅时,我们倾向于选择提供优质食物、良好环境以及良好服务的餐厅。

总之,麦当劳提供很多食物可供选择;去那里是一个不错的选择。

1. 这篇文章是关于什么的?
   (A) 快餐连锁店。
   (B) 连锁酒店。
   (C) 服装店。
   (D) 水果店。

2. 在麦当劳,我们点不到什么?
   (A) 汉堡。
   (B) 意大利食物。
   (C) 鸡肉。
   (D) 沙拉。

3. 对于麦当劳很受欢迎,作者列出了几条原因?
   (A) 一条。
   (B) 两条。
   (C) 三条。
   (D) 四条。

Unit 28 餐厅点餐 | Ordering

4. 麦当劳很受欢迎，不归功于下列哪项？
   (A) 良好的食物。
   (B) 服务生的礼貌。
   (C) 干净舒适的环境。
   (D) 良好的服务。

5. 下列哪项说法不正确？
   (A) 麦当劳提供甜点。
   (B) 麦当劳是世界上最大的快餐店。
   (C) 麦当劳最近开始引进食物。
   (D) 用餐时，麦当劳让顾客等待很久。

解析与答案

答案：1. (A)　2. (B)　3. (C)　4. (B)　5. (D)

1. 主旨题的答案通常会在最前面，可见第一段第一句 When it comes to fast food restaurants, we can't ignore McDonalds，因此答案选 (A)。
2. 从第一段第三句 ... McDonalds offered hamburgers, chicken, fried chips, salads... 以排除法可推论得知此题答案选 (B)。
3. 此题可见第二段下面列举的原因，First... Second... Last...，因此选 (C)。
4. 答案在倒数第二段第一句 Last, it contributes to their good food, clean and comfortable environment and good service，因此选 (B)。
5. 此题可见第四段中列举的第二条原因 Second, their service very fast. After ordering food, you can usually get your food within ten minutes or twenty minutes at most，因此选 (D)。

单词 Vocabulary

chain [tʃeɪn] n 连锁店，系列，拘禁 v 拘禁，束缚
salad [ˈsæləd] n 沙拉
dessert [dɪˈzɜːt] n 甜点
cater [ˈkeɪtə(r)] v 迎合，提供饮食，承办宴席
plenty [ˈplenti] n 足够，丰富，充足 a 足够的
era [ˈɪərə] n 时代，年代
another [əˈnʌðə(r)] a 又一，另外的
contribute [kənˈtrɪbjuːt] v 捐款，捐助，贡献，投稿
environment [ɪnˈvaɪrənmənt] n 环境，自然环境，包围
general [ˈdʒenrəl] a 普遍的，一般的，全体的 n 将军

Unit 29
餐厅内场 | Cooking Area

New TOEIC

Picture 29

情境中可明确指出的单词

1. **bowl** [bəʊl] n 碗
2. **colander** [ˈkʌləndə(r)] n 漏勺
3. **cook** [kʊk] n 厨师
4. **cooking utensil** ph 厨具
5. **counter top** ph 柜台面
6. **spatula** [ˈspætʃələ] n 抹刀
7. **stove** [stəʊv] n 炉灶,（做）菜用的小炉
8. **tap** [tæp] n 水龙头

情境中可延伸记忆的单词

1. **bake** [beɪk] n 烘烤,烘烤成的食品 v 烘烤,烤面包或糕饼
2. **condiment** [ˈkɒndɪmənt] n （辛辣）调味品,佐料
3. **cookie** [ˈkʊki] n 甜饼干
4. **heat** [hiːt] n 热度,温度 v 把……加热
5. **ingredient** [ɪnˈɡriːdiənt] n 食材,原料
6. **oven mitt** ph 隔热手套
7. **purchase** [ˈpɜːtʃəs] v 采购
8. **tomato** [təˈmɑːtəʊ] n 番茄

Unit 29 餐厅内场 | Cooking Area

bowl [bəʊl] n. 碗
After having dinner, you should help clean the bowls.
吃完晚餐，你应该帮忙洗碗。
- bowler n. 圆顶礼帽 / chopsticks n. 筷子

---

colander ['kʌləndə(r)] n. 漏勺
The chef put the colander in the pot.
厨师长把漏勺放进锅里。
- filter n. 滤器 v. 过滤 / strain v. 过滤 / ladle n. 勺子 / scoop n. 勺子

---

cook [kʊk] n. 厨师
The man and the lady in caps are cooks.
戴帽子的男士和女士是厨师。
- cookery n. 烹调术 / cookbook n. 食谱 / cooked a. 煮好的

---

cooking utensil ph. 厨具
The shelf is piled with cooking utensils.
架子上堆满了厨具。
- cookware n. 厨具 / cooker n. 烹调器具 / kitchenware n. 厨房用具

---

counter top ph. 柜台面
The cook got mad at the sight of plates and bowls on the counter top.
厨师看到台面上的盘子和碗，很生气。
- counter n. 柜台 / counter to ph. 相反地

---

spatula ['spætʃələ] n. 抹刀
I will buy a spatula this afternoon.
我今天下午会买一把抹刀。
- spatulate a. 抹刀型的 / smear v. 涂抹

---

stove [stəʊv] n. 炉灶，做菜用的小炉
He just put the pot on the stove.
他刚才把锅放在炉子上。
- gas stove ph. 煤气炉 / stovepipe n. 火炉的烟囱 / oven n. 炉 / fireplace n. 壁炉

---

tap [tæp] n. 水龙头
You forgot to turn off the tap this morning.
你今天上午忘记关水龙头了。
- tap into ph. 挖掘 / tap water ph. 自来水 / tap dance ph. 踢踏舞

291

bake [beɪk] n. 烘烤，烘烤成的食品 v. 烘烤，烤面包或糕饼

It takes a long time to bake cakes.
烤蛋糕需要很长一段的时间。
● bakery n. 面包店 / bakehouse n. 面包厂

condiment ['kɒndɪmənt] n. （辛辣）调味品，佐料

The dishes will be delicious with a few added condiments.
加入适量的佐料的菜就会很美味。
● seasoning n. 调料品 / sauce n. 调味酱，酱汁

cookie ['kʊki] n. 甜饼干

You know the chef is good at making cookies.
你知道，这个厨师擅长做甜饼干。
● tough cookie n. 非常坚强的人 / cookie cutter n. 千篇一律的东西

heat [hiːt] n. 热度，温度 v. 把……加热

Adjust the heat of the fire by turning the regulating valve.
通过调节阀来调节温度。
● heater n. 加热器 / heat stroke n. 中暑 / heat up v. 把……加热

ingredient [ɪn'griːdiənt] n. 食材，原料

The ingredients in the restaurant must be kept fresh.
餐厅的食材必须保持新鲜。
● food ingredient n. 食品配料成分

oven mitt ph. 隔热手套

While cooking, the cook needed to wear a pair of oven mitts.
做菜时，厨师需要带上隔热手套。
● ovenproof a. 耐高温的 / microwave oven n. 微波炉

purchase ['pɜːtʃəs] v. 采购

The purchasing agent needed to asked the chef before purchasing.
采购员采购食材前需要询问主厨的意见。
● purchaser n. 买方 / buy v. 购买 / sell v. 销售

tomato [tə'mɑːtəʊ] n. 番茄

The cook is showing how to cut a tomato into slices.
厨师正在展示如何将番茄切片。
● tomato sauce n. 番茄酱 / tomato juice n. 番茄汁

听力测验 | Part 1 图片描述题

题目
(A) There is only a chef in the cooking area.
(B) The chef is wearing a chef's hat.
(C) The chef is cooking Chinese food.
(D) The chef is cooking western food.

中译
(A) 餐厅内场只有一位厨师。
(B) 厨师戴着厨师帽。
(C) 厨师在做中国菜。
(D) 厨师在做西餐。

解析与答案
答案：(D)
从图片中可以看出，餐厅内场不止一个厨师，看得最清楚的是这位厨师没戴厨师帽，他在做西餐，所以选 (D)。

听力测验 | Part 3 简短对话题

NEW TOEIC

1. What doesn't the man want Elisa to do?
   (A) To wash vegetables.
   (B) To peel some potatoes.
   (C) To slice the potatoes and dice the meat.
   (D) To serve customers.

2. Why is the man in such a hurry?
   (A) Because he has something else to do.
   (B) Because the customer has been waiting for a long time.
   (C) Because the boss has been nagging at him.
   (D) Because he wants to finish his work quickly.

3. Will Elisa have dinner with the chef tonight?
   (A) Yes, she will.
   (A) Yes, but she wants to invite someone else.
   (C) No, because she has a date with someone else.
   (D) No, because she thinks it is the right thing to do.

Chef: Elisa, are you busy now? I'm badly in need of an assistant. Would you mind helping me?

Elisa: Sure, I'm not busy now. What can I do?

Chef: Please help me wash the vegetables on the table. The customers have been waiting for a long time, so I need it done quickly.

Elisa: OK.

Chef: And then peel these potatoes over there. Also, could you slice the potatoes and dice the meat for me?

Elisa: No problem. Leave it to me. The oil is running short, maybe I should get some oil first.

Chef: OK, thank you very much. I will treat you to dinner tonight.

Elisa: That would be my pleasure. But I have a date with someone else tonight.

Chef: OK. Maybe we can have dinner next time.

Unit 29 餐厅内场 | Cooking Area

中译

1. 男子不希望伊莉莎做什么？
   (A) 洗菜。
   (B) 削马铃薯皮。
   (C) 切马铃薯和肉。
   (D) 给顾客上菜。

2. 男子为什么如此着急？
   (A) 因为他还有其他事情要做。
   (B) 因为顾客已经等了很长时间了。
   (C) 因为老板一直在催他。
   (D) 因为他想快点完成工作。

3. 伊莉莎今天晚上会和厨师一起去吃晚饭吗？
   (A) 她会去。
   (B) 她会去，但是她还想邀请其他人。
   (C) 她不会去，因为她已经有约了。
   (D) 她不会去，因为她觉得她应该这样做。

厨　师：伊莉莎，你现在忙吗？我急需一个帮手。你能否帮我一下？
伊莉莎：当然，我现在不忙。我要做点什么？
厨　师：你先帮我把桌子上的菜洗洗。顾客都等了很长时间了，你必须动作快点。
伊莉莎：好的。
厨　师：你帮我削掉马铃薯的皮。另外，你能不能帮我把马铃薯切成片，把肉切成丁？
伊莉莎：没问题，交给我了。油快用完了，我觉得我应该先去给你拿些油。
厨　师：好的，太感谢你了。今天晚上我请你吃饭。
伊莉莎：不客气。我今天晚上已经有约了。
厨　师：好吧，或许下次我们可以一起吃晚餐。

解析与答案

答案：1. (D)　2. (B)　3. (C)

1. 根据听力内容可知，(A)、(B)、(C) 选项都有提到，只有 (D) 选项没有提到，所以选 (D)。
2. 根据 The customers have been waiting for a long time, so I need do it quickly 可知，答案选 (B)。
3. 根据 But I have a date with someone else tonight 可知，伊莉莎今晚不会去，原因是她已经有约了，所以答案选 (C)。

单词 Vocabulary

peel [piːl] n 皮　v 削，剥
slice [slaɪs] n 薄片，菜刀，部分　v 把……切成薄片
dice [daɪs] n 骰子　v 掷骰子，切成块状

295

阅读测验 | Part 7 文章理解题

New Decorations for Our Restaurant

I am happy to announce that our restaurant is reopening again. It is decorated inside and outside with a new appearance and a new atmosphere. You know that our old restaurant was famous for a relaxed atmosphere. Our new restaurant is more beautiful, fashionable and modern.

The cold colors and dull uniforms of our old restaurant are gone. However, the good service and high-quality food and drinks remain. One of our old chefs, Nathan Wood, will be in charge of American cuisine, while our new chef, Ken Green, will be in charge of French and German cuisine. I believe that you will certainly be satisfied with our food, drinks and service. Our restaurant still provides the best Asian food, the manager says. You can get your meal in ten minutes, which makes our restaurant popular with customers.

There is a parking lot near our restaurant. You can park your car there. It is located on the street in front of our restaurant. Every weekend, we provide a shuttle service from the parking lot to our restaurant. The shuttle buses depart every ten minutes.

You are welcome at any time. We are located on the second block of this district. If you come here by car or on foot, you go onto Lincoln Street from the park and walk straight. Turn right at the second block and you will see us on your right-hand side.

1. What is the announcement about?
   (A) A restaurant.
   (B) A parking lot.
   (C) A conference building.
   (D) A shuttle bus.

2. What is the restaurant famous for according to the first paragraph?
   (A) Expensive food.
   (B) Cheap food.
   (C) A Relaxed atmosphere.
   (D) Drinks.

3. Which of the following is NOT provided according to the second paragraph?
   (A) American cuisine.
   (B) African cuisine.
   (C) German cuisine.
   (D) French cuisine.

4. How soon can you get your food in this restaurant?
   (A) Within five minutes.
   (B) Within ten minutes.
   (C) Within fifteen minutes.
   (D) Within twenty minutes.

5. How often does the shuttle bus depart each weekend?
   (A) Every ten minutes.
   (B) Every fifteen minutes.
   (C) Every twenty minutes.
   (D) Every twenty-five minutes.

我们餐厅的新装修

我非常高兴宣布我们的餐厅重新开张。里里外外都装修了,新面貌、新氛围。你们知道,我们的旧餐厅因轻松的环境氛围而出名。我们新餐厅更加漂亮、时尚、现代化。

我们旧餐厅的冷色调以及呆滞的制服已经成为过去。不过,提供优质食物以及饮料的良好服务保留了下来。我们老厨师南森·伍德提供美式菜肴,我们的新厨师肯·格林提供法式、德式菜品。我相信您对我们餐厅的食物、饮料以及服务肯定会满意。经理说我们餐厅仍然提供最好的亚洲食物。十分钟内就可以上菜,这点让我们餐厅十分受顾客欢迎。

我们餐厅附近有一个停车场,您可以将车停到那里,它在我们餐厅前面的那条街。每周的周末,我们都会提供从停车场到我们餐厅的公交车往返服务。往返公交车每十分钟发一次。

随时欢迎您的光临。我们坐落在本区的第二条街区。如果您开车或步行来这里,您可以从公园那边走过来,走到林肯街,直走,在第二个街区右转,您就可以看到我们了,就在您的右手边。

1. 这则公告是关于什么的?
   (A) 餐厅。
   (B) 停车场。
   (C) 会议大楼。
   (D) 往返公交车。

2. 根据第一段,这家餐厅因什么而著名?
   (A) 昂贵的食物。
   (B) 便宜的食物。
   (C) 轻松的环境氛围。
   (D) 饮料。

3. 根据第二段,下列哪一项是不提供的?
   (A) 美式菜色(肴)。
   (B) 非式菜色(肴)。
   (C) 德式菜色(肴)。
   (D) 法式菜色(肴)。

4. 在这家餐厅,多快可以上餐?
   (A) 五分钟之内。
   (B) 十分钟之内。
   (C) 十五分钟之内。
   (D) 二十分钟之内。

Unit 29 餐厅内场 | Cooking Area

5. 每周末，往返公交车多久往返一次？
   (A) 每十分钟。
   (B) 每十五分钟。
   (C) 每二十分钟。
   (D) 每二十五分钟。

解析与答案

答案：1. (A) 2. (C) 3. (B) 4. (B) 5. (A)

1. 此题可见文章的题目 New Decoration for Our Restaurant，由此可知这篇文章的主题是餐厅，因此选 (A)。
2. 餐厅知名的原因通常会在前面提起。可见第一段第三句 ... our old restaurant was famous for a relaxed atmosphere，因此答案选 (C)。
3. 此题可见第二段第三句 One of our old chefs, Nathan Wood, will be in charge of American cuisine, while our new chef, Ken Green, will be in charge of French and German cuisine，因此答案选 (B)。
4. 在第二段最后一句 You can get your meal within ten minutes... 讲到顾客十分钟可以拿到餐点，因此是十分钟内上菜，选 (B)。
5. 此题可见第三段最后一句 The shuttle buses depart every ten minutes，因此答案选 (A)。

单词 Vocabulary

reopen [ˌriːˈəʊpən] v 重新开始，继续
inside [ˌɪnˈsaɪd] ad 在里面 n 内部 a 里面的
atmosphere [ˈætməsfɪə(r)] n 气氛，情趣，大气
relaxed [rɪˈlækst] a 放松的
fashionable [ˈfæʃnəbl] a 时尚的，流行的
modern [ˈmɒdn] a 时尚的，现代（化）的 n 现代人
certainly [ˈsɜːtnli] ad 无疑地，当然地
meal [miːl] n 膳食，玉米粉 v 进餐
popular [ˈpɒpjələ(r)] a 流行的，受欢迎的，大众的，通俗的
park [pɑːk] n 公园，停车场 v 停放（车辆）
shuttle [ˈʃʌtl] n 往返 v 短程往返
depart [dɪˈpɑːt] v 出发，离开，背离，违反，去世
district [ˈdɪstrɪkt] n 辖区，地区，区域
straight [streɪt] a 笔直的，正直的 ad 直接地，正直地

Unit 30
结账 | Payment

Picture 30

情境中可明确指出的单词

1. **apron** [ˈeɪprən] n 围裙
2. **bankcard** [ˈbæŋkkɑːd] n 银行信用卡
3. **coffee** [ˈkɒfi] n 咖啡
4. **cashier** [kæˈʃɪə(r)] n 收银员
5. **pay** [peɪ] v 支付
6. **glassware** [ˈglɑːsweə(r)] n 玻璃器具
7. **plaid** [plæd] a 有格子图案的
8. **shelf** [ʃelf] n 货架

情境中可延伸记忆的单词

1. **discount** [ˈdɪskaʊnt] n 折扣 v 打折
2. **coffee shop** ph 咖啡厅
3. **cash** [kæʃ] n 现金，现款
4. **invoice** [ˈɪnvɔɪs] n 发票 v 开发票
5. **separate** [ˈseprət] a 单独的，分开的 [ˈsepreɪt] v 分隔
6. **spend** [spend] v 花费
7. **swipe** [swaɪp] v 刷（磁卡）
8. **meet** [miːt] v 遇见

Unit 30 结账 | Payment

apron ['eɪprən] n 围裙
All the waiters and waitresses are supposed to wear aprons.
所有的男服务生与女服务生都应该穿围裙。
- apron string n 围裙带

bankcard ['bæŋkkɑːd] n 银行信用卡
The man passed his bankcard to the cashier.
男子把他的银行卡递给收银员。
- credit card n 信用卡 / cash card n 现金卡 / ATM card n 提款卡

coffee ['kɒfi] n 咖啡
The lady with long curly hair is holding a cup of coffee.
留有长卷发的女子手里拿着一杯咖啡。
- caffeinic a 咖啡酸的 / caffeic a 咖啡（因）的 / cafeteria n 自助餐厅 / café n 咖啡

cashier [kæ'ʃɪə(r)] n 收银员
The couple went to the cashier.
那对夫妇走向收银员。
- cash n 现金 / cash-in-hand a 当场付清的 / cashless a 无现款的

pay [peɪ] v 支付
They are paying for two cups of coffee.
他们正在为两杯咖啡付钱。
- payment n 付款 / pay back n 报答 / pay a visit to n 参观

glassware ['glɑːsweə(r)] n 玻璃器具
You should pay for the glassware you broke.
你应该为你打碎的玻璃器具付钱。
- glass n 玻璃，玻璃制品 / glassy a 像玻璃的 / glasswork n 玻璃制品

plaid [plæd] a 有格子图案的
All of the employees are dressed in plaid blouses.
所有雇员都穿着格子衬衫。
- plaid shirt n 格子衬衫 / plaided a 有格子图案的 / check n 方格图案

shelf [ʃelf] n 货架
He fetched a bottle of juice from the shelf.
他从货架上取来一瓶果汁。
- on the shelf 被搁置的 / shelve v 倾斜

discount ['dɪskaunt] n 折扣 v 打折

You can get it at a ten percent discount.
你可以九折带走它。

⊕ discounter n 折扣商店 / discountable a 可打折的 / discount card n 优惠卡

---

coffee shop ph 咖啡厅

He ordered a coffee to-go in the coffee shop.
他在一家咖啡厅点了一杯外带咖啡。

⊕ coffee bean ph 咖啡豆 / coffee house ph 咖啡厅

---

cash [kæʃ] n 现金，现款

The cashier asks the guest, "Will that be cash or card?"
收银员会问客人："您付现金还是刷卡？"

⊕ cash in ph 兑现 / cash debit ph 现金收入 / cash desk ph 商店付款处

---

invoice ['ɪnvɔɪs] n 发票 v 开发票

The cashier has to issue an invoice to the guests.
收银员应该开发票给顾客。

⊕ tax invoice ph 税务发票 / receipt n 收据

---

separate ['sɛprət] a 单独的，分开的 ['sɛpreɪt] v 分隔

I think that their bill will not be separate.
我想他们不会分开付账。

⊕ separatist n 分离主义者 / divide v 分割，分开 / segregate v 分离

---

spend [spend] v 花费

He always spends a lot of money on coffee.
他总是在咖啡上花很多钱。

⊕ spending n 花费，开销 / spender n 挥霍者 / consume v 消耗，花费

---

swipe [swaɪp] v 刷（磁卡）

The cashier will swipe the man's card through the POS.
收银员会在 POS 机上刷这位男士的卡。

⊕ swipe at ph 击打 / swipe card ph 磁卡 / swiped out ph 磁卡失效

---

meet [miːt] v 遇见

I met Mary while I was paying the bill.
我结账时遇见了玛丽。

⊕ meet with ph 符合 / meet up ph 遇到 / meeting n 会议

听力测验 | Part 1 图片描述题

题目
(A) The woman and the man are having a meal in a room.
(B) There are two cups of coffee on the table.
(C) They are going to pay for the bill.
(D) There is a square table in front of them.

中译
(A) 女子和男子在室内吃饭。
(B) 桌子上有两杯咖啡。
(C) 他们准备付账。
(D) 他们面前是一张方桌。

解析与答案

答案：(C)

从图片中可以看出，这位男子和女子是在室外，他们喝的不是咖啡，而是香槟；另外他们面前是一张圆玻璃桌，从他们都打开钱包可知，他们准备付账了，所以选 (C)。

听力测验 | Part 3 简短对话题

NEW TOEIC

1. What's the exchange rate for Korean Won?
   (A) One USD to 1,158.2 Korean Won.
   (C) One USD to 178. 285 3 Korean Won.
   (B) One hundred USD to 17,929.53 Korean Won.
   (D) One hundred USD to 17,828.53 Korean Won.

2. What's the difference if the woman pays with a Visa card?
   (A) She can get a 15% discount only.
   (B) She can get a 50% discount and 10% surcharge for tax.
   (C) She can get a 15% discount and 10% surcharge for tax.
   (D) She can get a 10% discount and 15% surcharge for tax.

3. How did the woman pay the bill?
   (A) She paid it with traveler's check.
   (B) She paid it with check.
   (C) She paid it with Visa card.
   (D) She paid it in cash.

Customer: I would like the bill please.

Waiter: Here is your bill. Would you like to pay in cash or with bank card?

Customer: In cash. Do you accept USD?

Waiter: Yes, but we only have Korean Won for change. And the exchange rate is one USD to 1 158.2 Korean Won.

Customer: Well, can I pay it with credit card?

Waiter: Sure. Do you have a Visa card?

Customer: Yes. Why?

Waiter: You get a 15% discount, if you pay it with a Visa card, but there is a ten percent surcharge for tax.

Customer: OK, here is my Visa card.

Waiter: Please sign the bill.

Unit 30 结账 | Payment

中译

1. 美元兑韩元的汇率是多少？
   (A) 1 美元兑换 1 158.2 韩元。
   (B) 1 美元兑换 178.285 3 韩元。
   (C) 100 美元兑换 17 929.53 韩元。
   (D) 100 美元兑换 17 828.53 韩元。

2. 女子用 Visa 卡付款有什么不同？
   (A) 她可以享受仅 15% 的折扣。
   (B) 她可以享受 50% 的折扣并收取 10% 的附加费。
   (C) 她可以享受 15% 的折扣并收取 10% 的附加费。
   (D) 她可以享受 10% 的折扣并收取 15% 的附加费。

3. 女子最后是以何种方式结账的？
   (A) 她是用旅行支票结账的。
   (B) 她是用支票结账的。
   (C) 她是用 Visa 卡结账的。
   (D) 她是用现金结账的。

顾　客：请结账。
服务生：这是你的账单，你是要付现金还是刷银行卡？
顾　客：现金。你们收美元吗？
服务生：收，但是我们找零只有韩元。其汇率是一美元兑换 1 158.2 韩元。
顾　客：那么我可以用信用卡吗？
服务生：当然。你有 Visa 卡吗？
顾　客：有啊，怎么了？
服务生：如果你用 Visa 卡支付的话，你可以享受 15% 的折扣，但是你要缴 10% 的附加费。
顾　客：好的，给你 Visa 卡。
服务生：请在账单上签名。

解析与答案

答案：1. (A)　2. (C)　3. (C)

1. 根据 And the exchange rate is one USD to 1 158.2 Korean Won 可知，正确答案选 (A)。
2. 根据 You get a 15% discount, … , but there is a ten percent surcharge for tax 可知，正确答案选 (C)。
3. 根据女子说的最后一句 here is my visa card 可知，她是用 Visa 卡付账，所以选 (C)。

单词 Vocabulary

bill [bɪl] n 账单，法案，广告　v 开账单，宣布，用海报宣传
change [tʃeɪndʒ] n 零钱，变化，更换　v 改变，兑换
discount ['dɪskaʊnt] n 折扣　v 打折，忽视，贴现
percent [pə'sent] n 百分比　a 百分之……的　ad 以百分之……地
surcharge ['sɜːtʃɑːdʒ] n 附加费，超载　v 追加罚款，使……负担过重

阅读测验 | Part 7 文章理解题

I'd like to discuss the question: Who should pay for the first date, men or women? Most people think it is the man's responsibility. A survey was done among five hundred lovers and the data shows that more than eighty percent of them think that it is the man's responsibility to pay for the first date, not women. It is very shocking, isn't it?

In the past, the reason why men were likely to pay is that women had no jobs and were not financially independent. However, nowadays, more and more women get jobs and can be financially independent. More and more women can be independent now and don't need to rely on men any longer. Some of them even become the breadwinners. It's women's pride. It has been reported that the proportion of two-parent families, in which mothers earn more than fathers are five times more than that of the last decades.

But why are men still expected to pay for the bill now? An expert said that, While the social roles have begun to change, it is more likely to accept the changes which can make life more convenient or easier, and refuse the changes which may make life more difficult. However, on this question, women are more likely to resist than men.

I think it can't always be only men or only women that pay for the bill. That is to say, sometimes, men can pay for the bill, and sometimes women.

What do you think of this question? We would like to invite you to express your ideas.

Unit 30 结账 | Payment

1. **What is this article about?**
   (A) Where do people have the first date?
   (B) Who pays for the first date?
   (C) When do people have the first date?
   (D) How to have the first date?

2. **What does the survey reveal?**
   (A) Most people think it is the man's responsibility to pay for the first date.
   (B) Most people think it is the woman's responsibility to pay for the first date.
   (C) Ninety percent of people think it is the man's responsibility to pay for the first date.
   (D) Nobody thinks it is the woman's responsibility to pay for the first date.

3. **Why were men more likely to pay in the past?**
   (A) Because men have lots of money.
   (B) Because their parents taught them to do so.
   (C) Because women had no jobs and were not financially independent.
   (D) Because men like spending money than women.

4. **What is the view of the writer on the payment question?**
   (A) Men should always pay for bills.
   (B) Women should always pay for bills.
   (C) Sometimes, men should pay for the bill, and sometimes women.
   (D) Not mentioned in the text.

5. **Which of the following is NOT right?**
   (A) Nowadays, the majority still think it's the man's responsibility to pay for bills.
   (B) Nobody thinks women should pay for bills.
   (C) People are more likely to accept the changes which can make their life easier.
   (D) People are more likely to resist the changes which may make their life more difficult.

我想讨论一个问题：第一次约会谁应该买单，男子还是女子？大多数人认为这是男子的责任。在五百名情侣中做了一份调查，资料表明 80% 以上的人认为第一次约会买单是男子的责任。这份调查结果让人十分震惊，不是吗？

过去，男性更可能买单的原因是女性没有工作，经济不独立。然而，现今，有工作的女性越来越多，不需要再依赖男性。其中，一些女性甚至是负担生计的人。这是女性的骄傲。据报道，母亲比父亲赚钱更多的双亲家庭是前十年的五倍。

但是，为什么现在还是期待男性买单？一位专家说："社会角色转变时，人们更可能接受那些让生活更方便、简单的变化，而排斥那些让生活更加困难的变化。"然而，在这个问题上，女性比男性更容易排斥。

我认为不应该总是只由男性或由女性来买单。也就是说，有时男性买单；有时女性买单。

你如何看待这个问题？我们想邀请你表达你的看法。

1. 这篇文章是关于什么的？
   (A) 在哪里进行第一次约会。
   (B) 谁应该为第一次约会买单。
   (C) 什么时候进行第一次约会。
   (D) 如何进行第一次约会。

2. 调查显示了什么？
   (A) 大多数人认为第一次约会买单是男性的责任。
   (B) 大多数人认为第一次约会买单是女性的责任。
   (C) 百分之九十的人认为第一次约会买单是男性的责任。
   (D) 人们认为第一次约会买单不是女性的责任。

3. 在过去，为什么男子更可能买单？
   (A) 因为男性有很多钱财。
   (B) 因为他们的父母教他们这么做。
   (C) 因为女性没有工作，经济不独立。
   (D) 因为男性比女性更喜欢花钱。

4. 作者对付款问题的观点是什么？
   (A) 应该总是由男性买单。
   (B) 应该总是由女性买单。
   (C) 有时由男性买单；有时由女性买单。
   (D) 文中未提及。

Unit 30 结账 | Payment

5. 下列哪项不正确？
   (A) 现今，大多数人仍然认为买单是男性的责任。
   (B) 人们认为女性不应该买单。
   (C) 人们更可能接受那些让生活更加方便、简单的变化。
   (D) 人们更可能排斥那些让生活更加困难的变化。

解析与答案

答案：1. (B) 2. (A) 3. (C) 4. (C) 5. (B)

1. 文章的第一段第一句就点出想讨论的问题：I'd like to discuss the question: Who should pay for the first date, men or women? 因此选 (B)。

2. 此题可见第一段第三句 ... the data shows that more than eighty percent of them think that it is men's responsibility to pay for the first date, not women，因此答案选 (A)。

3. 从第二段第一句可知 In the past, the reason why men were likely to pay is that women had no jobs and were not financially independent，以前的女性没有工作且经济不独立，因此选 (C)。

4. 作者在倒数第二段倒数第一句表达了自己的意见，即 That is to say, sometimes, it is men can pay for the bill; and sometimes, women，因此选 (C)。

5. 此题可见第一段第三句 ... the data shows that more than eighty percent of them think that it is man's responsibility to pay for the first date... 以及全文，因此选 (B)。

单词 Vocabulary

discuss [dɪ'skʌs] v. 讨论，商谈，论述
among [ə'mʌn] p. 在……之间
data ['deɪtə] n. 数据，资料
financially [faɪ'nænʃəli] ad. 经济上，财政上
independent [ˌɪndɪ'pendənt] a. 独立的，单独的，分开的
nowadays ['naʊədeɪz] ad. 现今
rely [rɪ'laɪ] v. 依赖，依靠，信赖
decade ['dekeɪd] n. 十年
meal [miːl] n. 膳食，玉米粉 v. 进餐
role [rəʊl] n. 角色，作用
resist [rɪ'zɪst] v. 拒绝，抵抗，反抗
express [ɪk'spres] v. 表达，陈述 n. 快递 a. 快的，专门的

学 习 重 点

页 数   **笔记内容**

NEW TOEIC

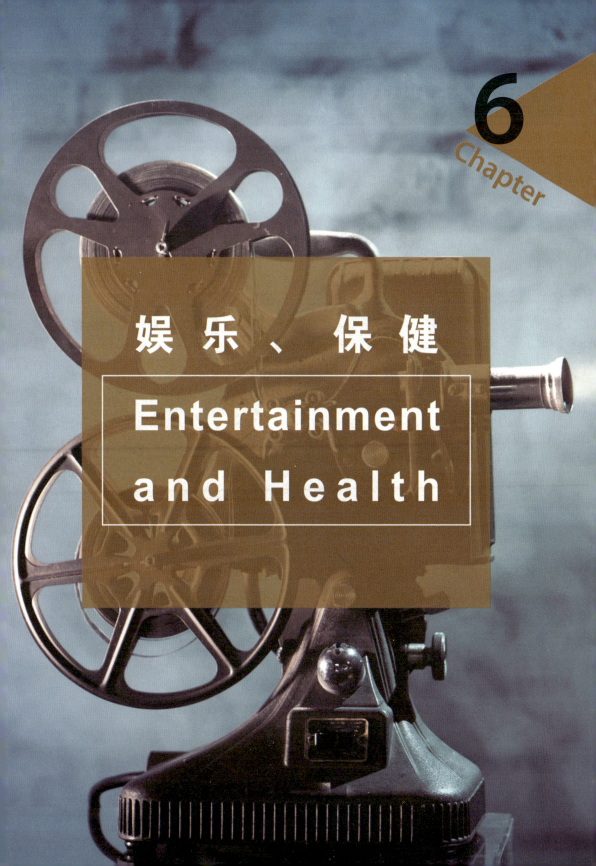

Unit 31
电影 | Movies

New TOEIC

Picture 31

情境中可明确指出的单词

1. **cap** [kæp] n 帽子
2. **cashier desk** ph 收银台
3. **coke** [kəʊk] n 可乐
4. **popcorn** [ˈpɒpkɔːn] n 爆米花
5. **POS** abbr 刷卡机
6. **talk thru window** ph 服务窗的对讲机
7. **uniform** [ˈjuːnɪfɔːm] n 制服
8. **straw** [strɔː] n 吸管

情境中可延伸记忆的单词

1. **director** [dəˈrektə] n 导演
2. **lover** [ˈlʌvə] n 情人，爱人
3. **movie ticket** ph 电影票
4. **romantic comedy** ph 浪漫喜剧片
5. **cinema** [ˈsɪnəmə] n （英）电影院
6. **show** [ʃəʊ] v 放映
7. **usher** [ˈʌʃə] n 领位员
8. **watch** [wɒtʃ] v 观看

Unit 31 电影 | Movies

cap [kæp] n. 帽子
You should not wear a cap indoors.
室内不应该戴帽子。
- capper n. 封口机 / cap and coat ph. 衣帽 / cap it all off 完成

---

cashier desk ph. 收银台
Please go to cashier desk No. 5 to pay the bill.
请到五号收银台付账。
- money n. 钱，货币 / scanner n. 扫描器

---

coke [kəʊk] n. 可乐
Both of the guests are holding a cup of coke in their hands.
这两位顾客每人手里都拿着一杯可乐。
- soft drink ph. 汽水 / Coca-Cola n. 可口可乐

---

popcorn ['pɒpkɔːn] n. 爆米花
The lady is holding a big bag of popcorn in her arms.
这位女子抱着一大袋爆米花。
- corn n. 玉米 / sweet a. 甜的 / salt a. 咸味的 / Churros 吉事果

POS abbr. 刷卡机
Nowadays, almost all the restaurants have POS.
现如今，几乎所有的餐厅都有刷卡机。
- Master n. 万事达卡 / Visa n. Visa 卡 / signature n. 签名

---

talk thru window ph. 服务窗的对讲机
Every employee is equipped with a talk thru window.
每名雇员都配备一部服务窗的对讲机。
- windscreen n. （英）汽车挡风玻璃

---

uniform ['juːnɪfɔːm] n. 制服
All staff are supposed to wear uniforms while working.
所有雇员上班期间都应穿制服。
- uniformity n. 一致性 / uniformed a. 穿着制服的

---

straw [strɔː] n. 吸管
How can you drink your coke without a straw?
你没有吸管怎么喝可乐？
- straw hat ph. 草帽

director [dəˈrektə(r)] n. 导演
They must know who the director of the film is.
他们一定知道这部电影的导演是谁。
- direct v. 导演，指挥 / directory n. 指导的 / producer n. 制作人

lover [ˈlʌvə(r)] n. 情人，爱人
I guess the woman and the man are lovers.
我猜这位女士和这位男士是情侣。
- lovely a. 可爱的 / loveseat n. 双人小沙发 / couple n. 一对（情侣或夫妇）

movie ticket ph. 电影票
Please show me your movie tickets.
请出示你们的电影票。
- the stub of a ticket ph. 票根

romantic comedy ph. 浪漫喜剧片
My friend invited me to see a romantic comedy.
我的朋友邀请我看浪漫喜剧片。
- horror film n. 恐怖片 / martial arts film n. 武侠片 / documentary film n. 纪录片

cinema [ˈsɪnəmə] n. （英）电影院
The man will sit next to the woman in the cinema.
在电影院这位男子会坐在这位女士旁边。
- cinematographer n. 放映技师 / movie theater n. 电影院

show [ʃəʊ] v. 放映
The movie will show tonight at 8 p.m.
这部电影将在今晚八点放映。
- show up ph. 露面 / show bill ph. 海报 / show off ph. 卖弄

usher [ˈʌʃə(r)] n. 领位员
We appreciated the usher leading us to our seats.
引座员将我们引领到座位上，我们十分感激。
- usherette n. 女引座员 / usher in 领进

watch [wɒtʃ] v. 观看
It is impolite to make noises while watching a film in a cinema.
在电影院看电影的时候发出噪声是不礼貌的。
- watchfulness n. 警觉性 / watch for ph. 等待 / view v. 观看，眺望

听力测验 | Part 1 图片描述题

(A) There are a few people in this cinema.
(B) People here are watching a comedy.
(C) People here are watching a tragedy.
(D) Each woman has a barrel of popcorn in her hand.

(A) 电影院里的人很少。
(B) 这些人看的是一部喜剧。
(C) 这些人看的是一部悲剧。
(D) 每个女子手里都有一桶爆米花。

答案：(B)

从图片中可以看出，电影院里有很多人，从这些人的表情（微笑，无惊恐、害怕、难过）可以推测出他们观看的是一部喜剧；另外，有的女子拿的是爆米花，有的女子拿的是可乐，所以答案选 (B)。

听力测验 | Part 3 简短对话题

NEW TOEIC

1. Which movie does the woman want to watch at first?
   (A) *Rise of the Planet of the Apes*.
   (B) *The Little Prince*.
   (C) *The Danish Girl*.
   (D) All of the above.

2. Why doesn't the woman want to watch *The Little Prince*?
   (A) Because she doesn't want to watch an animated cartoon.
   (B) Because she is afraid of crying when she watches a movie in the cinema.
   (C) Because she thinks the movie is boring.
   (D) Because she wants to watch *The Danish Girl*.

3. Will they go to a movie this weekend?
   (A) Yes, they will watch *The Danish Girl*.
   (B) Yes, they will watch the *Rise of the Planet of the Apes*.
   (C) No, but they will have a dinner together.
   (D) No, they will make it another time.

Sam: Kelly, Would you like to watch a movie with me this weekend?

Kelly: Sure! What is showing?

Sam: I heard there are several movies that are out. For example, *Rise of the Planet of the Apes*, *The Little Prince* and *The Danish Girl*.

Kelly: *The Rise of the Planet of the Apes* sounds good.

Sam: I don't think so. That one sounds terrible. How about *The Little Prince*?

Kelly: Oh, no. I think that one is a tragedy. I don't want to keep crying in the cinema.

Sam: Well, *The Danish Girl* would be the last choice.

Kelly: Yes, but that one doesn't exactly sound fascinating to me. So, maybe we can watch a movie next time?

Sam: Sure! We can make it another time.

Kelly: OK. I will invite you out if there is a good movie.

♪ 316

Unit 31 电影 | Movies

1. 女子刚开始想要看哪一部电影？
(A) 《猩球崛起》。
(B) 《小王子》。
(C) 《丹麦女孩》。
(D) 所有的都想看。

2. 女子为什么不想看《小王子》？
(A) 因为她不喜欢看卡通片。
(B) 因为她担心会在电影院看电影时忍不住哭泣。
(C) 因为她认为这部电影很无聊。
(D) 因为她想看《丹麦女孩》。

3. 他们这个周末会一起去看电影吗？
(A) 会，他们会一起去看《丹麦女孩》。
(B) 会，他们会一起去看《猩球崛起》。
(C) 不会，但是他们会一起吃饭。
(D) 不会，他们会另约时间。

山姆：凯莉，这周末能否和我一起去看电影？
凯莉：好呀！有什么电影要上映？
山姆：我听说有好几部呢，比如说《猩球崛起》《小王子》，还有《丹麦女孩》。
凯莉：《猩球崛起》听起来还不错。
山姆：我不这么认为，我觉得《猩球崛起》有一点点可怕。《小王子》怎么样？
凯莉：不好。《小王子》应该是一部悲剧吧。我可不想在电影院里一直哭着看电影。
山姆：那么，就只剩下《丹麦女孩》了。
凯莉：对，但是我觉得《丹麦女孩》也不是很好看。所以，也许我们下次再去看电影？
山姆：好！我们可以另约时间。
凯莉：好的，如果有好看的电影我就邀请你。

解析与答案

答案：1.(A) 2.(B) 3.(D)

1. 当男子（山姆）列举出几部电影的时候，女子（凯莉）的第一反应是说《猩球崛起》还不错，所以她刚开始是想看《猩球崛起》，答案选 (A)。
2. 凯莉说《小王子》是一部悲剧，她怕看电影时会哭，所以答案选 (B)。
3. 根据对话内容可知，他们的意见不一，最后只剩《丹麦女孩》，但是凯莉说感觉不太好看，提议另约时间，山姆也同意了，所以答案选 (D)。

单词 Vocabulary

several ['sevrəl] a 各自的，几个的
tragedy ['trædʒədi] n 悲剧，惨案，灾难
cinema ['sɪnəmə] n 电影，电影院
choice [tʃɔɪs] n 选择（权），精选品 a 精挑细选的，仔细推敲的
fascinating ['fæsɪneɪtɪŋ] a 迷人的，吸引人的

阅读测验 | Part 7 文章理解题

The American Davis International Movie Festival this year will start on Sep. 19th and will last for about seven days at the American Davis Center. I think it makes movies more available to the audience than before and easier to be shown at different places all over the world. If you are interested in it, you can buy tickets on the American Davis Center official website at www.adimf.tickets.com starting tomorrow. The movies will begin at 6 p.m.

Mission Impossible

It's a movie about teamwork. Teamwork is very important in a team and it is essential to success or failure. This movie will make you very nervous when you see it, but it is also exciting. Ethan, the hero in the movie, is bound to make a difference.

Saturday, Sep. 19th and Sunday Sep. 20th

Jurassic World

This is a science fiction movie about dinosaurs. Some people make man-made dinosaurs which are much smarter than human beings. These people open a dinosaur park to be visited by people, but there is danger in it. This movie will attract many young people.

Sunday Sep. 20th

The Nature

The heroine inherits a large sum of money from her parents and she donates the money to a disaster stricken area. And she appeals to society to make donations. Many journalists have interviews with her and what she does makes her rise to fame overnight. You will be shocked by what the heroine does. This movie encourages us to help those people who are in need of help.

Saturday, Sep. 19th and Sunday Sep. 20th

1. What is this poster about?

    (A) New Year.

    (B) Christmas Eve.

    (C) A Movie Festival.

    (D) A Competition.

2. When does the movie festival begin according to the poster?

    (A) On Sep. 19th.

    (B) On Sep. 20th.

    (C) On Sep. 21st.

    (D) On Sep. 22nd.

3. How long will the movie festival last?

    (A) One day.

    (B) About one week.

    (C) About one month.

    (D) About one season.

4. Where can we buy tickets according to the poster?

    (A) In the ticket-hall.

    (B) In the cinema.

    (C) In the convention center.

    (D) On the official website at www.adimf.tickets.com.

5. What is the movie *Jurassic World* about according to the poster?

    (A) Dinosaurs.

    (B) Donation.

    (C) Teamwork.

    (D) Love.

今年,美国戴维斯国际电影节将于9月19日开始,在美国戴维中心举办,时间将会持续七天左右。我认为这使得电影比过去更接近观众,更易于展现在全世界的不同角落。如果你感兴趣,从明天开始,你可以在美国戴维斯的官方网站 www.adimf.tickets.com 购票。电影从下午六点开始上映。

《不可能的任务》

这是一个关于团队合作的电影。团队合作在一个团队中十分重要,对于成败十分重要。当你看这场电影时,你会十分紧张,但是也会十分兴奋。电影中男主角伊森注定会有所作为。

9月19日,星期六;9月20日,星期日

《侏罗纪世界》

这是一场关于恐龙的科幻电影。一些人制造出人造恐龙,这些恐龙比人类聪明许多。这些人开设一家恐龙公园,供人们观赏,但是其中却隐藏着危险。这场电影一定会吸引许多年轻人。

9月20日,星期日

《本质》

女主角从父母那边继承许多钱财,她将这些钱财贡献给灾区,并呼吁整个社会进行捐赠。许多记者采访了她,这使她一夜成名。女主角的所作所为一定会震撼到你。这场电影鼓励我们去帮助那些需要帮助的人。

9月19日,星期六;9月20日,星期日

1. 这张海报是关于什么的?
   (A) 新年。　　　　　　　　　　(B) 圣诞夜。
   (C) 电影节。　　　　　　　　　(D) 竞赛。

2. 根据海报,电影节什么时候开始?
   (A) 9月19日。　　　　　　　　(B) 9月20日。
   (C) 9月21日。　　　　　　　　(D) 9月22日。

3. 电影节将会持续多久?
   (A) 一天。　　　　　　　　　　(B) 大约一周。
   (C) 大约一个月。　　　　　　　(D) 大约一个季度。

4. 根据海报所说，我们可以在哪里买票？
  (A) 售票厅。
  (B) 电影院。
  (C) 会议中心。
  (D) 官方网站 www.adimf.tickets.com。

5. 根据海报，《侏罗纪世界》这场电影是关于什么的？
  (A) 恐龙。
  (B) 捐赠。
  (C) 团队合作。
  (D) 爱情。

答案：1. (C) 2. (A) 3. (B) 4. (D) 5. (A)

1. 此题考信息获取能力，海报的开头就提到此次主题关于电影节，因此选 (C)。
2. 此题考细节，从第一段的第一句 American Davis International Movie Festival this year, will start on Sep. 19th... 可知答案选 (A)。
3. 此题考细节以及换算能力，从第一段的第一句 American Davis International Movie Festival... will last for about seven days 可知电影节持续大约七天，也就是一周，因此选 (B)。
4. 此题考信息获取能力，可见第一段的倒数第二句 ... you can buy tickets on the American Davis Center official website at www.adimf.tickets.com...，因此选 (D)。
5. 此题考细节，可见第二段，第二段都是在讲述关于《侏罗纪世界》这场电影的内容主要关于恐龙，因此答案选 (A)。

单词 Vocabulary

American [ə'merɪkən] n 美国人 a 美国的
available [ə'veɪləbl] a 可获得的，有空的，可得到的
audience ['ɔːdiəns] n 观众，听众
website ['websaɪt] n 网址
essential [ɪ'senʃl] a 必要的，本质的 n 要素，要点
science ['saɪəns] n 科学
dinosaur ['daɪnəsɔː(r)] n 恐龙
heroine ['herəʊɪn] n 女主角，女英雄
inherit [ɪn'herɪt] v 继承，成为财产的继承人
appeal [ə'piːl] v 吸引，呼吁，求助

Unit 32
音乐 | Music

New TOEIC

Picture 32

情境中可明确指出的单词

1. **drum** [drʌm] n 鼓 v 打鼓
2. **electronic organ** ph 电子琴
3. **frame** [freɪm] n 画框，架构
4. **guitar** [gɪˈtɑː(r)] n 吉他
5. **lamp** [læmp] n 灯 v 照亮
6. **microphone** [ˈmaɪkrəfəʊn] n 麦克风
7. **music** [ˈmjuːzɪk] n 音乐，乐谱
8. **stereo** [ˈsteriəʊ] n 立体声音响设备
   a 立体声的

情境中可延伸记忆的单词

1. **band** [bænd] n 乐团
2. **enthusiastic** [ɪnˌθjuːziˈæstɪk] a 狂热的，热烈的
3. **lead singer** ph 主唱
4. **melody** [ˈmelədi] n 旋律，歌曲
5. **pop** [pɒp] n 流行音乐
6. **stage** [steɪdʒ] v 演出
7. **tap** [tæp] v 轻拍 n 节拍
8. **tone** [təʊn] n 色调，光度

Unit 32 音乐 | Music

drum [drʌm] n 鼓 v 打鼓
The lady on the stool is playing the drums.
坐在凳子上的那位女子正在打鼓。
▶ drummer n 鼓手 / drum kit ph 一套鼓乐器 / drumbeat n 鼓声

electronic organ ph 电子琴
My mother advised me to play the electronic organ.
妈妈建议我学电子琴。
▶ electronic a 电子的 / piano n 钢琴

frame [freɪm] n 画框，架构
I want to buy a new frame for this painting.
我想给这幅画买新画框。
▶ photo frame ph 相框 / frame of mind ph 心情

guitar [gɪ'tɑː(r)] n 吉他
The man standing in front of the poster is playing a guitar.
海报前的那位男子正在弹吉他。
▶ guitar player ph 吉他手 / guitarist n 吉他手 / chord n 和弦

lamp [læmp] n 灯 v 照亮
The lamp is silhouetted against the glass of the frame.
灯从画框的玻璃里反射出影像。
▶ wall lamp n 壁灯 / lamp post ph 灯柱 / light n 光线 v 点亮

microphone ['maɪkrəfəʊn] n 麦克风
The woman is singing and dancing while holding a microphone.
女子正手拿麦克风，载歌载舞。
▶ wireless microphone n 无线麦克风 / speaker n 扩音器，喇叭

music ['mjuːzɪk] n 音乐，乐谱
Put the music on the music stand.
把乐谱放上乐谱架。
▶ pop music ph 流行音乐 / music box ph 音乐盒 / musical a 音乐的

stereo ['steriəʊ] n 立体声音响设备 a 立体声的
Behind the young man, we can see a stereo.
在那位年轻男子的后面，我们可以看到一个立体声音响设备。
▶ stereophonic a 立体声的 / stereo system ph 立体声音响系统

band [bænd] n 乐团
The band's success is owed to their teamwork.
乐队的成功归功于队员之间的团队合作。
- bandage n 绷带 / chorus n 合唱团

enthusiastic [ɪnˌθjuːziˈæstɪk] a 狂热的，热烈的
They must be enthusiastic music lovers.
他们一定是狂热的音乐爱好者。
- enthusiast n 狂热者 / ardent a 热烈的，激动的 / interested a 感兴趣的

lead singer ph 主唱
The lead singer is standing in the middle of the stage.
主唱站在舞台中间。
- harmony n 和声

melody [ˈmelədi] n 旋律
I was attracted by her beautiful melody.
我被她那优美的旋律吸引住了。
- melodious a 悦耳的 / tune n 旋律，曲调，和谐 / song n 歌曲

pop [pɒp] n 流行音乐
A majority of young people like pop music.
大部分年轻人喜欢流行音乐。
- popularity n 普及 / pop art n 流行艺术 / pop cans n 易拉罐

stage [steɪdʒ] v 演出
We are staging a play this weekend.
我们这个周末将要演出戏剧。
- stage n 舞台 / stage by stage 逐步地 / performance n 演出，演奏

tap [tæp] v 轻拍 n 节拍
They tapped their feet while they played.
演奏期间，他们会用脚打着拍子。
- tap into ph 挖掘 / tap out ph 敲打出

tone [təʊn] n 色调，光度
I don't like the dark tone of this film.
我不喜欢这影片的暗色调。
- toneless a 沉闷的 / tone in with ph 与……相配 / tone up ph 加强，提高

听力测验 | Part 1 图片描述题

题目

(A) There are many snacks and CDs on the table.
(B) The two women are wearing short-sleeved shirts.
(C) The music makes them very happy.
(D) They are singing at a KTV.

中译

(A) 桌子上有很多的小吃和光碟。
(B) 这两位女子都穿着短袖。
(C) 音乐让她们非常开心。
(D) 她们正在 KTV 唱歌。

解析与答案

答案：(C)
从图片中可以看出，这两位女子是在家里，音乐让她们感到非常开心，桌子上有小吃和饮料，看不出来有光碟；另外，她们一个穿的是短袖，一个穿的是长袖，所以选 (C)。

听力测验 | Part 3 简短对话题

1. What does the man want the woman to do?
   (A) He wants Amy to keep shop for him.
   (B) He wants Amy to invite him to watch a musical performance.
   (C) He wants Amy to do the delivery for him.
   (D) He wants Amy to ask someone else to keep shop for him.

2. What does the woman offer the man?
   (A) Amy gives up the chance to watch a musical performance.
   (B) Amy is willing to do the delivery for David.
   (C) Amy invites David to watch a musical performance.
   (D) Amy asks someone else to keep shop for David.

3. What can we learn from this conversation?
   (A) Amy is selfish.
   (B) Amy is kind-hearted.
   (C) David is decisive.
   (D) David is ungrateful.

David: Amy, I have to go out on a delivery tomorrow, would you like to keep shop for me for a while?

Amy: Oh, I'm afraid not. My daughter invited me to watch a musical performance. She has been preparing for nearly a whole month. I don't want to let her down.

David: OK. I understand.

Amy: Can't you put off the delivery date? I can help you anytime, except tomorrow.

David: No, I can't. The customer has been waiting for her order for several days.

Amy: I'm sorry about that. But I can ask someone else to keep shop for you.

David: Are you sure?

Amy: Of course.

David: I owe you one.

Unit 32 音乐 | Music

中译

1. 男子想让女子做什么？
   - (A) 他想让艾咪帮他看店。
   - (B) 他想让艾咪邀请他去看音乐剧表演。
   - (C) 他想让艾咪替他去送货。
   - (D) 他想让艾咪找人替他看店。

2. 女子将为男子做什么？
   - (A) 艾咪将放弃看音乐剧的机会。
   - (B) 艾咪愿意替大卫去送货。
   - (C) 艾咪邀请大卫一起去看音乐剧表演。
   - (D) 艾咪将请其他人帮大卫看店。

3. 从这段对话中我们可以得出什么？
   - (A) 艾咪是一个自私的人。
   - (B) 艾咪是一个热心肠的人。
   - (C) 大卫是一个果断的人。
   - (D) 大卫是一个忘恩负义的人。

大卫：艾咪，我明天必须出去送货，你能帮我看一下店吗？
艾咪：恐怕不行。我女儿邀请我去看她的音乐剧表演。她为此准备了差不多一个月的时间，我不想让她失望。
大卫：好的，我可以理解。
艾咪：你不能把发货日期延后吗？除了明天，我都可以来帮你。
大卫：不能，因为顾客已经等订单很久了。
艾咪：非常抱歉。不过我可以找人替你看店。
大卫：真的吗？
艾咪：当然。
大卫：太感谢你了。

解析与答案

答案：1. (A) 2. (D) 3. (B)

1. 根据 would you like to keep shop for me for a while 可知，男子（大卫）是想让女子（艾咪）帮他看店，所以答案选 (A)。
2. 根据 But I can ask someone else to keep shop for you 可知，艾咪可以找人帮大卫看店，所以答案选 (D)。
3. 听力内容是讲大卫有事，希望艾咪帮他看店，但是艾咪答应女儿要去看音乐剧表演，尽管如此，她还是找人帮大卫看店，由此可以推论艾咪是一个热心的人，答案选 (B)。

单词 Vocabulary

musical [ˈmjuːzɪkl] a 悦耳的，音乐的 n 唱片
performance [pəˈfɔːməns] n 表演，绩效，执行，性能
owe [əʊ] v 感激，把……归功于

阅读测验 | Part 7 文章理解题

To: Penny Hofstadter

From: Mary Winkle

Subject: Impressions of the Maroon 5 concert

Dear Hofstadter,

    When was the last time you saw a concert? What kind of concerts have you seen? Whose concert have you been to? Have you ever seen a Maroon 5 concert? Here are my impressions of the Maroon 5 concert I saw near my home the day before yesterday.

    As of the end of this month, I will have been to more than ten concerts, but I think this show was the most engaging that I have ever seen. The concert was held in a strange place, but Maroon 5 showed great intimacy and energy. I am crazy about them and I have collected all their albums. It is crazy, isn't it? To be honest, I was surprised by the scene of the concert.

    It fascinated me. I didn't know they are so lively and talkative with fans. If they were trying to set a good relationship with fans, it worked. Fans knew every note, word and rhythm. The show was really interesting and exciting. The atmosphere was a compliment to the concert. All the fans had a great time there! Do you have the same feelings as me? I think the answer is absolutely positive.

    I hope to see another show on their next tour! Let's look forward to it together!

Mary Winkle

New York

November 25th, 2017

Unit 32 音乐 | Music

1. What is the e-mail about?
   (A) A concert.
   (B) A movie.
   (C) A play.
   (D) A game.

2. How many concerts has Mary been to?
   (A) One.
   (B) Two.
   (C) Five.
   (D) More than ten.

3. What does Mary think of the Maroon 5 concert she saw?
   (A) Great.
   (B) So-so.
   (C) Bad.
   (D) Terrible.

4. Where was the concert held?
   (A) In a strange place.
   (B) In a gymnasium.
   (C) In a business center.
   (D) In a conference center.

5. What does Mary expect at last?
   (A) To see a show on the next Maroon 5 tour.
   (B) To see a rock concert.
   (C) To see a Taylor Swift concert.
   (D) To buy the albums of all singers.

收件人：佩妮·霍夫施塔特
寄件者：玛丽·温克尔
主题：魔力红的音乐会观后感

亲爱的霍夫施塔特：

　　你上次看音乐会是什么时候？你看过什么类型的音乐会？你看过谁的音乐会？你看过魔力红的音乐会吗？前天我在我家附近看了魔力红音乐会，这是我的观后感。

　　截止到这个月月底，我已经看过十多场音乐会，但是我认为这场演出才是我看过那么多场中最吸引人的音乐会。这场音乐会在一个陌生的地方举行，但是魔力红将他们的亲切感和能量展现得淋漓尽致。我对他们十分狂热，而且我收集了他们所有的专辑。很疯狂，不是吗？说实话，我为音乐场面所震撼，并且被深深地吸引。

　　我从未见过他们对待粉丝如此活泼、健谈。如果他们是想要与粉丝建立良好的关系的话，他们做到了。粉丝们了解每一个音符、歌词以及节奏。演出真有趣、真令人兴奋。气氛就是对音乐会的致意。所有粉丝在那里都很开心！你跟我有同样的感受吗？我认为答案绝对是肯定的。

　　我希望看他们下一次巡回演出！让我们一起期待吧！

玛丽·温克尔

纽约

2017 年 11 月 25 日

1. 这封邮件是关于什么的？
   (A) 音乐会。
   (B) 电影。
   (C) 话剧。
   (D) 游戏。

2. 玛丽看过多少场音乐会？
   (A) 一场。
   (B) 两场。
   (C) 五场。
   (D) 十多场。

3. 玛丽认为她看的魔力红音乐会怎么样？
   (A) 很棒。
   (B) 一般般。
   (C) 糟糕。
   (D) 糟糕极了。

Unit 32 音乐 | Music

4. 这场演唱会是在哪里举行的？
   (A) 陌生的地方。
   (B) 体育馆。
   (C) 商业中心。
   (D) 会议中心。

5. 最后，玛丽期望什么？
   (A) 看魔力红下一场巡回演出。
   (B) 摇滚演唱会。
   (C) 泰勒·斯威弗特的演唱会。
   (D) 购买所有歌手的专辑。

解析与答案

答案：1. (A)　2. (D)　3. (A)　4. (A)　5. (A)

1. 询问邮件的主题，答案就在邮件标题里，可见 Subject: Impressions of Maroon 5 Concert，因此选 (A)。
2. 在第二段第一句中，玛丽提到 I will have been to more than ten concerts...，因此答案选 (D)。
3. 此题可见第二段第一句 ... this show was the most engaging that I have ever seen，因此答案选 (A)。
4. 从第二段第二句 The concert was held in a strange place... 可知演唱会在陌生的地方举办，因此答案选 (A)。
5. 期望的内容通常会在后半部提到，见最后一段第一句 I hope to see another show on their next tour，因此答案选 (A)。

单词 Vocabulary

concert [ˈkɒnsət] n 音乐会　v 商议，协调
impression [ɪmˈpreʃn] n 感想，印象，影响，效果
attractive [əˈtræktɪv] a 吸引人的，引人注目的
among [əˈmʌŋ] p 在……之间
strange [streɪndʒ] a 奇怪的，陌生的
collect [kəˈlekt] v 收集，聚集
album [ˈælbəm] n 专辑，唱片
talkative [ˈtɔːkətɪv] a 健谈的，喜欢说话的，饶舌的
rhythm [ˈrɪðəm] n 韵律，节奏，节拍
positive [ˈpɒzɪtɪv] a 积极的，肯定的，确定的，确信的

Unit 33
饭店 | Hotel

Picture 33

情境中可明确指出的单词

1. **consult** [kən'sʌlt] v 咨询
2. **plant** [plɑːnt] n 植物
3. **point** [pɔɪnt] v 指
4. **posy** ['pəʊzi] n 花束
5. **receptionist** [rɪ'sepʃənɪst] n 接待员
6. **service counter** ph 服务柜台
7. **trunk** [trʌŋk] n 旅行箱
8. **vase** [vɑːz] n 花瓶

情境中可延伸记忆的单词

1. **accommodation** [ə,kɒmə'deɪʃn] n 住宿，住处
2. **bellboy** ['belbɔɪ] n 行李员
3. **choose** [tʃuːz] v 挑选
4. **considerate** [kən'sɪdərət] a 体贴的，周到的
5. **check-in** [tʃek in] n 登记入住
6. **document** ['dɒkjumənt] n 证件，单据
7. **luxurious** [lʌɡ'ʒʊəriəs] a 奢华的
8. **service guide** ph 服务指南

Unit 33 饭店 | Hotel

consult [kən'sʌlt] v 咨询
You can **consult** our receptionist if you have any problems.
如果你有问题的话，可以咨询我们的柜台人员。
● **consultant** n 顾问 / **consultation** n 咨询 / **consult with** 交换意见

plant [plɑ:nt] n 植物
It's better to place some **plants** in our room.
往我们房间里放些植物比较好。
● **plantation** n 绿植 / **vegetation** n （总称）植物，草木

point [pɔɪnt] v 指
The man **pointed** at the hotel and told me this was the one he was looking for.
男子指着这家饭店对我说这就是他在找的饭店。
● **key point** n 关键点 / **point out** 指出 / **point to** 表明 / **in point of** 就……而言

posy ['pəʊzi] n 花束
A **posy** is standing in the vase on the counter.
柜台上的花瓶里插着花束。
● **bunch** n 束 / **bouquet** n 花束，一束花

receptionist [rɪ'sepʃənɪst] n 接待员
The **receptionist** explained the rules and regulations of the hotel to us.
接待员向我们解释饭店的规章制度。
● **reception** n 接待 / **receptivity** n 感受性

service counter ph 服务柜台
The surface of the **service counter** is made of marble.
服务柜台的台面是大理石制成的。
● **reception personnel** n 接待人员 / **registration office** n 登记处

trunk [trʌŋk] n 旅行箱
You can keep your **trunk** at the registration desk.
你可以将你的旅行箱放在登记台。
● **tree trunk** n 树干 / **suitcase** n 小型旅行箱 / **portmanteau** n 旅行皮箱

vase [vɑ:z] n 花瓶
The **vase** should be placed carefully on the counter.
应当小心把这只花瓶放在柜台。
● **crystal vase** n 水晶花瓶 / **flower arranging** n 插花艺术

accommodation [əˌkɒməˈdeɪʃn] n 住宿，住处

The company will arrange **accommodations** for the staff on the business trip.
公司会为出差人员安排住宿。
accommodate v 容纳 / **lodging** n 住宿，住所 / **lodging house** n 公寓

---

bellboy [ˈbelbɔɪ] n 行李员

The **bellboy** will take your luggage to your room.
行李员将会把你的行李送到你的房间。
porter n 行李员 / **housekeeper** n 女管家

---

choose [tʃuːz] v 挑选

The hotel has many kinds of rooms to **choose** from.
饭店有多种类型的房间供选择。
choose from ph 挑选 / **choice** n 选择 / **have no choice** ph 别无选择

---

considerate [kənˈsɪdərət] a 体贴的，周到的

The service of this hotel must be very **considerate**.
这家饭店的服务一定很周到。
considerate towards ph 体谅 / **considerate of** ph 体贴 / **thoughtful** a 体贴的

---

check-in [ˈtʃek ɪn] n 登记入住

They are going through the **check-in** procedure at the registration desk.
他们正在登记台办理入住手续。
check out ph 退房

---

document [ˈdɒkjumənt] n 证件，单据

The manager needs to submit the **documents** to the boss by this Friday.
经理应该在本周五前将文件递交给老板。
documentary n 纪录片 / **documental** a 文件的 / **docket** n 事项表，备忘录

---

luxurious [lʌɡˈʒʊəriəs] a 奢华的

The hotel hall is not only **luxurious** but also tasteful.
这家饭店的大厅不只奢华而且很有品位。
luxury n 奢侈（品）/ **luxury goods** n 奢侈品 / **gracious** a 雅致的

---

service guide ph 服务指南

He took a glimpse at the **service guide** on the desk.
他瞥了桌上的服务指南一眼。
guide n 指南 / **guidebook** n 旅行指南 / **tour guide** n 导游

听力测验 | Part 1 图片描述题

(A) This room is tiny and chaotic.
(B) There is a single bed in this room.
(C) There is lots of food and drinks on the table.
(D) Hotel staff is cleaning the room.

(A) 这个房间又小又乱。
(B) 房间里有一张单人床。
(C) 桌子上有很多的食物和饮料。
(D) 饭店人员在打扫房间。

答案：(C)
从图片中可以看出，这个房间很大，收拾得很干净，里面有一张双人床，桌子上摆放了很多的食物和饮料，房间里没有任何人员，所以答案选 (C)。

听力测验 | Part 4 简短独白题

1. When will Sam probably leave for his trip?
   (A) On June 6th.
   (B) On June 8th.
   (C) On June 10th.
   (D) On June 13rd.

2. What isn't Sam suggested to do?
   (A) To confirm the booking one day in advance.
   (B) To pay in full on arrival.
   (C) To retain the original receipts.
   (D) To file a claim.

3. What could the hotel do if Sam doesn't confirm the booking in time?
   (A) The hotel could call Sam back.
   (B) The hotel could assign the room to another guest.
   (C) The hotel could charge more.
   (D) The hotel could file a claim.

Hello, Sam. To meet your requirements, I have booked an executive suite for you at the Hilton Hotel. You can check in at the hotel on June 8th and will stay until the 13th. The scheduled time parallels your business trip. If you want to know more about the room, you can search for it on the Internet. There is one important thing. You must confirm the booking one day in advance, otherwise the hotel is entitled to assign the room to another guest. Also, you need to pay the bill in full on arrival. Just in case, you need to keep your original receipts so that you can maintain your own rights in case of problems. Lastly, you can call me if you have any question. Enjoy your business trip.

Unit 33 饭店 | Hotel

中译

1. 山姆可能什么时候开始他的旅行？
   (A) 6 月 6 日。
   (B) 6 月 8 日。
   (C) 6 月 10 日。
   (D) 6 月 13 日。

2. 说话者不建议山姆做的是什么？
   (A) 提前一天确定房间预订。
   (B) 住宿费需要一次性付清。
   (C) 保留原始收据。
   (D) 要求索赔。

3. 如果山姆没有及时确定房间预约，酒店可以怎么做？
   (A) 酒店人员可以回电话给山姆。
   (B) 酒店人员可以把房间转让给其他房客。
   (C) 酒店人员可以索要更高的住宿费。
   (D) 酒店人员可以要求索赔。

山姆，你好。按你的要求，我已经在希尔顿饭店为你预订了商务套房。你的入住时间是 6 月 8 日到 13 日。酒店的预订时间和你的商务旅行时间是一致的。如果你想对你的房间有更多的了解，你可以在网上查询。还有重要的一点，你必须提前一天确认你的房间预订，否则酒店有权将房间转让给其他人。此外，你应该一次付清费用。以防万一。为了你能维护自己的权益，你最好保留你的原始收据。最后，如果你有任何疑问，可以打电话给我。祝你旅途愉快。

解析与答案

答案：1. (B) 2. (D) 3. (B)

1. 文章中提到房间的预订时间是 6 月 8 日至 6 月 13 日，这和山姆的商务旅行时间一致，所以据此可推测山姆是从 6 月 8 日开始旅行，答案选 (B)。
2. 听力中 (A)、(B)、(C) 选项都有提到，只有 (D) 选项没有提到，所以选 (D)。
3. 根据 you must confirm the booking..., the hotel is entitled to assign the room to another guest 可知，答案选 (B)。

单词 Vocabulary

requirement [rɪˈkwaɪərəmənt] n 要求，必需品，必要条件
executive [ɪgˈzekjətɪv] a 行政的，执行的 n 执行者，总经理
check [tʃek] v 检查，制止，打钩 n 支票，检验
parallel [ˈpærəlel] v 使……与……平行 n 平行线 a 类似的，平行的
confirm [kənˈfɜːm] v 确认，批准，使巩固
maintain [meɪnˈteɪn] v 维护，主张，供养，继续

阅读测验 | Part 7 文章理解题

Dear Sir,

We have something important to tell you before checking in.

First, before checking in:

Check-in starts at 12:00 noon every day. If you check in before 12:00, you will have to pay extra fees. If you arrive before 12:00, but you wish to wait, you can keep your luggage at the reception desk and wait in the lobby until 12:00.

All our suite rooms are fully equipped with a bathroom, hair dryer, television, computer and so on.

If you park your car here, you will be charged $8 per day.

We are near underground stations and bus stops here. For more details, you can read the timetable.

Second, before checking out:

Check-out ends at 12:00 noon.

Last but not least, we want to make sure you have had a pleasant stay here. We aim to provide every guest with an enjoyable stay here and would be happy for you to give us feedback after you experience our service. We would like to ask you to fill in this form today. If you have any suggestions, you can list them and we will try our best to improve everything. After finishing the form, please leave it on the table in the room. We will take it after you leave.

We look forward to seeing you again.

Regards,

May Green

Manager

Unit 33 饭店 | Hotel

1. Where can you most likely see this announcement?
   (A) In the restaurant.
   (B) In the hotel.
   (C) In the washing room.
   (D) In the bus.

2. What time is check-in and check-out?
   (A) 12:00 noon.
   (B) 1 p.m.
   (C) 2 p.m.
   (D) 3 p.m.

3. If guests want more details about the time of the underground or bus schedules, what can be done?
   (A) Ask the manager.
   (B) Ask the receptionists.
   (C) Ask May Green.
   (D) Read the timetable.

4. What does the hotel ask guests to fill in the form for?
   (A) Just for fun.
   (B) Getting feedback from guests to improve the management of the hotel.
   (C) Asking the guests to stay for another day.
   (D) Not mentioned in the announcement.

5. What does May Green do according to the announcement?
   (A) Assistant.
   (B) Receptionist.
   (C) Manager.
   (D) Cleaning staff.

尊敬的先生，

在您入住之前，我们有重要的事情要告诉您。

首先，入住前须知：

我们必须告诉您，入住时间于每日中午十二点开始。如果您在十二点之前入住，需要交纳额外的费用。如果您在十二点之前到达，但是想在十二点后入住，您可以将您的行李在接待柜台保存，在大厅等到十二点。

我们所有的套房设备齐全，配有浴室、吹风机、电视、电脑等。

如果您是开车到我们这里的，您每天需要交付八美元。

我们距离这里的地铁站与公交车站很近。欲知详情，请看时刻表。

其次，退房前须知：

退房时间在中午十二点结束。

最后一项要点是，我们想确认一下您在我们这里是否愉快。我们旨在使每一位宾客在这里度过愉快的时光，我们很高兴您在体验我们的服务之后，能给我们回馈。我们想知道今天是否可以占用您的时间填下表格。如果您有建议，可以写在表格上，我们必定尽力改善一切。在填完表格之后，您将它放在房间里的桌子上即可；在您离开之后，我们会去拿。

期待您的再次光临。

此致

敬礼！

梅·格林

经理

1. 你最可能在哪里能看到这份公告？
   (A) 餐厅。 (B) 酒店。
   (C) 洗手间。 (D) 公交车。

2. 入住与退房在什么时间？
   (A) 中午十二点。 (B) 下午一点。
   (C) 下午两点。 (D) 下午三点。

Unit 33 饭店 | Hotel

3. 如果客人想知道更多有关地铁或公交车到达时间的详情，可以怎么做？
(A) 问经理。　　　　　　　　　　(B) 问接待人员。
(C) 问梅·格林。　　　　　　　　　(D) 阅读时刻表。

4. 酒店为什么让宾客填写表格呢？
(A) 仅仅是为了娱乐。　　　　　　　(B) 获取宾客的回馈信息，提升饭店管理。
(C) 让宾客再住一天。　　　　　　　(D) 通告中并未提及。

5. 根据公告可知，梅·格林是做什么工作的？
(A) 助理。　　　　　　　　　　　　(B) 接待人员。
(C) 经理。　　　　　　　　　　　　(D) 清洁员工。

解析与答案

答案：1. (B)　2. (A)　3. (D)　4. (B)　5. (C)

1. 此题考信息提取能力，虽然文章中并没有直接说明是酒店，但看到第二段的第二条 All our suite rooms are fully equipped with a bathroom, hair dryer, television, computer and so on, 以及下面四个选项就可知选项 (B) 最符合题意。
2. 此题考细节，可见第二段的第一条 ... check-in starts at 12:00 noon..., 以及第三段的 Check-out ends at 12:00 noon, 因此选 (A)。
3. 此题考细节，可见第二段的第四条 We are near underground stations and bus stops here. For more details, you can read the timetable, 由此得知如果想要知道更多信息，可以看时刻表，因此答案选 (D)。
4. 此题考细节，从倒数第二段的第二句 ... would be happy for you to give us a feedback..., 以及第四句 If you have any suggestions, you can list them and we will try our best to improve everything 可知填写表格的目的是希望获得回馈，因此选 (B)。
5. 此题同样考信息判断能力，由这份公告最后的 May Green Manager 可知答案选 (C)。

单词 Vocabulary

notice ['nəʊtɪs] n 通知，公告　v 注意，通知，评论
start [stɑːt] v 开始，出发，发生
extra ['ekstrə] a 额外的，特大的　ad 另外，额外地　n 附加费用
luggage ['lʌgɪdʒ] n （英）行李
reception [rɪ'sepʃn] n 接待，接受，（英）接待处
underground ['ʌndəgraʊnd] a 地面下的，秘密的　n 地铁
　　　　　　　　[ˌʌndə'graʊnd] ad 在地下，秘密地
aim [eɪm] v 旨在，瞄准
guest [gest] n 宾客，客座教授　a 客座的　v 款待，招待，当特别来宾
enjoyable [ɪn'dʒɔɪəbl] a 享受的，快乐的
improve [ɪm'pruːv] v 提高，改进，改善

Unit 34
医院 | Hospital

New TOEIC

Picture 34

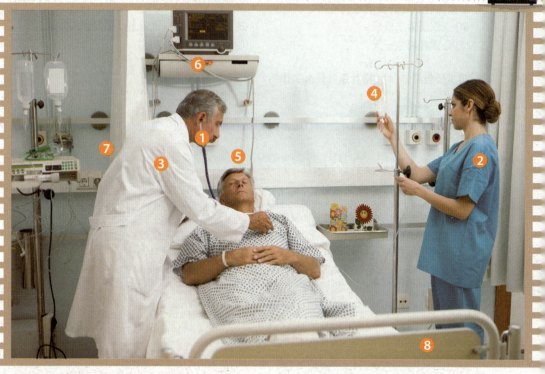

情境中可明确指出的单词

1. **auscultate** [ˈɔːskəlteɪt] v 听诊
2. **nurse** [nɜːs] n 护士
3. **doctor** [ˈdɒktə(r)] n 医生
4. **infusion** [ɪnˈfjuːʒn] n 输液
5. **patient** [ˈpeɪʃnt] n 住院病人 a 有耐心的
6. **wire** [ˈwaɪə(r)] n 电线
7. **bow** [baʊ] v 弯腰
8. **sickbed** [ˈsɪkbed] n 病床

情境中可延伸记忆的单词

1. **injection** [ɪnˈdʒekʃn] n 注射
2. **treat** [triːt] v 治疗,看待,请客
3. **cure** [kjʊə(r)] v 治愈
4. **remedy** [ˈremədi] n 疗法,治疗 v 治疗
5. **recover** [rɪˈkʌvə(r)] v 恢复
6. **nursing** [ˈnɜːsɪŋ] n 看护
7. **sterile** [ˈsteraɪl] a 无菌的,不生育的
8. **amputate** [ˈæmpjuteɪt] v 截肢

Unit 34 医院 | Hospital

auscultate [ˈɔːskəlteɪt] v 听诊
The doctor is auscultating the patient with a stethoscope.
医生正在用听诊器为病人听诊。
✪ auscultation n 听诊 / auscultatory a 听诊的 / stethoscope n 听诊器

nurse [nɜːs] n 护士
The nurse is adjusting the IV bottle.
护士正在调整输液瓶。
✪ nursing n 护理 / nurse through 细心照料 / head nurse n 护士长

doctor [ˈdɒktə(r)] n 医生
You need to see a doctor if you are not feeling well.
如果感觉不舒服，你需要去看医生。
✪ doctorate n 博士学位 / physician n 医生，内科医生 / surgeon n 外科医生

infusion [ɪnˈfjuːʒn] n 输液
This patient needs an infusion of blood.
这位病人需要输血。
✪ infuse v 灌输 / infusive a 令人鼓舞的

patient [ˈpeɪʃnt] n 住院病人 a 有耐心的
The nurse is patient with the patient.
这名护士对待病人有耐心。
✪ patience n 耐心 / invalid n 病人 / patient of n 能忍受 / patient with n 对……有耐心

wire [ˈwaɪə(r)] n 电线
Don't touch the wire, it's dangerous.
不要碰这条电线；很危险。
✪ wireless a 无线的 / wire netting n 铁丝网 / wire pole n 电线杆

bow [baʊ] v 弯腰
The patient bowed to the doctor after he recovered from his illness.
那名病人康复之后，向医生鞠躬。
✪ bow down n 鞠躬；压弯 / stoop v 屈身，弯腰

sickbed [ˈsɪkbed] n 病床
The general gave his orders from his sickbed.
这名将军在病床上下指令。
✪ hospital bed n 病床 / sick leave n 病假 / sick of 对……厌恶

injection [ɪnˈdʒekʃn] n 注射
The nurse will give the patient an injection.
护士会为病人注射。
- injector n 注射器 / inject v 注射 / shot n 注射

treat [triːt] v 治疗，看待，请客
The doctor will treat the patient properly.
医生会用适当的方法治疗病人。
- treatment n 治疗 / treatable a 能治疗的 / doctor v 治疗

cure [kjʊə(r)] v 治愈
The patient's sickness will be cured by the doctor's treatment.
在医生的治疗下，病人的病会治愈的。
- curable a 可治愈的 / cure-all n 万能药 / curer n 医疗者，治疗器

remedy [ˈremədi] n 疗法，治疗 v 治疗
The doctors have found a remedy for the patient's illness.
医生们已经找到治疗这个病人的疗法。
- remediation n 补救 / remedial a 治疗的 / therapy n 治疗，疗法

recover [rɪˈkʌvə(r)] v 恢复
The patient is recovering from an illness.
病人正在康复。
- recovery n 恢复 / retrieve v 恢复 / reinstate v 使恢复，使复原

nursing [ˈnɜːsɪŋ] n 看护
She decided she wanted to study nursing.
她决定她要读护理。
- nurture v 养育 / nursling n 哺育中的婴儿

sterile [ˈsteraɪl] a 无菌的，不生育的
The cuts must be protected by a sterile dressing.
伤口一定要用无菌纱布包扎保护。
- sterilization n 消毒 / aseptic a 无菌的，防腐性的

amputate [ˈæmpjuteɪt] v 截肢
The doctor amputated the patient's limbs as a last resort.
医生在万不得已时才会给病人截肢。
- amputee n 被截肢者 / amputation n 截肢术

听力测验 | Part 1 图片描述题

(A) The doctor is operating on a patient.
(B) Doctors are discussing the patient's condition.
(C) Doctors in this hospital all wear the same uniform.
(D) Doctors in this hospital are old.

(A) 医生在为患者做手术。
(B) 医生在商讨病人的病情。
(C) 这个医院里的医生都穿着一样的工作服。
(D) 这个医院里的医生年龄都比较大。

答案：(B)
从图片中可以看出，有人在排队看病，有三位医生在看病者的 CT 片，说明他们是在谈论病人的病情；另外，这三名医生看上去比较年轻，而且年龄不大，没有在做手术，所以选(B)。

听力测验 | Part 4 简短独白题

1. What will Susan do for these freshly graduated nurses?
   (A) She will guide them by herself.
   (B) She will ask someone else to guide them.
   (C) She will make some rules for them.
   (D) She will make them pass the probation successfully.

2. Which of the following factors won't be considered in the final evaluation?
   (A) Professionalism.
   (B) Love for patients.
   (C) Punctuality.
   (D) Bedside manners.

3. How long is the probation period?
   (A) One month.
   (B) Two months.
   (C) Three months.
   (D) Four months.

Welcome! I'm happy to have you employed at our hospital. I'm the head nurse here. You can call me Susan or by my title. Considering that you are freshly graduated nurses, I will ask the senior staff to guide you for the first three months. There are some rules you should follow in the hospital. Your salary and evaluation depend on your performance. During this time, these factors will be considered in your final evaluation, including professionalism, affection for patients, and punctuality. Now, I will take you to the office. You will meet your respective mentors there. I hope you can pass the probation period successfully.

Unit 34 医院 | Hospital

1. 苏珊会为毕业新生做些什么？
   (A) 她会亲自指导这些新生。
   (B) 她会安排人指导这些新生。
   (C) 她会为这些新生订下一些规则。
   (D) 她会让这些新生顺利通过试用期。

2. 最终评价不包括下列哪一个因素？
   (A) 专业精神。
   (B) 对病人的关爱。
   (C) 守时。
   (D) 临床态度。

3. 试用期有多长时间？
   (A) 一个月。
   (B) 两个月。
   (C) 三个月。
   (D) 四个月。

非常开心你们被录取了，欢迎你们成为这个医院的一员。我是这里的护士长。你可以称呼我为苏珊，或称呼我为护士长。考虑到你们都是毕业新生，前三个月我会让资深员工指导你们。在医院里，你们需要遵守很多规则。你的薪水和评价取决于你自己的表现。在此期间，你的专业性、对病人的关爱和守时等因素都会是你的最终评价中的考虑因素。现在，我带你们到办公室，你会与你们各自的导师会面。希望你们都能顺利通过试用期。

答案：1. (B) 2. (D) 3. (C)

1. 根据 I will ask the senior staff to guide you for the first three months 这句话可知，苏珊会安排人对他们进行指导，所以答案选 (B)。

2. 根据 these factors..., including professionalism, affection for patients, and punctuality 可得出答案为 (D)。

3. 根据 I will ask the senior staff to guide you in the first three months 可推测出他们的试用期是三个月，所以选 (C)。

单词 Vocabulary

evaluation [ɪˌvæljuˈeɪʃn] n 评价，估价，估算
professionalism [prəˈfeʃənəlɪzəm] n 专业主义，专业精神
affection [əˈfekʃn] n 感情，喜爱，感染，疾病
punctuality [ˌpʌŋktʃuˈæləti] n 守时，规矩，正确
mentor [ˈmentɔː(r)] n 良师益友，指导员 v 指导
probation [prəˈbeɪʃn] n 试用，缓刑，检验

阅读测验 | Part 7 文章理解题

Doctors in this hospital have reached an agreement with technology personnel about clarifying priorities and goals while running medical software, but have not yet agreed on the time of live tech support.

The study by the local association showed agreements and disagreements between doctors and technology personnel on their view of how to implement the software successfully. The local association shows that the survey is clear and definite for the purchasers and sellers, and it has already made a series of guide books to explain how doctors can guarantee the success of the software implementation.

Mike Bright, president of the local branch association, announced that successful software should be programmed according to the clear vision, intention, and goals for the usage of the software between the doctors and technology personnel. There should be a representative to direct usage of the software. Doctors and technology personnel agree that it is essential for technology personnel to state what is needed for successful implementation of the software. This includes necessary specifications.

However, both sides disagree on the significance of the software and the duration of how long technical support should be provided. Doctors say it is needed for a few years, while the technology personnel say it is only needed for weeks or months.

Unit 34 医院 | Hospital

1. What is this article mainly about?
   (A) Implementation of medical software.
   (B) Surgical operations.
   (C) Computers.
   (D) Books.

2. What do the doctors and technology personnel disagree on at first?
   (A) The place of technology support.
   (B) The people of technology support.
   (C) The time of technology support.
   (D) The software the technology personnel provided.

3. Who is Mike Bright?
   (A) A doctor in the hospital.
   (B) President of the local branch association.
   (C) A patient.
   (D) A nurse.

4. What does Mike Bright suggest?
   (A) Nobody should monitor the software.
   (B) All the doctors and technology personnel should direct the software.
   (C) There should be a representative to direct the software.
   (D) They should introduce the latest technology from overseas.

5. What do both sides disagree on according to the last paragraph?
   (A) When to implement the software.
   (B) How to implement the software.
   (C) The significance of the software and the duration of the technical support provided.
   (D) Where to implement the software.

中译

在阐明清楚的观点、优先事项以及目标方面，这家医院的医生与技术人员在运行医用软件时已经达成一致意见，然而在现场技术支持的时间方面却不能达成一致。

当地组织的研究显示医生与科技人员对于在软件成功运行的主要原因上有相同与不同的观点。当地组织表示，对于购头者与销售者而言的调查十分清晰；并在调查的基础上，已经制定了一系列指导书籍来解释医生如何能保证软件运行成功。

麦克·布朗特，当地分会的主席，宣称成功的软件应是基于医生与技术人员之间清晰的观点、意图以及目标而设计的程序。应该有代表人员来讲解软件的使用方式。医生与技术人员都认为技术人员要说明软件成功运行的要素是十分重要的，这也包括必要的规格。

然而，双方在软件的意义与提供技术支援的期限上有异议。医生说需要几年，但是技术人员说只需要几周或几个月。

1. 这篇文章主要关于什么？
   (A) 医用软件的运行。
   (B) 外科手术。
   (C) 电脑。
   (D) 书籍。

2. 起初，医生与技术人员在什么方面意见不一致？
   (A) 技术支援的地点。
   (B) 技术支援的人员。
   (C) 技术支援的时间。
   (D) 技术人员提供的软件。

3. 麦克·布朗特是谁？
   (A) 这家医院的医生。
   (B) 当地组织分支的主席。
   (C) 患者。
   (D) 护士。

4. 麦克·布朗特的建议是什么？
   (A) 不应有人监控软件。
   (B) 全体医生与技术人员都应指导软件。
   (C) 应当有代表人员来指导软件。
   (D) 他们应当从海外引进最先进的技术。

Unit 34 医院 | Hospital

5. 根据最后一段可知，双方在什么方面意见不统一？
   (A) 运行软件的时间。
   (B) 运行软件的方式。
   (C) 软件的意义与提供技术支援的期限。
   (D) 运行软件的地点。

解析与答案

答案：1. (A) 2. (C) 3. (B) 4. (C) 5. (C)

1. 此题可见第二段第一句 ... implement the software successfully，因此答案选 (A)。
2. 从第一段第一句 ... but have not yet agreed on the time of live tech support... 可推测出答案选 (C)。
3. 答案在第三段第一句 Mike Bright, president of the local branch association...，直接表明麦克·布朗特的身份，答案选 (B)。
4. 此题可见第三段第二句 There should be a representative to direct usage of the software，因此答案选 (C)。
5. 题目已经点出最后一段，所以直接在最后一段中找答案。由 ... both sides disagree on the significance of the software and the duration of how long technical support should be provided 可知其对于期限的意见不同，因此答案选 (C)。

单词 Vocabulary

personnel [ˌpɜːsəˈnel] n （总称）人员，人事部门
clarify [ˈklærəfaɪ] v 澄清，阐明，使清楚
vision [ˈvɪʒn] n 观点，视力 v 显现
support [səˈpɔːt] n 支持，支撑，扶养
ought [ɔːt] v 应该
association [əˌsəʊsiˈeɪʃn] n 结合，联盟，协会
implementation [ˌɪmplɪmenˈteɪʃn] n 实施，运行，成就
survey [sɜːˈveɪ] v 调查，测量 [ˈsɜːveɪ] n 调查，调查报告，检视
program [ˈprəʊɡræm] v 设计程序
representative [ˌreprɪˈzentətɪv] a 代表（性）的，典型的 n 代表（物），代理人
usage [ˈjuːsɪdʒ] n 用法，使用，习惯
essential [ɪˈsenʃl] a 本质的，必要的，基本的 n 要素，本质，必需品
specification [ˌspesɪfɪˈkeɪʃn] n 明细，说明书，详述
significance [sɪɡˈnɪfɪkəns] n 重要性，意义，含义
duration [djuˈreɪʃn] n （时间的）持续，期间

Unit 35
看医生 | Seeing a Doctor

Picture 35

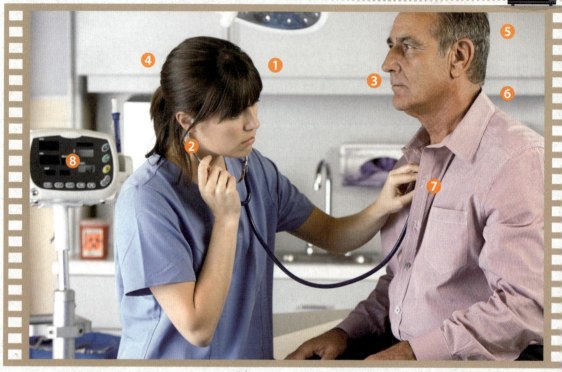

情境中可明确指出的单词

1. **diagnose** [ˈdaɪəgnəʊz] v 诊断
2. **stethoscope** [ˈsteθəskəʊp] n 听诊器
3. **breathing** [ˈbriːðɪŋ] n 呼吸
4. **seriously** [ˈsɪərɪəsli] ad 认真地，严肃地
5. **ahead** [əˈhed] ad 在前，事前
6. **unhealthy** [ʌnˈhelθi] a 不健康的
7. **chest** [tʃest] n 胸部，胸
8. **instrument** [ˈɪnstrəmənt] n 仪器

情境中可延伸记忆的单词

1. **recover** [rɪˈkʌvə(r)] v 恢复
2. **faint** [feɪnt] n / v 晕倒 a 头晕的
3. **headache** [ˈhedeɪk] n 头疼
4. **emergency** [ɪˈmɜːdʒənsi] n 紧急情况
5. **antiseptic** [ˌæntiˈseptɪk] n 消毒剂 a 抗菌的
6. **regularly** [ˈregjələli] ad 按时，定期地
7. **thermometer** [θəˈmɒmɪtə(r)] n 体温计，温度计
8. **hospitalization** [ˌhɒspɪtəlaɪˈzeɪʃn] n 住院

Unit 35 看医生 | Seeing a Doctor

diagnose [ˈdaɪəgnəʊz] v. 诊断
The doctor is **diagnosing** the patient.
医生正在诊断病人的病情。
⊕ diagnosis n. 诊断 / diagnostic a. 诊断的 / diagnostician n. 诊断者

stethoscope [ˈsteθəskəʊp] n. 听诊器
The doctor hears the patient's heartbeat with a **stethoscope**.
医生用听诊器听病人的心跳。
⊕ heartbeat n. 心跳

breathing [ˈbriːðɪŋ] n. 呼吸
The patient kept **breathing** steadily while being checked.
在检查时病人保持着平稳的呼吸。
⊕ breathlessness n. 呼吸急促 / breath n. 呼吸 / breathing capacity n. 肺活量

seriously [ˈsɪərɪəslɪ] ad. 认真地，严肃地
The man won't see the doctor unless he is **seriously** ill.
除非病得特别严重，否则他不会去看医生。
⊕ seriousness n. 严重性 / serious-minded a. 热心的

ahead [əˈhed] ad. 在前，事前
We have to make an appointment with the doctor **ahead** of time.
我们必须提前和医生预约。
⊕ ahead of n. 在……的前方 / ahead of schedule n. 提前，提早

unhealthy [ʌnˈhelθɪ] a. 不健康的
The patient looks pale and **unhealthy**.
这个病人脸色苍白，精神不振。
⊕ unhealthful a. 影响健康的 / unhealthiness n. 有病 / healthy a. 健康的

chest [tʃest] n. 胸部，胸
The doctor puts the stethoscope on the patient's **chest**.
医生把听诊器放在病人的胸口上。
⊕ chest cavity n. 胸腔 / chest of drawers n. 五斗柜，衣柜 / breast n. 胸部，乳房

instrument [ˈɪnstrəmənt] n. 仪器；设备
The hospital introduced advanced **instruments** last month.
上个月，医院引进了先进设备。
⊕ instrumentality n. 手段，工具 / instrument board n. 仪表板

recover [rɪˈkʌvə(r)] v 恢复
The patient will **recover** soon after doctor's treatment.
经过医生的治疗，病人很快就恢复了。
▶ recovery n 恢复 / recover from phr 从某病中恢复

faint [feɪnt] n / v 晕倒 a 头晕的
The doctor is checking the reasons why the patient suddenly **fainted**.
医生正在查找病人突然昏厥的原因。
▶ faintness n 模糊 / pass out phr 晕倒 / swoon n / v 昏厥，昏倒

headache [ˈhedeɪk] n 头疼
The patient tells the doctor that he is suffering from a **headache**.
病人告诉医生他正遭受着头疼的折磨。
▶ stomachache n 胃痛 / backache n 背痛

emergency [iˈmɜ:dʒənsi] n 紧急情况
The doctor on duty must have the ability to deal with **emergency** situations.
值班医生必须有处理紧急情况的能力。
▶ emergence n 出现 / emergent a 紧急的，意外的

antiseptic [ˌæntiˈseptɪk] n 消毒剂 a 抗菌的
The nurse uses the **antiseptic** to bathe the cut.
护士用消毒剂清洗伤口。
▶ antisepticize v 杀菌 / cleanser n 清洁剂

regularly [ˈregjələli] ad 按时，定期地
It is necessary to have a physical examination **regularly**.
定期做身体检查是有必要的。
▶ regularize v 调整 / usually ad 通常地 / on schedule phr 按照预订时间

thermometer [θəˈmɒmɪtə(r)] n 体温计，温度计
The nurse takes the patient's temperature with a **thermometer**.
护士用体温计给病人测体温。
▶ clinical thermometer n 体温计

hospitalization [ˌhɒspɪtəlaɪˈzeɪʃn] n 住院
The **hospitalization** fees are a really huge cost.
住院费真是一笔巨大的开销。
▶ hospitalize v 就医，住院治疗 / hospital n 医院

听力测验 | Part 1 图片描述题

[图片]

(A) The doctor is treating a little girl.
(B) There are many patients in this room.
(C) The little girl starts to cry when she is treated.
(D) The doctor is terrible.

(A) 医生在为一个小女孩看病。
(B) 房间里有很多的病人。
(C) 小女孩因为要看病开始哭泣。
(D) 这位医生很可怕。

答案：(A)
从图片中可以看出，房间里只有一名医生和一位病人，从医生的面容可以看出她很和善，这位病人是一个小女孩，她在看病的时候不哭不闹，非常勇敢，所以答案选 (A)。

听力测验 | Part 3 简短对话题

1. Is the woman ill?
   (A) Yes, she has a fever.
   (B) Yes, she has a cold.
   (C) No, she just feels tired and has no appetite.
   (D) No, she just doesn't want to work overtime.

2. Why does the man mention Dr. Smith?
   (A) Because he knows Dr. Smith.
   (B) Because he heard Dr. Smith is a good doctor.
   (C) Because Dr. Smith is Jessica's boss.
   (D) Because Dr. Smith is their friend.

3. Will the woman go to see a doctor?
   (A) Yes, she will go to see a doctor by herself.
   (B) Yes, she will go to see a doctor with the man.
   (C) No, she will stay at home.
   (D) No, she just wants to have a good sleep.

Ben: Hello, Jessica! You look exhausted. How are you feeling?

Jessica: Terrible. I have felt uncomfortable for a few days.

Ben: You must be ill. Do you have a fever or cold?

Jessica: No, I don't think I'm ill. But I feel tired and don't want to do anything.

Ben: Maybe you have too much stress. Do you often work overtime?

Jessica: Yes. I don't have enough time to sleep and I don't have any appetite.

Ben: I think you should go to see a doctor. The doctor will prescribe some medicine for you. I heard that Dr. Smith is good.

Jessica: OK. Would you like to come with me? I will feel better if you're there.

Ben: OK. I will come with you.

Unit 35 看医生 | Seeing a Doctor

中译

1. 女子生病了吗？
   (A) 是的，她发烧了。
   (B) 是的，她感冒了。
   (C) 没有，她只是觉得疲惫，没有胃口。
   (D) 没有，她只是不想加班。

2. 男子为什么提到了史密斯医生？
   (A) 因为他认识史密斯医生。
   (B) 因为他听说史密斯医生是好医生。
   (C) 因为史密斯医生是洁西卡的老板。
   (D) 因为史密斯医生是他们的朋友。

3. 女子会去看医生吗？
   (A) 会，她会一个人去看医生。
   (B) 会，她会和男子一起去看医生。
   (C) 不会，她想待在家。
   (D) 不会，她只想好好睡一觉。

班：你好，洁西卡！你看起来好憔悴，你怎么了？
洁西卡：很糟糕。我最近一直觉得不舒服。
班：你肯定是生病了。你是不是发烧或者感冒了？
洁西卡：不是，我觉得我没有生病。我就是容易疲劳，什么事也不想做。
班：你或许是压力太大。你最近是不是经常加班？
洁西卡：是的。我经常睡眠不足，还总是没有胃口。
班：你应该去看看医生，让医生给你开一些针对你症状的药。我听说史密斯医生的医术不错。
洁西卡：的确。你能和我一起去吗？我觉得你在会好一点。
班：好的。我和你一起去。

解析与答案

答案：1. (C) 2. (B) 3. (B)

1. 根据 I don't think I'm ill. But... 可知女子（洁西卡）没有发烧、感冒，只是疲劳、没有胃口，所以答案选 (C)。
2. 对话中，男子（班）提到史密斯医生是在他建议洁西卡去看医生之后，而且根据 I heard that Dr. Smith is good 可知，他是听说史密斯的医术比较好，所以向洁西卡推荐史密斯医生，答案选 (B)。
3. 班建议洁西卡去看医生，洁西卡也认为如此，并且想请男子陪她一起，班答应了，所以答案选 (B)。

单词 Vocabulary

exhausted [ɪgˈzɔːstɪd] a 疲惫的，耗尽的，精疲力竭的
fever [ˈfiːvə(r)] n 发烧，狂热 v 使发烧，使狂热
stress [stres] n 压力，重要性，强调 v 加压，使紧张
appetite [ˈæpɪtaɪt] n 食欲，胃口，欲望
prescribe [prɪˈskraɪb] v 开药方，规定

阅读测验 | Part 7 文章理解题

When it comes to illness, we think of doctors. They are lifesavers. In my point of view, being a doctor is the most respectable profession in the world. Let's talk about seeing a doctor.

People can see a doctor in a private clinic in the west. There is usually a receptionist and a nurse in the clinic. The receptionist helps to answer phone calls, and the nurse assists the doctor. There is a lab in the clinic, sometimes. There may be a few doctors working in the same building and sharing the same lab. It is a universal phenomenon in the west.

People often choose a doctor in their phone books or one is recommended by others. Many people think being a doctor is a well-paid profession, but it takes an attentive person to be a doctor. A careless person can never be a doctor, because it involves the health or even life of patients. Nowadays, the medical field has become more and more modern, and doctors are more and more in demand.

If you are not feeling well and the doctor is too busy to take care of you, you can get quick medical care at the emergency room. But this kind of treatment is very expensive. If you can't go to the emergency room on your own, you can have an ambulance to take you there.

Unit 35 看医生 | Seeing a Doctor

1. What is the text about?
   (A) Becoming a doctor.
   (B) Seeing a doctor.
   (C) Choosing a career.
   (D) Looking for a job.

2. What profession does the author think is the most respectable?
   (A) Teacher.
   (B) Doctor.
   (C) Professor.
   (D) Policeman.

3. How do people choose a doctor?
   (A) Asking the hospital.
   (B) Check the phone book or one is recommended by others.
   (C) Asking his parents.
   (D) Not mentioned in the text.

4. What does it take to be a doctor?
   (A) Money.
   (B) Wisdom.
   (C) Attentiveness.
   (D) Carelessness.

5. What can you do if you can't go to the emergency room on your own?
   (A) Call an ambulance.
   (B) Invite a doctor to your home.
   (C) Call your friends.
   (D) Have a rest in bed.

中译

当谈到生病时,我们会想起医生。他们是人类的拯救者。在我看来,医生是世界上最受尊敬的职业。让我们谈一下看医生的事情吧。

在西方,人们可以去私人诊所看医生。诊所里通常会有一名接待员和一名护士。接待员接听电话,护士协助医生。有时,诊所里会有实验室。同时,一栋楼中也可以有好几个医生工作,共用一个实验室。在西方,这是普遍现象。

人们经常通过电话簿或别人的推荐来选择医生。很多人认为,医生是一份高薪职业,但是当医生要更细心。粗心的人绝不能当医生,因为这涉及患者的健康,甚至是生命。现如今,医学领域越来越现代化,对医生的要求也越来越多。

如果你感觉不舒服,而医生特别忙,无法顾及你,你应该去急诊室,在那里可获得快速治疗。但是,这种治疗费用十分昂贵。如果你自己去不了急诊室,你可以叫救护车带你去那里。

1. 文章是关于什么的?
   (A) 当医生。
   (B) 看医生。
   (C) 选择生涯。
   (D) 找工作。

2. 作者认为什么职业最受尊敬?
   (A) 教师。
   (B) 医生。
   (C) 教授。
   (D) 警员。

3. 人们如何选择医生?
   (A) 问医院。
   (B) 查看电话簿或者别人推荐。
   (C) 问父母。
   (D) 文中未提及。

4. 当医生需要什么?
   (A) 钱财。
   (B) 智慧。
   (C) 细心。
   (D) 粗心。

Unit 35 看医生 | Seeing a Doctor

5. 如果你自己去不了医院，你会怎么做？
   (A) 叫救护车。
   (B) 在家请医生。
   (C) 打电话给朋友。
   (D) 躺床上好好休息。

解析与答案

答案：1. (B) 2. (B) 3. (B) 4. (C) 5. (A)

1. 整篇文章都在讲"医生"，但是关于"当医生"还是"看医生"，可见第一段最后一句 Let's talk about seeing a doctor，从中得知要讨论"看医生"，因此答案选 (B)。

2. 从第一段 In my point of view, being a doctor is the most respectable profession in the world 中可知，作者认为医生最值得尊敬。

3. 在第三段第一句中提到人们找医生的方式有 People often choose a doctor in their phone books or one being recommended by others，因此选 (B)。

4. 由第三段第二句 ... it takes an attentive person to be a doctor 可知当医生需要细心，所以答案选 (C)。

5. 此题可见最后一段最后一句 If you can't go to the emergency room on your own, you can have an ambulance to take you there，因此答案选 (A)。

单词 Vocabulary

illness ['ɪlnəs] n 生病，身体不适
doctor ['dɒktə(r)] n 医生，博士 v 治疗，修理
respectable [rɪ'spektəbl] a 尊敬的，名声好的
profession [prə'feʃn] n 职业，同业，声明
clinic ['klɪnɪk] n 诊所
assist [ə'sɪst] v 帮助，协助，支持
universal [ˌjuːnɪ'vɜːsl] a 普遍的，一般的，众所周知的
phenomenon [fə'nɒmɪnən] n 现象，奇迹
choose [tʃuːz] v 挑选，选择，决定
attentive [ə'tentɪv] a 注意的，倾听的，体贴的
involve [ɪn'vɒlv] v 涉入，牵扯，包含，需要，使专注
demand [dɪ'mɑːnd] n 要求，需求 v 要求，需要，查问
treatment ['triːtmənt] n 治疗（法），对待，处理
ambulance ['æmbjələns] n 救护车

Unit 36
药房 | Pharmacy

New TOEIC

Picture 36

情境中可明确指出的单词

1. **pill** [pɪl] n 药丸
2. **colorful** ['kʌləfl] a 色彩缤纷的
3. **kit** [kɪt] n 药盒包装
4. **white-coated** [waɪt 'kəʊtɪd] n 白色医师袍
5. **pocket** ['pɒkɪt] n 口袋
6. **prescription** [prɪ'skrɪpʃn] n 处方
7. **dispensary** [dɪ'spensəri] n 药房
8. **medicine bottle** n 药瓶

情境中可延伸记忆的单词

1. **sick** [sɪk] a 生病的
2. **overdose** ['əʊvədəʊs] n / v 用药过量
3. **ointment** ['ɔɪntmənt] n 软膏
4. **painkiller** ['peɪnkɪlə(r)] n 止痛药
5. **pharmacist** ['fɑːməsɪst] n 药剂师
6. **hypnotic** [hɪp'nɒtɪk] n 安眠药 a 催眠的
7. **allergy** ['ælədʒi] n 过敏
8. **anticoagulant** [ˌæntikəʊ'æɡjələnt] n 抗凝血剂

Unit 36 药房 | Pharmacy

pill [pɪl] n 药片
You must take these pills on time, three times a day.
你必须按时吃药,一天三次。
- sleeping pills 安眠药 / bitter pill to swallow 不得不忍受的苦事 / tablet n 药片

colorful [ˈkʌləfl] a 色彩缤纷的
The drug shelf is full of colorful medicine bottles and cases.
药架上摆满了色彩缤纷的药瓶和药盒。
- color 色彩,颜色 / coloration 着色 / multicolored 彩色的

kit [kɪt] n 药盒包装
We couldn't see the contents of the kit clearly.
我们看不清药盒包装上的内容。
- tool kit 工具箱

white-coated [waɪt ˈkəʊtɪd] n 白色医师袍
The pharmacist in a white-coated is famous for his excellent medical skills.
那位穿着白色医师袍的药剂师因医术高明而出名。
- gown n 医生穿的手术衣

pocket [ˈpɒkɪt] n 口袋
The pharmacist always has a pen in his pocket.
药剂师口袋中总是带一支笔。
- pocket money 零用钱 / out of pocket 赔钱

prescription [prɪˈskrɪpʃn] n 处方
The pharmacist is dispensing the medicine according to the prescription.
药剂师正在按处方配药。
- prescribe v 开药方 / prescript 规定的 / formula n 处方,配方

dispensary [dɪˈspensəri] n 药房
You can buy the medicine recommended to you in the dispensary.
你可以在药房买医生推荐给你的药。
- pharmacy n 药房,药店 / drugstore 兼卖杂货的药房

medicine bottle ph 药瓶
The pharmacist put all of the pills into a medicine bottle.
药剂师把所有的药片放到药瓶里。
- medicine n 药 / medicine chest 药箱

sick [sɪk] a 生病的
The sick man should go see a doctor.
这生病的男子应该去看医生。
sickness n 疾病 / sick and tired of 对……十分厌倦 / ill a 生病的，虚弱的

---

overdose [ˈəʊvədəʊs] n / v 用药过量
Follow the instructions so you do not take an overdose.
按照说明书服用就不会用药过量。
overdrive v 过度驱使

---

ointment [ˈɔɪntmənt] n 软膏
Most ointments can be bought at a pharmacy.
大部分软膏都能在药房买到。
salve n 软膏，药膏 / application n 敷用擦剂

---

painkiller [ˈpeɪnkɪlə(r)] n 止痛药
Painkillers should not be taken frequently.
止痛药不应该频繁服用。
anodyne n 止痛剂，镇痛剂 / analgesic n 止痛剂

---

pharmacist [ˈfɑːməsɪst] n 药剂师
Pharmacists may not have much knowledge about medicine.
药剂师也许没有太多的医学知识。
druggist n 药剂师，药商 / chemist n （英）药剂师

---

hypnotic [hɪpˈnɒtɪk] n 安眠药 a 催眠的
People are not allowed to buy too many hypnotics at one time.
个人不允许一次性购买过多的安眠药。
sleeping pills n 安眠药 / hypnosis n 催眠 / hypnoidal a 催眠状的

---

allergy [ˈælədʒi] n 过敏
Doctors should ask patients to take an allergy test before the use of penicillin.
在使用青霉素前，药剂师应该让病人做过敏测试。
allergist n 过敏症专科医生 / hypersensitivity n 过敏症

---

anticoagulant [ˌæntikəʊˈæɡjələnt] n 抗凝血剂
Pharmacists shouldn't give patients anticoagulant drugs at random.
药剂师不应该随便给病人开抗凝血性的药物。
anticoagulation n 抗凝作用

听力测验 | Part 1 图片描述题

题目
(A) There are all sorts of pharmaceuticals in this pharmacy.
(B) There are many people buying drugs.
(C) People in the pharmacy all wear uniforms.
(D) The staff is sorting out pharmaceuticals on the shelf.

中译
(A) 这个药房里面有各种各样的药品。
(B) 有很多人在买药。
(C) 药房里的人都穿着工作服。
(D) 员工在整理架子上的药物。

解析与答案

答案：(A)
从图片中可以看出，药房的架子上有各种各样的药物，但是没有人在整理，这里的人穿着也很随意，并不是工作服，买药的人也很少，所以选 (A)。

听力测验 | Part 3 简短对话题

1. Why does the man want to buy medicine?
   (A) Because he is sick.
   (B) Because he wants to know how to therapy headache.
   (C) Because he thinks it's too much trouble to see a doctor.
   (D) Because he thinks he can take the medicine anytime.

2. Which of the following suggestions is offered by the woman?
   (A) Taking medicine once a day.
   (B) Take the medicine after meal.
   (C) Paying more attention to the customer's diet.
   (D) Buying some Chinese medicine.

3. How many times should the man take the medicine a day?
   (A) Once a day.
   (B) Twice a day.
   (C) Three times a day.
   (D) Anytime he wants.

Pharmacist: Hello, what can I do for you?

Customer: Hello! I want to get some medicine for the liver.

Pharmacist: OK. Here is your medicine. You should take this medicine twice a day.

Customer: OK. Anything else that I should pay attention to?

Pharmacist: Yes, you need to watch your diet.

Customer: I see. Thank you!

Unit 36 药房 | Pharmacy

中译

1. 顾客为什么想要买药？
   (A) 因为他生病了。
   (B) 因为他想知道如何治疗头痛。
   (C) 因为他认为看医生太麻烦了。
   (D) 因为他认为他可以随时吃药。

2. 药剂师提出下列哪一个建议？
   (A) 坚持每天吃一次药。
   (B) 餐后吃药。
   (C) 注意饮食。
   (D) 买一些中药。

3. 顾客每天应该吃几次药？
   (A) 一天一次。
   (B) 一天两次。
   (C) 一天三次。
   (D) 想吃就吃。

药剂师：你好，我能为你做些什么呢？
顾　客：你好！我想买一些治疗肝脏的药。
药剂师：好的。这是你的药。你一定要坚持一天吃两次。
顾　客：好。还有什么是我需要注意的吗？
药剂师：有，你要注意你的饮食。
顾　客：我知道了。谢谢！

解析与答案

答案：1. (A)　2. (C)　3. (B)

1. 听力中男子说他要拿治疗肝病的药，在答案选项中并没有直接提到肝病的选项，最接近的答案是 (A)。
2. 对话中，药剂师建议每天吃两次药，并注意饮食，选项 (A) 的内容错误，可删去，选项 (B)、(D) 在对话中都没有提到，所以答案要选 (C)。
3. 根据药剂师说的 You should take this medicine twice a day 可知一天要吃两次药，所以答案选 (B)。

单词 Vocabulary

liver ['lɪvə(r)] n 肝脏，居住者
attention [ə'tenʃn] n 注意力，立正状态，照顾，关心
diet ['daɪət] n 饮食，食物 v 节食，给病人指定饮食

阅读测验 | Part 7 文章理解题

We have opened a new pharmacy here and introduced a new kind of capsule.

I will give an introduction to all of our customers. These are white powder capsules. They contain American barley, which is superior to Spanish barley. You can take the capsules with a cup of warm water rather than juice, milk or something else. Barley is very beneficial for our health, so it is good to take some. These capsules can help to alleviate fever, inflammation of tonsil, etc. There are many other excellent effects that you don't know about. If you want to know more details, please read the instructions on the bottle.

One thing we need to emphasize is that you should take three capsules a day, when you need it. But you should never take it continuously for more than two months, or you will experience side effects. Side effects include slight nausea, and you may feel like vomiting, but these will disappear soon. There is only a small chance of experiencing these side effects. Don't be too nervous about the side effects, as they are very slight.

If you have any question, visit us directly and we will help you. You can check our official website www.barleycapsules.com on the Internet. We can also be reached at 666-6868.

We wish you good health!

Unit 36 药房 | Pharmacy

1. Where may we read this announcement?
   (A) In the restaurant.
   (B) In the office.
   (C) In the factory.
   (D) In a pharmacy.

2. What is the article talking about?
   (A) Capsules.
   (B) Computers.
   (C) Food.
   (D) Fruit.

3. What kind of illness can the capsules cure according to the article?
   (A) Cough.
   (B) Fever.
   (C) Nausea.
   (D) Fever and inflammation of the tonsils.

4. What side effect can the capsules have according to the article?
   (A) Allergy.
   (B) Stomachache.
   (C) Headache.
   (D) Feeling nausea and vomiting.

5. Which of the following approaches is NOT mentioned to reach the pharmacy?
   (A) To go to the pharmacy directly.
   (B) To check their official website on the Internet.
   (C) To make a telephone call to them.
   (D) To write letters to them.

我们在这里开了一家新药房，并引进了一种新胶囊。

我将为所有的顾客做一些介绍。这是内装白色粉末的胶囊，其中包含美国大麦的成分，这些成分优于西班牙大麦。用温开水服用胶囊，而不能用果汁、牛奶或者其他东西服用。大麦对我们的健康十分有益，因此服用一些是有益处的。这种胶囊能够帮助清热解毒、治愈扁桃体发炎等。它们还有一些您不知道的优良功效。欲知详情，请阅读瓶子上的说明书。

我们必须强调的是您需要一天服用三粒。但是记住，决不能连续服用两个月以上，否则会产生副作用。副作用就是您可能会感到轻微的恶心、想吐，但是很快会消失。产生副作用的概率非常小。不要对副作用太焦虑，副作用十分轻微。

如果您有任何问题，直接来我们这里即可，我们将会帮助您解决。您也可以在网上搜寻我们的官方网站 www.barleycapsules.com，也可以拨打 666-6868 联系我们。

希望您身体健康！

1. 我们在哪里可以看到这则公告？
　　(A) 餐厅。
　　(B) 办公室。
　　(C) 工厂。
　　(D) 药房。

2. 文章谈及什么？
　　(A) 胶囊。
　　(B) 电脑。
　　(C) 食物。
　　(D) 水果。

3. 根据这则文章可知，胶囊能治愈什么疾病？
　　(A) 咳嗽。
　　(B) 发烧。
　　(C) 恶心。
　　(D) 热毒以及扁桃体发炎。

4. 根据这则文章可知，胶囊会产生什么副作用？
　　(A) 过敏。
　　(B) 胃疼。
　　(C) 头疼。
　　(D) 感觉恶心、想吐。

Unit 36 药房 | Pharmacy

5. 联系药房，下列哪种方法未提及？
   (A) 直接去药房。
   (B) 在网上搜寻官方网站。
   (C) 打电话给他们。
   (D) 写信给他们。

解析与答案

答案：1. (D) 2. (A) 3. (D) 4. (D) 5. (D)

1. 此题考信息提取能力，可见第一段第一句 We have opened a new pharmacy here and introduced a new kind of capsule，由此可知这是药房的公告，因此选 (D)。

2. 此题十分简单，整篇文章都在讨论胶囊，因此选 (A)。

3. 此题考细节，可见第二段的倒数第三句 These capsules can help to alleviate fever, inflammation of tonsil, etc.，因此答案要选 (D)。

4. 此题考信息提取能力，从第三段第三句 Side effect include slight nausea, and you may feel like vomiting... 可知，副作用为恶心、想吐，答案选 (D)。

5. 此题考信息提取能力，从倒数第二段 If you have any question, just come to us directly and we will help you to solve it. You can also search our official website www.barleycapsules.com on the Internet. We can also be reached at 666-6868 可逐步删除选项，文中提到直接找他们、上官方网站、打电话，但没有讲到写信，所以此题的答案要选 (D)。

单词 Vocabulary

pharmacy [ˈfɑːməsi] n 药房，制药业

capsule [ˈkæpsjuːl] n 胶囊，小盒

introduction [ˌɪntrəˈdʌkʃn] n 介绍，引进，序言

superior [suːˈpɪəriə(r)] a 优越的，较好的 n 上司，长官，优胜者

beneficial [ˌbenɪˈfɪʃl] a 有益的，有利的

tonsil [ˈtɒnsl] n 扁桃体

instruction [ɪnˈstrʌkʃn] n 说明，教导，命令

continuously [kənˈtɪnjuəsli] ad 连续地，连续不断地

official [əˈfɪʃl] a 官方的，官员的 n 官员，公务员

学习重点

| 页数 | 笔记内容 |

版权专有　侵权必究

图书在版编目（CIP）数据

全面突破新托业NEW TOEIC 660分 / 廖迪安著. —北京：北京理工大学出版社，2019.7
ISBN 978-7-5682-7238-4

Ⅰ.①全… Ⅱ.①廖… Ⅲ.①英语—词汇—水平考试—自学参考资料 Ⅳ.①H313

中国版本图书馆CIP数据核字（2019）第134993号

北京市版权局著作权合同登记号图字：01-2017-2409
简体中文版由我识出版社有限公司授权出版发行
全面突破新多益NEW TOEIC 660分，Dean Liao著，2016年，初版
ISBN：9789869267809

出版发行 / 北京理工大学出版社有限责任公司	
社　　址 / 北京市海淀区中关村南大街5号	
邮　　编 / 100081	
电　　话 / (010)68914775（总编室）	
(010)82562903（教材售后服务热线）	
(010)68948351（其他图书服务热线）	
网　　址 / http://www.bitpress.com.cn	
经　　销 / 全国各地新华书店	
印　　刷 / 天津久佳雅创印刷有限公司	
开　　本 / 710毫米×1000毫米　1/16	
印　　张 / 24	责任编辑 / 梁铜华
字　　数 / 536千字	文案编辑 / 梁铜华
版　　次 / 2019年7月第1版　2019年7月第1次印刷	责任校对 / 刘亚男
定　　价 / 92.00元	责任印制 / 李志强

图书出现印装质量问题，请拨打售后服务热线，本社负责调换